D1064326

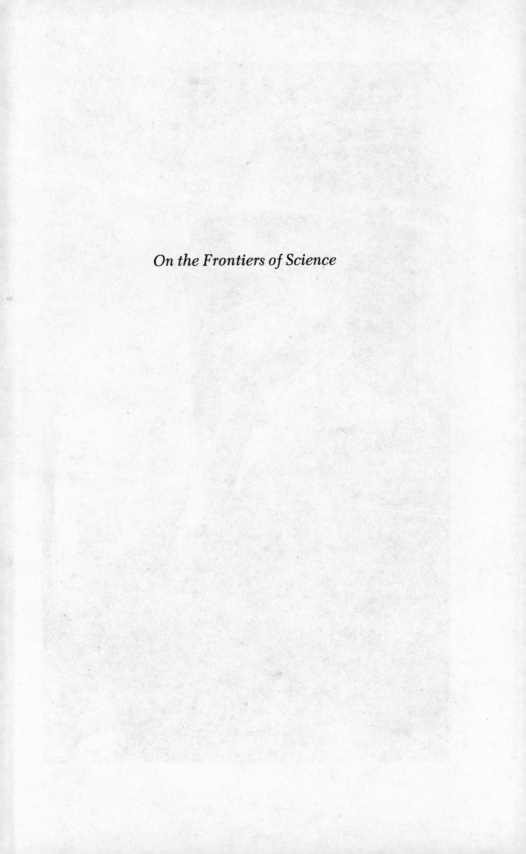

On the Frontiers of Science

J. B. Rhine: On the Frontiers of Science

K. Ramakrishna Rao, Editor

McFarland 1982

Jefferson, North Carolina, and London

Library of Congress Cataloging in Publication Data

Main entry under title:

J. B. Rhine, on the frontiers of science.

Papers presented at a conference sponsored by the
Foundation for Research on the Nature of Man and Duke
University's Psychology Dept., Nov. 28, 1980.
Bibliography: p.
Includes index.
1. Rhine, J. B. (Joseph Banks), 1895–1980 – Congresses.
2. Psychical research – Congresses. I. Rao, K. Ramakrishna.
II. Foundation for Research on the Nature of
Man. III. Duke University. Psychology Dept.
BF1027.R48J16 1982   133.8′092′4 [B]   82-17206

ISBN 0-89950-053-6

Manufactured in the United States of America

McFarland & Company, Inc., Publishers
  Box 611, Jefferson, North Carolina 28640

With Much Love and Admiration to
LOUISA E. RHINE
Life and Laboratory Partner to
J. B. RHINE
for Sixty Years

Contents

Introduction

The passing away of Dr. Joseph Banks Rhine on February 20, 1980, marks the end of an era which began with the publication of his *Extra-Sensory Perception* in 1934 — a book of such a scope and "of such promise as to revolutionize psychical research and to make its title literally a household phrase" (Mauskopf and McVaugh, 1980). For almost half a century he was the undisputed leader of the field in determining its course. He gave it its concepts and methods, defined its scope, mapped out its territory, and provided the instrumentalities necessary for its professionalization — including the establishment of the *Journal of Parapsychology* and the formation of the Parapsychological Association. His admirers as well as his adversaries agree that parapsychology is what it is today largely because of him. It is difficult to find a parallel situation in the development of any other science.

Joseph Banks Rhine was born on September 19, 1895, in Juniata County, Pennsylvania. He had retired from his professorship in psychology at Duke University in 1965 and had since been professor emeritus there and the executive director of the Foundation for Research on the Nature of Man.

J. B. Rhine was educated at Ohio Northern University, the College of Wooster and the University of Chicago, where he received his M.A. (1923) and Ph.D. (1925) degrees in botany. After three years of teaching and research in plant physiology, Rhine, with his wife, Louisa, went to Harvard in 1926 and, a year later, moved to Duke to work under Professor William McDougall. There, in the Department of Psychology, he began the studies that helped to develop parapsychology as a branch of science.

The results of his early work at Duke were summarized in 1934 in *Extra-Sensory Perception*. Rhine was the author of three other books and coauthor of two. In collaboration with his colleagues, he edited four books and published numerous research reports.

Around Dr. Rhine grew a center for research in psychical phenomena. In 1935 this center became the Parapsychology Laboratory with Rhine as its director. For the next 28 years the Parapsychology Laboratory continued as part of Duke University, at first in the Department of Psychology, but after 1950, as a separate unit.

Along with William McDougall, Rhine founded the *Journal of Parapsychology* in 1937 and remained on its staff for forty years. In 1957 he initiated the Parapsychological Association, the professional society of the field which now has some 300 members in various parts of the world. Then, in 1962, as his mandatory retirement age approached, he established the Foundation for Research on the Nature of Man to take over the Duke Parapsychology Laboratory and reorganized it as the Institute for Parapsychology.

One of Rhine's principal contributions to parapsychology was the development of standardized research procedures for testing psychic ability. Along with Dr. Zener, he developed a deck of 25 cards consisting of five simple geometric designs. Using these cards he was able to test subjects under conditions where sensory information was adequately shielded. His efforts first centered around ESP, culminating in the Pearce-Pratt experiment which provided strong evidence in support of ESP. Rhine next turned his attention to the study of psychokinesis (PK), the direct action of mind on matter. He developed an experimental method in which falling dice were used as targets. After nine years of investigation Rhine concluded in 1943 that the psychokinetic effect had been demonstrated. Among other things, Rhine's work provided evidence in support of the notion that ESP is not constrained by time and space, that it is unconscious and somewhat elusive, and that it is not limited to a few rare individuals but is common among ordinary people.

Throughout his research career, Rhine's commitment to scientific method was total and unreserved. He had supreme faith in the promise of science to provide answers to most of our questions. One example of his profound belief in and irrevocable adherence to the empirical approach may be found in the way he dealt with the question of the possibility of the survival of human personality after bodily death, a question which had brought him into psychical research. When he found, after ten years of research with mediums, that there was no way to determine the actual source of the medium's information, he unhesitatingly relegated the survival question to the back shelf, waiting for a more discriminating method which would provide an unambiguous answer.

Rhine's greatest accomplishment was his contribution toward the naturalization of the supernatural, bringing psychical phenomena from the closed seance rooms of mediums into the open laboratories of experimental psychology. Over the years Rhine and his center became the Mecca for all those who had an interest in this area. The careers of many of the present leaders in parapsychology have been launched from his laboratory and almost every serious researcher in the world today has spent some period of time studying and working with Rhine.

J.B., as friends called him, was a warm and affectionate person, able to inspire confidence in his coworkers. He worked hard, sometimes under very adverse conditions. He was attacked, criticized and even ridiculed. But he would not bend and was never bitter. He was passionate about what he believed in without becoming dogmatic.

He sincerely believed that parapsychological findings shed new light on human nature and are a starting point of a new order of investigation. To those who followed him, his work is of historic significance and in due time, J. B. Rhine will be classed among those who, like Freud and Jung before him, gave a new perspective for a fuller understanding of the nature of humankind.

Dr. Rhine lived a full and fruitful life. His accomplishment as a scientist is significant and lasting. Yet, he died as a man who felt that his mission was incomplete. His last words were: "We must go on." In some of his unpublished notes he briefly indicated what he considered should be the main thrust: "The major challenge that stands out increasingly in parapsychology research today," he wrote, "is the great elusiveness of this psi, or psychic, ability. It has functions wide and useful enough to allow a minimal grasp and scientific verification. Yet it evades most of the controlled application all the known sensorimotor abilities permit. Every researcher in the field is keenly challenged to bring the ability under easier control and repeatable demonstration."

Though he pursued psi research with total devotion, parapsychology for J. B. R. was not an end in itself. It was the implications of the existence of psi that fascinated him most. "Like many of the founders of parapsychology," he once said, "I am searching for light on man's nature with respect to the physical order. I had found it hard to hold on to a religious view that rested on the supernatural." The science of parapsycholgoy, he hoped, would answer questions about "man's transcendent nature."

His contributions were not limited to research. The leadership he gave to the field is unparalleled in its history. Most of us who are active in parapsychology today came into the field and stayed in it because of J. B. Rhine. He gave fifty years of his life to the field. During fifteen of these years he received no salary. In addition, he and Louisa Rhine gave to the FRNM close to 500 acres of beautiful land which will fetch for parapsychology at least a million dollars.

Any tribute to Dr. Rhine would be incomplete without a word about his wife, Dr. Louisa Rhine. She shared with him the tribulations, the challenges and frustrations of working in a controversial field. J. B. R. was able to accomplish what he did because of the support and understanding he received from Louisa at home and at work.

The Foundation for Research on the Nature of Man and Duke's Psychology Department, where J. B. Rhine was professor emeritus, jointly sponsored a conference on November 28, 1980. This volume brings together all the papers presented at the conference and a few that were written specially for this volume. The latter include those by Professor C. T. K. Chari, Dr. Frederick Dommeyer and Ms. Diana Robinson.

To all the authors who have written for this volume and to those who contributed in other ways to the Rhine conference I am deeply grateful. I am also indebted to Mrs. Dorothy H. Pope, Mr. Jay Showers, and Ms. P. Spivey, who provided valuable assistance in editing this volume, to Ms. Rhea White for her help with the bibliography and to Sylvia Corless for secretarial help. Finally, my thanks are due to the members of the Board of Directors of the FRNM and its chairman, Dr. Russell Moores, for their encouragement and support.

K. Ramakrishna Rao
January 1982

Mauskopf, S. H., and McVaugh, M. R., *The Elusive Science* (Baltimore: Johns Hopkins University Press, 1980), p. 101.

Rhine, J. B. *Extra-Sensory Perception* (Boston: Branden Press, 1973; originally published, 1934).

Some Important Events
in the Life of J. B. Rhine

1895 Born on September 29 in Waterloo, Pennsylvania

1914–1915 Ohio Northern College, Ada, Ohio

1915–1916 College of Wooster, Wooster, Ohio

1917–1919 Served in World War I with the United States Marine Corps

1920 Married Louisa Ella Weckesser

1920 Entered the University of Chicago

1922 Received Bachelor of Science degree in biology from the University of Chicago

1923 Received the Master of Science degree in biology from the University of Chicago

1923–1924 Research fellow in plant physiology at Boyce Thompson Institute

1924–1926 Instructor in plant physiology at West Virginia University

1925 Received Doctor of Philosophy degree from the University of Chicago

1926–1927 Studied philosophy at Harvard University

1927 Came to Duke University to work with Dr. William McDougall

1928–1929 Instructor in philosophy and psychology at Duke University

1934 Publication of *Extra-Sensory Perception*

1937 Became a full professor of psychology at Duke University

1937 Publication of *New Frontiers of the Mind*

1937–1938 Founder and coeditor (with William McDougall) of *The Journal of Parapsychology*

1938 First report of experiments on precognition begun in 1933

1938 Symposium on parapsychology at the American Psychological Association at Columbus, Ohio

1940 Publication (with colleagues) of *Extrasensory Perception After Sixty Years*

1942–1957 Senior editor, *Journal of Parapsychology*

1943 Report of experiments in psychokinesis begun in 1934

1947 Publication of *The Reach of the Mind*

1950 Address to the Royal Society of Medicine in London

1953 Publication of *New World of the Mind*

1957 Publication (with J. G. Pratt) of *Parapsychology: Frontier Science of the Mind*

1957 Founding of the Parapsychological Association

1962 Formation of the Foundation for Research on the Nature of Man

1965 Publication of *Parapsychology from Duke to FRNM*

1965 Granada Guildhall Lecture: London

1966 Gift of 460 acres of land in Orange County to the Foundation for Research on the Nature of Man

1968 Publication (with Robert Brier) of *Parapsychology Today*

1971 Publication of *Progress in Parapsychology*

1978 Smithsonian Institution lecture

1978 Taught a course on Parapsychology and Religion at Southern Methodist University, Dallas, Texas

1980 Elected president of the Society for Psychical Research (London)

1980 Died on February 20 at Hillsborough, North Carolina

J. B. Rhine: Man and Scientist

Louisa E. Rhine

A few introductory remarks seem especially in order in connection with the personality of J. B. Rhine and his scientific work. I think that to an extraordinary degree some of his particular personality characteristics were responsible for the specific work he accomplished. I want to mention a few of these.

These particular characteristics, of course, were both hereditary and environmental. Heredity is a complex subject and I will not enlarge on it here except to mention one characteristic which I think all those who knew him will recognize and agree was inborn. That was a serious and one-track cast of mind, which meant that he was not much interested in trivialities and that to topics that interested him he gave full and consistent attention.

Not so generally known, however, are some aspects of his early environment, which it would appear left their marks on his personality. One of the earliest of these is recorded in an autobiographical sketch he once wrote for a college class. In it he tells that he was born in a log cabin in the mountains of southern Pennsylvania and that there were no near neighbors, so that for the first five years of his life he had no playmates except his sister, two years older than he. As a consequence, he was, he says, "as shy as a wild turkey," and so, instead of people, he early felt at home with the great out-of-doors. He writes, "I learned to love the big blue mountains, the rich dark woods, and the great brown hills. Even to this day," he continues, "I feel that I belong more to them than to the crowded cities." Again, I think all those who came to know him personally can readily see that the twig so bent foreshadowed the man he became.

It was not only the love of nature and the out-of-doors that was a life-long characteristic of J. B. Rhine. Another was what I might call his aloneness: a marked and definite independence of mind, a freedom from, and even an unawareness of, social pressures,

1

especially in regard to the opinions of others. He felt no need to be influenced by them unless, after consideration, he could approve. And so, any ideas, opinions, or conclusions he held were the result of his own careful and logical scrutiny. They were not copied from anyone else and were as likely as not to run counter to those of others. The result was that he was inherently a skeptic, not a follower, and his opinions were not casually changed or easily abandoned. They were modified only by new evidence.

Another circumstance of his childhood and boyhood should be mentioned, even in a brief sketch like this, for it was one that it would seem must have helped mould the personality that could sustain a decades-long struggle to pursue unchanged the direction of his interest however unpopular and controversial it might be. This was the fact that because of his father's unrest and unending search for a better opportunity, J. B.'s family moved eleven times, he says, during his school years before high school. This meant that repeatedly, nearly every year in fact, he was the "new boy" on the school playground. Because of what seems to be an unwritten law of juvenile male behavior in such situations, a new boy must fight his way to social acceptance by the crowd. And this is what this perennial new boy had to do. As those school years passed, he had to do it not only for himself but, as they came along, for his younger brothers too. As he says, to pick on them was his own prerogative and he shared it with no others.

As one can see now, along with the need to fight when challenged, went the corollary that you don't give up when attacked. Instead you stand your ground and battle through to peace and eventual acceptance. He may not have been aware of learning this lesson, but it must have been stamped indelibly into his unconscious.

These personality characteristics, of course, affected also his choice of topic for research. That topic, briefly stated, began as the question: Does the human spirit survive the death of the body? Eventually it took the more general form: Does human nature include any aspect other than the physical? As you all may know, his interest in what came to be the problem can be traced back to adolescence when he came to feel deeply the dominant religious attitudes of his community. With the intensity and single-mindedness of his nature, that religious response colored his outlook and directed his aspirations until his college days. As he characterized it, that period was his "age of feeling." Later, in college, came the "age of reason," when he began to look critically at the religious beliefs he had held since boyhood. This led to complete disillusionment, which he took with all the seriousness of his nature. It resulted in a thorough-going mechanistic outlook, an outlook that persisted for a period of years, including several in the Marine Corps.

But when, the war over, he returned to college and heard of the field of psychical research, it rearoused in him the old interest in the question of survival. Entirely skeptical as he was, he nevertheless had to find out what the people in these societies for psychical research reported. He found, of course, that the question of survival was still open, although some evidence supporting the possibility was reported. But the main method of inquiry had depended on the use of mediums, and that, to him, did not seem good enough to support so weighty a conclusion as that the deceased survive and can communicate with the living.

Since by then he was in graduate-school days and deep into the use of strict objective scientific method, he wondered what that method might produce if applied to the great question of survival. With his mechanistic outlook challenged by some of the results reported by the SPR, his very nature and background required that he look for the answer without any question about the length of time it might take. This is something of J. B.'s background when, in 1926, college days and a few years of teaching over, he decided to turn full time to his basic interest.

We all know of the quandary many young persons, and men especially, face when they come to the crossroads of career selection. In J. B.'s case any such uncertainty vanished once he realized that the question of man's total nature could be attacked by the same method used universally in the study of man's physical nature.

It was after this that the problem, first phrased as that of "survival," became more broadly thought of as the question whether human nature includes any aspect beyond the physical. Once J. B. was launched on that investigation — and given his nature — he never, I am sure, considered for himself any other field of endeavor.

However, I can think of at least two possible deterrents that, given a different kind of personality, might have diverted or deterred him, either at the beginning or somewhere along the way. One of them he was aware of then; the other, certainly not. The one of which he was aware was simply a matter of economics. In those graduate-school days, soon after he first heard of psychical research, he had tried to find a way by which he could turn from plant chemistry to the investigation of psychic phenomena. On June 27,

1923, he wrote three letters of inquiry for scholarships or positions in which he might get support while training to become an investigator in the area of psychical research. In each letter he made it clear that he would leave the field in which he was about to get a Master's, the Ph.D. to follow, and change to the other if he could find support.

The first letter went to Frederick K. Edwards, president of the ASPR in New York. The answer was encouraging as to the need for workers with an educational background like J. B.'s, but no financial aid was available. He advised J. B. to read up on his own and he gave advice as to what to read.

The second letter went to Dr. William McDougall, head of the Psychology Department at Harvard, asking if a fellowship was available by which J. B. could maintain himself if he left plant chemistry for full-time training in psychical research. The answer was that only one such fellowship had been established and it was held by Gardner Murphy. There was some money at Stanford University, but it did not seem to be available.

The third letter was addressed to Prof. Joseph Jastrow, Psychology Department, University of Wisconsin. The reply was a recommendation against J. B.'s leaving his present field for psychical research, which, Jastrow said, was "largely concerned with the elucidation of error, partly with the explanation of obscure phenomena." He said, "Positions are few and often the critical attitude is the very obstacle."

J. B., therefore, was fully aware that psychic research offered no monetary return. The fact that it was an unpopular field was very clear, and even Dr. Jastrow's emphasis on the critical attitude with which it was often met, could have been a deterrent. All that, however, did not count against the importance of the topic for humanity as well as for J. B. himself. As in the past, he assumed that such considerations as the financial one would take care of themselves incidentally, once the major objective was undertaken.

The other possible deterrent, as I said, was one which he did not then suspect: that to any positive results that might be secured in the investigation, the general reaction of scientists — some psychologists especially — would be as strongly negative as it turned out to be. This, of course, he did not know; nor, I think, did he ever imagine it until after the publication of his monograph, *Extra-Sensory Perception*, when it fell on him over succeeding years like unending tons of bricks. In his preface to that book he says, in a tone that anyone launching a new idea might use:

It is to be expected, I suppose, that these experiments will meet with a considerable measure of incredulity and perhaps even hostility from those who presume to know, even without experiment, that such things as they indicate simply cannot be.

And so, he was prepared for "a considerable measure of incredulity and perhaps even hostility," but not for the viciousness or durability of it. He did not know then or even faintly foresee that, even decades later, what he called in his preface "the inevitable reactionary response to all things new and strange" would be resounding against his investigations just about as stridently as ever; nor could he have guessed that his last effort, even in old age and failing health, would have to be expended in defense of even his own basic honesty. No, he certainly did not foresee that. Instead, he thought already in 1934 when the monograph was published, that he would see signs of decline in this reaction when, as he said, the world turns "a scientific attitude toward the new facts." But he did not foresee then that that time—if it ever does come—would not come during his lifetime. And, without that dogged, unquestioning devotion to the solution of the problem—which he thought of as benefiting humanity as well as himself—he might have been discouraged and diverted somewhere along the way. But to a personality combination of hereditary single-mindedness and early training in meeting adversity head-on, such turning back or away was unthinkable. I'm sure it would have been so, if he could have known it, even at the start.

But he did not know then, either, that those same characteristics that kept him from being diverted when the obstacles were greater than he had foreseen, could also account for his success in eliciting from his subjects, even in the unpracticed beginning of his research, the evidence that would lead to the answer to his basic question.

As we all know now, but no one knew then, psi ability is particularly fragile and elusive in its expression and dependence on the psychological "atmosphere." In the list of well-known human abilities, I think of it as somewhat like humor, which also depends on certain not easily defined conditions. Few people can fulfill, on demand, the request, "Now be funny. See if you can make me laugh."

As we all know, too, in the attempt to discover and understand almost any unknown, the first attempts to unravel the secret often seem by hindsight to have been clumsy, if not actually counterproductive. But in J. B.'s attempt to unravel this secret, it did not turn out that way, for the very seriousness and intensity with which he asked the question of his student subjects affected them with something like contagion so that they took the task he set for them in the same way. Neither teacher nor student knew that such an attitude was necessary; but once they caught the spirit and became involved, the proper attitude resulted and together they got the answer, or what was then at least the promise of an answer. And as it seems now, they got it because the spirit which they brought to it supplied what one could call the "yeast," the ferment necessary in this recipe for a psi experiment.

Later, when other experimenters often failed to duplicate the results, even though they followed carefully all the points of technique J. B. had described, they were baffled; and for a time and to an extent, J. B. was too. But the fact was that in this recipe the "yeast," the necessary spirit, was not mentioned. I went back then to the account of the tests reported in that first book and found not the slightest mention of it.

Possibly the atmosphere in which these early subjects worked was all the more effective because they and the experimenter too were unaware of this ingredient. But as it appears now, it had been unconsciously created by the nature of the experimenter and the combination of factors that defined his personality. Together they created the yeast that was such an important ingredient of the test.

And so, as I said, I think it was certain particular characteristics of J. B.'s personality that made him able to accomplish his particular scientific work, which then became the basis on which many others have carried on the investigation. This was true in the beginning when an important condition for a successful psi test was unknown and he unwittingly supplied it. It was true also over the years when obstacles greater than he had ever contemplated confronted him. Because of those characteristics, he never dreamed of turning aside. Just as when, as the new boy on the playground, he could not give up or dodge the struggle, in this larger arena too, he could only face it and go on. And as a consequence, in his last days, I know he took a large measure of satisfaction in believing, as he did, that psi ability in the human personality is now established. He knew it was the answer to his question.

J. B. as Family Man

This book looks at J. B. Rhine from many points of view. My contribution is about J. B. as a family man. I am his eldest daughter, the second of his four children. I was born during the first decade of his work at Duke, perhaps the busiest and most exciting period of the ESP investigation. How my parents managed four small kids as well as they did during that time when they were already well into their thirties and on a rather limited income is still a mystery to me. I now know that my mother quietly did more than her share of the parenting in the same matter-of-fact way that she displayed in all their joint endeavors. This account might well be the story of both my parents and their remarkable partnership of almost sixty years — but that is a story which deserves its own attention elsewhere.

I hope that a focus on J. B. as seen within his family will provide a clearer understanding of him as a person, although understandably it will be biased, for which I make no apology. I will include some information about J. B.'s own father and mother which I obtained from him during the last six months, when, in his eighty-fourth year, he finally was persuaded that he had a personal story worth telling.

My earliest memories of my father are a blur of sensations: the feel and smell of his large bushy head of hair as he carried me piggyback, the thrill of being tossed up in the air as he greeted me coming home from work at night, the sound of the little tune he'd hum to lull me to sleep at night, though he never knew that I often quieted down simply out of sympathy for him and not because of the quality of his music. J. B. had no end of interesting aspects for children — he could peel an apple in one long unbroken peel, he could lead us to hidden springs back in the deep woods, and he could play wonderful marching music on his accordion which he would also use to march us off to bed at night. There was never any doubt that we cared for and were cared about by J. B.

7

Early in childhood I discovered that my playmates too had a real fascination and affection for J. B. I can still visualize my friend Leah Lloyd at age 7 telling me sadly that she wished J. B. was her father, and I got my first awareness that not everyone was so blessed. My parents were consistently kind to and interested in our friends, and our house and yard were always a congregating place for the neighborhood children, as it was also for the Lab staff and students on weekends. Only much later did I stop to wonder how my mother ever managed all of that so well! Our large backyard at 908 Club Boulevard contained special attractions handmade by J. B. There were the usual swings, but also a slide built with a bump in the middle for extra excitement, and even more thrilling, a large disc-shaped merry-go-round which spun around on an axle and made us the envy of all our friends until we finally wore it out. It was not until this year, listening to J. B.'s memories of his own childhood, that I realized that he had essentially repeated what his own father had done for him years before in the hills of Pennsylvania, including the merry-go-round. In J. B.'s words, "I'm right there. I can see where the swing was that Dad built for us out of a whiskey barrel stave over on the hill under an apple tree. The fact that I can remember these things so well indicates that he made them interesting." Well, I would add, not any more interesting than his son did for his own children.

As his father had done for him also, J. B. constantly encouraged us to inquire and to be curious about the world around us, particularly about the unusual and the unexplored. He recalls his father reading to him from a prized adventure book, Stanley's *Travels in Darkest Africa*; years later he got this book from his father to pass along the excitement to my brother Robbie and me in our early years. And for all of us there was a standing offer of a penny for every really unusual and interesting sight we could spot along the way on a long car trip. Visitors may recall that his office always contained a variety of interesting objects, like the rock which would bend or the wooden puzzles that simply couldn't be explained. Of course, ESP stories and reports were commonplace topics at the supper table. Our home was a frequent meeting place for fascinating people, both those connected with work at the lab, and others, like Mr. Joseph, who could put a pin through the skin of his hand without making it bleed, or Mr. Wallace, the local magician who loved to hoodwink us by talking doubletalk.

J. B. took an active role in advising us, as well as all inquiring young people, about how to broaden our outlook on the world. Science in the broad sense was his deepest love. He completely turned around my distaste for high school chemistry by essentially reteaching it to me at night with all the wonder and excitement of Madame Curie explaining the inner workings of the atom. I can remember the very spot on a walk along Club Boulevard where J. B. explained to me the beauty and necessity of the scientific method as the highest achievement of man's rational mind in learning the basic facts of nature.

Again following the example of his father before him, J. B. provided an excellent model of the moral, healthy, and self-disciplined man, although he was no doubt totally unaware of the impact he was having on us. I never knew him to do anything dishonest, unethical, or shoddy, nor to overindulge in any strong food or drink. (He always stopped the delicious apple cider he made from becoming too alcoholic.) I never recall his saying a harsh word to us or to Mother, although I am sure we children often tested his patience. Still, he was frequently very firm. Being sent in to "talk" to J. B. about some misdeed was a far greater deterrent than any corporal punishment. Some insight into his control of temper comes from a short autobiography that he wrote in college, where he reflects upon the pain he suffered as a child at a time when his parents were quarreling. He resolved at that time never to inflict upon his wife and family that trauma he felt so intensely as a child. And he never did.

Fun for J. B., and in turn for the rest of us growing up, usually involved getting outdoors, sometimes by playing softball, croquet, or badminton in our own backyard, but usually going off on a hike in the woods or a swim in the Eno River. If we were lucky we might pack a picnic and go off to Crystal or Hogan's Lake, where water fights with J. B. were a matter of course. Another source of fun for him was music, either playing the mouth organ or accordion by ear as his mother had, or sitting trancelike in his big chair listening to classical music on record or radio. I used to resent having to be quiet on Sunday afternoons while the opera was on, but indeed I am grateful for his taking me so often to the Duke concerts and symphonies, and most especially for his patient attention and encouragement of my own attempts to play the piano. His interest in my playing "with feeling" helped me utilize music as an emotional outlet, as I believe it was for him. I think J. B. was indeed a very emotional man, well-controlled or even overcontrolled as he often appeared on the surface.

I could speak of many other endearing and inspiring qualities of J. B. as a father and grandfather, but the picture is not complete without some of the irritating aspects of his character. One of them was that he was often so busy or preoccupied with this ESP business that it's a wonder we didn't all hate the subject. Other little girls' fathers would be home early in the evening, certainly on weekends, and definitely all day on holidays, but not our father. He was always at "the Lab." And it was several years before I realized that "Seminar" was not some far-off place which he seemed to be forever visiting. No doubt my annoyance today at being kept waiting stems from the many hours I had to wait for J. B. when we were to ride or walk home from the lab with him. Probably it was only due to Mother's calm acceptance of the situation that we learned to accept my father as well as we did. Somehow we grew up knowing that something "important" was going on, although just what it all meant then was a mystery to the child mind. I know we often half-jokingly wished we had a "normal" family.

Figuring out what "famous" or "important" meant was another problem for me as a child. I can remember kindly Mrs. McDougall mildly reprimanding us three girls for some sort of misbehavior, probably making too much noise, "Now you must remember, your father is an important person!" But J. B. himself wasn't much help in figuring out what that meant. When asked, he would pooh-pooh anything personal with his strange and bothersome sense of modesty, and instead describe, at some length, the importance of ESP. (An interesting sideline here is my recollection of J. B.'s telling me in hushed tones about Dr. McDougall: "This is the greatest man you will ever meet." At the time, I felt a strange conflict in my own mind at having to choose between this man and my own father on that score.)

Actually, it was not until much later as a teenager that the full impact of what "important" meant came home to me in a strange and frightening way. One day during World War II, J. B. became suddenly very ill with what we later learned was spinal meningitis. Because of Mother's strong insistence, the family doctor came out a second time to the house when she was unable to rouse my father from what had seemed like a very bad cold. After taking a quick look, Dr. Spikes hurried to the phone, making sure that Mother was out of earshot. Hiding behind the door, I overheard the chilling words of the doctor as he argued forcefully with the hospital people who obviously had no beds, "But you *have* to admit him. This is Dr.

Rhine. He's an important person, and it's a matter of life and death!"
I never was sorry he was "important" after that.

One habit of J. B.'s which was a source of some trouble for me
was his slow and laborious manner of speech, no doubt a reflection of
his careful, one-track mind. I think my own impatience and
frequent tendency to interrupt surely stems from having to sit quietly
and wait for a break in his dinnertable conversation, especially since
he rarely looked at his audience. Often I marvelled at Mother's
seemingly angelic qualities of patience as she would wait for J. B. to
make a point in paragraph rather than sentence form.

But when the overall measure is taken, J. B. has surely been a
powerful positive force in my life, as he has been for my siblings, his
grandchildren, and even the little great-granddaughter whom he
loved so much during his last years. Last Christmas (1979), when he
was already quite ill, six of his grandchildren happened to be sitting
in my living room after a family gathering, reminiscing spontaneously about the impact this man had already made in their
young lives. One spoke of one of J. B.'s mottoes: "If you just add 15
minutes more each time you practice, you can accomplish almost
anything." Another spoke of how J. B. had served as a real father
figure to him and how he hated to do things which would disappoint
J. B.'s high expectations of him. Several of them spoke enthusiastically of how they owed their love of the outdoors to J. B. All of them
laughed at the crazy fun they had had with J. B. and his old Jeep
truck in the woods. They all marvelled at the breadth and depth of
knowledge on practically any subject which J. B. still had at the age
of 84, even with practically all of his senses failing him. And so on
and on. I daresay no man has left behind a more devoted following
within his own family or set a pace so inspiring to them.

One of his greatest legacies has been the example of his determination. J. B. spoke of his own father much as I might speak of
him: "Anything he tried, he tried hard." Clearly J. B. was a much-
loved son of both his parents who early on was expected to make his
mark on the world. He recalls his mother telling neighbors when he
was only four, "Banks is going to be a preacher someday," which was
the highest achievement a religious mother could want for her son in
those days. And there was the constant reminder from his father to
do well in school. "You're going to need that knowledge someday.
You're going to amount to something." Whether from these expectations or his own desire to stand out among classmates, where because
of family moves he was frequently a newcomer or stranger, J. B.

always did well in school, often despite fairly big obstacles. Even when there was not a challenge he seems to have created one, as he did in the Marines when he decided to be the best rifleman that he could rather than go off into town with the others and drink. His determination led to his winning the big national Presidential Rifle Match in 1919, a fantastic achievement for a man who never shot a gun before or since.

But I think the most poignant and meaningful statement of this philosophy of life-as-a-challenge was what he said to me a little over a year ago today. I had gone to J. B.'s Watts Street office to console him when I heard the sad news that his blindness was not going to be correctable by surgery. As I knelt beside his big easy chair where he was sitting quietly in the dusk, I found my tears rising. Then J. B. consoled me with these words: "Well, I am a person who has always had to have a challenge in order to find out how much I could do, and this is just another of life's challenges which will be a good test for me." As I wept silently, I thought to myself how all men, even my own dear father, have their limitations, and that this challenge would surely be one not even he could surmount.

Often since his death in February, I have wished that J. B.'s own original interest in the question of survival had had a more positive outcome, for it would be so comforting to have some evidence that his spirit survives in some way yet. Yet the most important lesson I have gotten from J. B. is that of unswerving devotion to truth and reality as a man can know it, using the best methods of science, rather than belief, fantasy, or wish. And so I must be content to know that he survives in his impact on me, his family, and on so many others. I must hope that the discoveries he made, though different from what he supposed at the outset, will help to enlarge our view of the human mind. And I think that all of his modesty aside, for a "plain son of the hills" as he characterized himself, J. B. Rhine would have to agree that he did lead a rich and fulfilling life, that he did make a significant contribution to mankind, and last but not least, that he was a great success as a father, husband, and family man.

Joseph Banks Rhine:
Teacher and Friend

ELIZABETH A. McMAHAN

Most of us can point to outstanding persons we have known who, through special challenge, encouragement, or support at crucial points in our careers, profoundly influenced our lives. For many of us this role belongs to Doctors J. B. and Louisa E. Rhine. Their *separate* influences cannot easily be distinguished, for in both their professional and their personal lives, the Rhines were a totally integrated team. I will continually refer to Louisa Rhine in these pages, for without her, my memories of J. B. Rhine are only half complete.

This account is necessarily a personal one, drawing on memories from over 37 years of close association, but I think I represent the many students who have been drawn into the Rhines' orbit. Often we were first attracted by their exciting investigations into ESP and PK, but on closer acquaintance we found that the Rhines were special in their own right. We came to know them as wise friends to whom we took our triumphs and our defeats. They could be counted on for comforting words when our egos were shattered, for pats-on-the-back when jobs were well done, and for straight-from-the-shoulder admonitions when we deserved them. They inspired our research efforts. They provided a big part of our recreation and our social life. They made us believe that we were important to them, and we valued their opinions above all others. In their presence we were ashamed to be petty, unjust, or mean. We knew that they tended to see the best in us, and so unconsciously we *did* our best.

I was 18 and a sophomore at a small teacher's college in western North Carolina when I first made contact with the Rhines. I had learned about the Duke work in parapsychology the previous year from my freshman faculty advisor, Burke Smith (a former research

13

assistant at the Parapsychology Laboratory), and immediately I had begun testing myself and my friends for ESP. By my sophomore year I had read *Extra-Sensory Perception, New Frontiers of the Mind*, and most of *ESP after Sixty Years*. One day I plucked up the courage to write to Dr. Rhine to tell him about my ESP tests (which were yielding results consistently above chance) and to ask his advice about certain testing procedures. I recall my delight at receiving an immediate response, one characteristic of Dr. Rhine's invariably encouraging attitude toward young people. In his letter, he complimented my initiative in experimentation, but he gently suggested that my testing procedures might have left open the possibility that unconsciously I could have obtained sensory cues from the backs of the cards. He suggested ways of eliminating this possibility and sent me a packet of testing materials. He also asked me to continue to let him know the results of my experiments. This direct exposure to scientific method, to the procedure of eliminating systematically all counterexplanations before claiming evidence for a given hypothesis (plus the heady experience of correspondence with a scientist of such international note) marked the beginning of my interest in a career in scientific research.

At the end of my sophomore year, Dr. Rhine invited me to spend a few weeks of the summer vacation period at the Duke Parapsychology Laboratory to see, as he put it, "if this kind of research continues to appeal to you." For me it was the beginning of 11 years as a research assistant and associate in the Parapsychology Laboratory, for I transferred to Duke that fall and began some of the most exciting years of my life.

Perhaps Dr. Rhine's role as teacher and friend can be most clearly shown through several anecdotes, which to me characterize his warmth, his generosity of spirit, his total integrity, his sense of justice, and his love of music and of nature.

He was a very kind and generous man. Not long after I came to the Parapsychology Laboratory in the summer of 1943, Dr. Rhine learned that my father was having great difficulty during those war years in finding field hands to help with harvesting the sorghum cane that was the major cash crop on the family farm. It appeared that much of the cane would have to go unharvested. Dr. Rhine immediately arranged to spend a two-week "vacation" on our farm, working daily in the cane fields from dawn until long after dark, stripping the stalks, loading the cane carts, feeding the mill, canning the molasses. He did the hard physical work of three or four regular field hands. I can recall the way he motivated the other workers with his cheerful bantering and by his headlong example. I remember his enjoyment of the watermelons we would eat in the fields, the smiling compliments he paid my mother's cooking, the easy camaraderie with the relatives and the neighbors who came to visit. That farming community still considers Dr. Rhine one of its own, and thanks to his all-out help, an economic crisis for our family was averted.

Dr. Rhine was a believer in human dignity, justice, and the rights of the underdog. He was a liberal in the best sense of that word. In the late 1940s a religious sect in Durham received much publicity for its use of rattlesnakes in its religious rituals. Outraged citizens and newspaper articles ranted against the practice and urged suppression by the police. Dr. Rhine wrote a letter to the editor of the Durham paper. He did not encourage activities dangerous to the public, but he urged a cooling of judgments and a warning against official suppression of sincere religious beliefs. It was a steadying voice in an inflamed situation, and it illustrates his way of looking at both sides of any controversy and trying to see that justice was impartial. He was never afraid to speak up on the unpopular side.

In the late 1950s the country was in turmoil following the Supreme Court's ruling on the desegregation of public schools. Newspapers carried pictures of angry whites clustered at school entrances hurling threats and insults at black children being escorted to school by federal marshals. Dr. Rhine wrote a letter to *Life* magazine, suggesting that it use its editorial pages to praise the courage of the black youngsters who daily had to run the gauntlet of hatred to reach their classes. His letter ended: "This may not yet be entirely the land of the free, but it is certainly the home of the brave." *Life* printed his letter, so expressive of his love of justice, in its entirety as the editorial itself.

The Rhines, by their example, underlined the importance of keeping up with local, state, national, and world affairs. They considered it a citizen's responsibility to cast an informed vote at election time. They were voracious readers, keeping abreast not only of happenings in the field of parapsychology, but subscribing to numerous newspapers, journals, and magazines in a variety of fields. It was in their home that I first encountered the *Saturday Review, Harper's Magazine, The New Statesman and Nation.* Several books were always in the process of consumption. Louisa Rhine, who never ate breakfast, often read aloud at the breakfast table from the latest volume of interest. Dr. Rhine especially enjoyed biographical and autobiographical literature. Frequently, he would ask his younger acquaintances if we had read this book or that article, launching a discussion of the ideas therein and encouraging our interest in broad topics.

Dr. Rhine was an unusually fine teacher. In addition to being director of the Parapsychology Laboratory he was also professor of psychology at Duke. He taught an undergraduate course on "human personality" and a graduate seminar in parapsychology. I consider them two of the very best courses I ever took. In "human personality" we discussed topics such as the mind–body problem, the cultural and biological bases of ethics, and the place of human personality in the universe. We used, as a starting point for discussion, Dr. William McDougall's analysis of personality into the factors of disposition, temperament, temper, intellect, and character, and we discussed the integration of all personality factors into a unified whole. Central to the course's philosophy was the mind–body problem: Can human personality be explained solely on the basis of physical laws that appear to govern the body, or is there another aspect, the mind, with additional attributes? Dr. Rhine's years of research in parapsychology had convinced him that there was evidence to support a belief in the existence of the nonphysical aspect, and he told us about this research and its bearing on an understanding of the nature of human personality.

One day he asked each of us to write an essay on the topic "My Philosophy of Life." In it we were to tell what gave our lives meaning, how we came by our particular sets of values, and the degree of our satisfaction with these beliefs as blueprints for guiding our lives. It was an exercise in self-revelation, and it had a more profound effect on our own insights and maturation than perhaps any other assignment of our college careers.

Dr. Rhine did not tell us what to believe. He challenged us to think, to refuse to accept beliefs passively, and to seek answers, using the methods of science. In his class we learned to view human personality in all its aspects as an integral part of the natural universe. If it should be shown to have nonphysical attributes, that would not make it any less a natural phenomenon, but would indicate a need for a reassessment of our view of nature.

Dr. Rhine's style of lecturing was not that of the showman (although his classroom demonstrations of hypnosis were truly fascinating). He spoke quietly, but he captivated us with the earnestness of his arguments, his deep sincerity and honesty, and his interest in our welfare. Since he embodied the truth that example is the best precept, his teaching was not confined to the classroom. For many of us he remains the model in our own lives as teachers and scientists.

Whenever we former students think of Dr. Rhine, we remember his love of music. He had never taken music lessons and he played the ocarina, mouth organ, and accordion by ear, but I never knew anyone who enjoyed music more. The Rhines had a good record library of classical music and folk songs. Even today when I hear certain music, such as Smetana's *The Moldau* or Mozart's *Eine kleine Nachtmusik*, I am at once transported in imagination to "the den" in the Rhines' house at 908 Club Boulevard. I can see Dr. Rhine (sitting in his easy chair by the record player) pause in his writing, lean back, close his eyes, and give himself up to the music.

The Rhines invariably bought several season tickets to the Duke Entertainment Series, always held in Page Auditorium, and their seats were chosen in the lower balcony section. Some of the Rhine children often accompanied them, and they frequently shared their tickets with students and colleagues. My first sight of Leonard Bernstein as a young conductor, my first exposure to *La Traviata*, my first view of *Swan Lake* was from that balcony in Page, seated alongside the Rhines in one of their reserved seats.

Dr. Rhine had a succession of accordions. On weekends when we students gathered (as we always did) at the Rhines' house, we would prevail on him to play. Seated around a campfire in the back yard we would join in singing as he made the woods ring with *Shenandoah*, *The Four Insurgent Generals*, *Sweet Betsy from Pike*, or *Du, Du liegst mir im Herzen*. He knew a variety of German songs and encouraged those of us taking German to learn them too. "It's a pleasant way to learn a language," he would say.

Whenever he heard a new song he liked he would have someone sing it until he knew the tune by heart and then he would play it. Some of his favorite accordion tunes were: *Meet Me in St. Louie, Louie* (always played with a twinkle in Mrs. Louie's direction), *Veni Sul Mar*, *The Little Silver Ring*, and *On Top of Old Smokey*. Once in a while the accordion would refuse to play a proper note, and then Dr. Rhine would break off and whistle the tune.

He reserved the ocarina for the haunting melodies that suited it best. He would play alone on a summer's evening from the lower end of the big backyard, the clear, sweet notes of *Drink to Me Only* or *The Last Rose of Summer* drifting up through the darkness.

Perhaps even more than music J. B. Rhine loved nature. He and

Louisa Rhine had taken their graduate degrees in botany at the University of Chicago and both loved the woods, the fields, and green growing things. Both had very green thumbs, and their gardens (both vegetable and flower) were always bountiful. Much of the wisdom I prize from them was received as we hoed the beans or dug the potatoes. With the Rhines one didn't discuss the latest fashions or the current movie idols. As we hoed we talked about the war news, the up-coming election, the newest proclamation by the City Council, ideas for a new PK experiment, the meaning of parapsychological findings for religion. We were hoeing the Rhine's garden, I recall, when the news of President Roosevelt's death was relayed from the newscast.

Dr. Rhine appeared to enjoy all outdoor chores, from gardening to chopping wood. An activity we students especially enjoyed was to accompany the Rhines on blackberry picking expeditions. These forays were for the purpose of obtaining a supply of berries for the magnificent pies that were a specialty of Louie Rhine, and also for the fun of it. We would start before daylight on a Saturday morning, armed with berry pails and permission from various farmers to pick from the gigantic sprawls of blackberry briars that grew wild in their pastures. The farms were at some distance from town and usually we had to hike a considerable way from the nearest road, keeping a sharp lookout for unfriendly cows. Dr. Rhine was the champion blackberry picker, a red bandana tied rope-like across his brow to keep the hair out of his eyes. We would all return home with brimming pails, a sense of vast accomplishment, and a multitude of chiggers.

Dr. Rhine's idea of relaxation was to lead a strenuous hike through the woods and along some rocky stream. During the World War II years we would pool our gasoline rationing coupons. Then on Sunday afternoons the Rhine family, plus several of us students, would pile into their big old blue DeSoto and drive out to a river of our choice. In the spring we looked for the pale lavender hepatica blooms on the slopes by the Eno or the yellow dog-toothed violets by New Hope Creek, or the dwarf iris and trailing arbutus by Little River. In the fall we shuffled through the drifts of red and yellow leaves and admired the brilliant seeds of the wahoo. In the summer we swam in the deeper pools of the Eno or New Hope. In the winter we crunched over the snow-covered trails and sometimes waded across the icy water to admire a bed of running cedar on the far bank. As we walked, the Rhines were constantly naming the trees and shrubs and flowers, showing us the tiny, hidden ginger vases, pointing out the seasonal wonders.

Dr. Rhine had a special fondness for natural springs, and he knew the location of a great many, most of them in very out-of-the-way places. Often he would direct a detour from the trail in order to visit one. Under his direction, we would clear out the leaves that choked it, look for salamanders and other denizens, and even take a drink from a folded leaf cup. In all our hikes, Dr. Rhine was always in the lead, choosing the trail. Staff in hand he would stride briskly along, we trooping behind. He would soon out-distance us, but he would wait at a bend in the river or at a forking of the trail until we were within sight of him, then off he would go again. We used to swear that he picked the steepest cliffs, the brushiest terrains, and the marshiest lowlands to lead us over. One of our birthday gifts to him was a pith helmet with these words emblazoned on the front:

No path or trail his feet will sully
While he can find a creek or gully

Dr. Rhine's birthdays were always occasions for thinking up outrageous but affectionate verse in his honor. Perhaps we teased him about letting his latest cider brew explode in the refrigerator, or we immortalized some other appropriate — or inappropriate — event in his life. These contributions were usually presented at the end of one of Louisa Rhine's fabulous birthday dinners to which we students seemed always to be invited. Dr. Rhine would open each card with feigned surprise, read it aloud with much expression, and then break off, laughing heartily, as he protested with mock indignation his outrage at some of the doggerel. His tolerance of our teasing and his appreciation of our efforts kept us composing.

The Rhines' house was always a center of much activity, which included not only the immediate family (and later the grand-children), but even peripheral students and colleagues, as I have mentioned. I held most of my "PK Parties" in their living-room, the Rhine children and their friends serving as subjects in these tests of psychokinesis. In the winter time there was a warm fire in the living-room fireplace, surrounded on most weekends by the ever-present students. The Rhines were magnets; we could not resist their attraction.

During the war years the Rhines were listed with the local USO as a family that welcomed soldiers in need of a place to stay. Some of the men who took advantage of this hospitality became almost like members of the family and returned as often as they could. Weekends were always Open House at the Rhines. Sunday afternoons were usually devoted either to hiking or to a rousing softball game in the backyard. Everyone, from master sergeants to the smallest Rhine daughter, played. Dr. Rhine was usually the pitcher for his team.

When I remember the soldiers, the students, the children of acquaintances needing direction, and all the other young people helped by the Rhines, I see a pattern of love. The Rhines took in anyone in need. Far from avoiding responsibility, they went to meet it. It seemed as though they felt a personal sense of responsibility for the next generation.

Dr. Rhine was always concerned about the future of those of us who wanted to make parapsychology our field of research. He used to tell us that we should get advanced degrees in some "orthodox" subject such as psychology, mathematics, or zoology, so that we would be eligible for jobs in those areas. He knew that parapsychology's future would be uncertain for an indefinite time to come. Most of us did get our degrees in other fields, but even when we left the Parapsychology Laboratory for other careers we never lost our interest in the subject or left behind the influence of the Rhines.

One of the great advantages of an association with the Parapsychology Laboratory and the Rhines was the opportunity to meet the many visitors who came to discuss psi phenomena. Noted authors, psychologists, philosophers, biologists — they came from all over the world. We students had an unparalleled chance to meet these outstanding thinkers and to get a sense of the deep excitement of the field. Naturally the Laboratory also attracted persons who believed themselves to have special psi abilities. They ranged from the internationally famous medium, Eileen Garrett, to small town fortune-tellers and palmists. Dr. Rhine welcomed anyone with a sincere interest in psi phenomena to come to the laboratory for testing. I recall one occasion when an unknown medium arrived to be tested while Dr. Rhine was away for several days on a speaking engagement. By the time he returned, we younger researchers were out of patience with this particular subject for what we felt was her petulance and her irritating personality. We were starting to react with disdain and impatience, which, of course, fed the spiral of discontent. When, on his return, we complained to Dr. Rhine, he lost no time in bringing us back to the tenets of the Laboratory: our job as laboratory personnel was to provide foolproof testing procedures under conditions that gave the best possible chance of releasing a subject's psi abilities. Antagonizing the subject was not that kind of proper condition. Dr. Rhine's policy for the testing of mediums was one of dignity. He knew that mediumship was associated with fraud and chicanery, but he did not want to discourage the participation by psychics in the laboratory's testing program. He let it be known that in the Parapsychology Laboratory we would not set hidden traps to confound fraudulent subjects. Our tests would be straightforward and entirely open in procedure and intent. The experimental procedures, however, would preclude any possibility of the occurrence of trickery or sleight-of-hand. This approach combined scientific integrity with dignity and epitomized for me Dr. Rhine's way of setting the tone of leadership in this difficult field.

As a pioneer in parapsychology, Dr. Rhine was continually in the public eye, sometimes being honored for his insight and courage; often being ridiculed, even viciously attacked, for his temerity in continuing studies pronounced "unscientific" by some would-be guardians of science. How he could endure the accusations and innuendos, I used to wonder. Knowing his high code of honor, I was incensed—no, infuriated—at the aspersions cast by lesser men on his integrity. But I came to believe that his serenity in the face of disdain and abuse was due to his certainty that his quest was of fundamental importance to humanity. He was by nature a challenger, and he had found the crux of a truly successful life: a commitment to something grand. No mere insults could diminish for him that high purpose.

I mentioned earlier that Dr. Rhine began his scientific career as a botanist. I have often speculated in my mind on the difference it would have made to him, and to science, had he continued professionally in that field. Instead of following Dr. McDougall to Duke and beginning the Parapsychology Laboratory under McDougall's auspices, what if he had become a professor of botany or of biology at Duke or elsewhere? What if he had become a plant physiologist in some great research laboratory? Knowing his abilities and his devotion to science, I am certain that he soon would have become one of the top men in his field. I have imagined, in my fantasy, the discoveries he would have made, the honors he would have won in the world of science. He would have received all the acclaim that a lifetime of single-minded devotion to science should have merited. No one would have accused him of being a crackpot, a sly manipulator of data, a naïve believer in the occult. Life would have been interesting, and his contributions to science would have been extensive, acknowledged, and satisfying. For his sake I have almost wished, sometimes, that this fantasy were true. But I am very certain that J. B. Rhine never regretted that long-ago decision that led him and Louisa Rhine into parapsychology. In their investigation of those aspects of human personality that do not fit into the common view of the physical universe, they have broadened the horizons of science far more profoundly than they ever could have done in any more conventional way. They made the choice that, given their natures, they had to make.

Perhaps these lines from the last verse of Robert Frost's *The Road Not Taken* say it best for the Rhines:

> Two roads diverged in a wood, and I —
> I took the one less travelled by,
> And that has made all the difference.

What a difference for science and for us all.

Rhine's Contributions
to Experimental Methodology
and Standards of Research

GERTRUDE R. SCHMEIDLER

When Dr. Rao invited me to join in this collection of tributes I felt grateful for the opportunity to express some of my great respect for Dr. Rhine — and was well pleased at the topic assigned me. It will be a pleasure to review both Rhine's contributions to experimental methodology and his specific innovative methods, and show how he continually maintained the highest possible research standards. His contributions were so basic that they set the research patterns for many of us. They have set my own for almost forty years. It does not seem too much to say that he both founded parapsychology and determined its direction.

Psychical research had existed before, of course, but an informal paper by LeShan and Margenau [in a private communication] argues persuasively that psychical research deserves to be considered a different field. Its methods are more varied than parapsychology's, and its topics cover a wider range. Its goals overlap with parapsychology's but its subgoals are different. It tries to evaluate and integrate even weak findings relevant to its problems, but parapsychology tries to study only topics where rigorous controls can be employed. If we agree with this argument, we can add that parapsychology emerged as a distinctive area because of Rhine's methods, his spectacular results, his theoretical approach (which developed the methods into a methodology), as well as his gift for eye-catching nomenclature and his skills in public relations and organization.

In thinking about his work, I keep remembering and wanting to paraphrase a quotation from the Roman emperor Octavius, who boasted that he found Rome a city of brick and left it a city of marble. Dr. Rhine was not a boastful man, but we can say for him what he did not say for himself: that when he began his life work he found the study of psychical research, and he left for us the science of parapsychology.

How did this come about? To trace it, let us put ourselves in imagination back in the 1920s. Suppose you were trained as a scientist then, and wanted to do research. (I am talking about J. B. Rhine, of course, but am asking you to identify with him and his decisions.) You wanted it to be good research, careful and definitive; all research workers do. But beyond that, what you really hoped was that it would be meaningful, would help toward resolving important issues. One such issue is the nature of life. Is life only inanimate matter in some particular patterns, or is it something more? And other issues follow from this one, dealing with our place in the universe. Are we only corporeal, or do our spirits survive bodily death?

Your own area of specialization was the physiology of plant cells. This is relevant to what you want to learn, because the basic processes of plant cells surely relate to the nature of all life and thus indirectly will bear on the larger issues that concern all thoughtful human beings. But is it relevant enough? Research on plant physiology demands concentrating on its own specialized technical problems. Is each such technical problem only a short detour that will soon lead back toward the important answers? Or does the whole topic relate to the larger issues so indirectly, so remotely, that its findings will not bear on them in the foreseeable future?

It must surely have been tempting for both J. B. and Louisa Rhine, with their doctorates in biology from the prestigious University of Chicago, to stay with the topics and the methods where they were already expert. But as we all know, they succumbed to the greater temptation of trying to study their most important problems as directly as possible. Their reading of prior work in psychical research made them think that psychical abilities had perhaps already been demonstrated; and this was where they turned. They hoped to check out that "perhaps" and, if they could eliminate it, go forward, to learn more.

Now another question arose. Psychical research was not a single, simple topic; the decision to work in it could not give anyone a specific directive. Rhine categorized its phenomena neatly (Rhine, J. B., 1934/1973) while describing his own research decisions. He listed four possible sources for psychic effects, ranging from those due to "simple corporeal agency" (the example he cited was telepathy) to those due to a simple incorporeal agency such as a spirit. And for each of these four classes he listed a varied set of phenomena to investigate: psychological effects, or physiological, or physical, or pathological. His four-by-four table, with its broad areas within psychical research, left many directions open.

Then where should his own investigation begin? His useful apprenticeship with Dr. Walter Franklin Prince had trained him in the strict standards set by the best methods of psychical research, but the time was largely spent in helping expose a fraudulent medium. Interesting and worthy though such exposure may be, it is obviously not the route to major scientific advances. Other early work with a psychic animal subject had seemed more promising. Rhine argued to himself — and to his readers, in this first book — that research on any of the 16 subtopics would have ramifications leading to the others. He then put forth the problem for his first major project in these words: "Are there really dependable evasions of psychological laws (as they are regarded today) by corporeal personalities? In other words, can we find persons able to demonstrate the more commonly reported sort of apparent exception to psychological laws — mainly, cognition of events without the usual sensory or rational experience required by our habitual concepts for the knowing act?" (Rhine, J. B., 1934/1973, p. 11).

He decided, in short, to begin by "contributing independent proof of E.S.P. as a primary objective" (p. 15). He would work in a most difficult field, but would start with what seemed the simplest part of it. He would do this by searching for gifted subjects, who could give firm, reliable results. His next questions were: Where would he find these subjects, and what methods should he use to obtain those results?

Let me break away from the narrative account of how his contributions developed, to pick it up later after introducing another theme — a theme which will make it easier for some of you to identify with Rhine, but perhaps harder for others to do so. Because his talks and writings emphasized general issues and theories, we may be slow to recognize that he was basically an empiricist; his thinking was more inductive than deductive. Often, perhaps almost always, his theory was not only suggested by observations, but was then built up and modified by further observations.

Consider, for example, because it is relevant to his next research decision, his emphasis on the need to evaluate data in mathematical terms, the need that led to his developing and advocating a forced-choice method for ESP tests. On what was the need based? On the observation that without such quantitative evaluation, controversy is endless. With a spontaneous case or other qualitatively interesting coincidence, a decision as to whether it was psychic or was due to chance or normal causes demands a subjective weighting of the alternatives. One person's private weighting may lead to one conclusion, but the next person's assessment can lead to the opposite. Again and again such qualitative judgments have been shown to be unconvincing to others; their appeal rests on the unscientific basis of personal judgment and personal authority. It was these observations about inconclusive controversies that gave him the prescription for his own basic research. It should be susceptible to statistical evaluation, because this is objective, public, and generally accepted.

Now to pick up the chronological account. A first suggestion for a possible source of gifted subjects came from the investigation conducted by the Rhines on a target of opportunity, the horse "Lady." They had found her responses initially showed telepathic success without sensory cues, but that later her telepathic scores declined and she eventually showed dependence on sensory cuing. Perhaps careful work with animals would give the solid base that was needed. Rhine began by trying to find such suitable subjects, but soon learned — the hard way — that gifted infrahuman animals were in short supply in his neighborhood. He therefore turned to testing the humans who were so amply available at Duke and its environs.

How was he to do his testing? He had, as we saw, laid down one rule for himself: there must be quantitative evaluation of whatever results he obtained. This was most readily achieved by forced choices within some specified sample of targets, because when a large sample of such targets was randomly arranged the theoretical odds of chance success were known. He naturally began with the targets which had come down to him from previous investigators: the digits from 0 to 9 and the letters of the alphabet.

But he was too keen an observer to stay with those targets for long. He saw what was not widely recognized then: that stimulus preference for certain of the digits or letters was so strong as to distort the responses. Further, sequence effects were a major source of response bias. After responding with a 2, a person would be all too likely to continue with 4, 6, 8, or with 3, 4, 5; and the tendency to use letters of the alphabet to spell words or parts of words is almost irresistible. Rhine recognized that the target population should consist of items with equal or nearly equal drawing power and that there should be no obvious, generally used way of ordering them.

His colleagues in the Department of Psychology at Duke were encouraged by the Department's chairman, Dr. William McDougall, to offer advice on these problems. One of them, Dr. Karl Zener, was especially helpful. Largely due to Zener's suggestions, a set of target cards was constructed. Each carried one of five symbols: a circle, rectangle, plus, five-pointed star, and set of two wavy lines. After some early exploration of ways to present them, they were arranged into packs of 25, with five of each symbol in a pack. Out of these Zener cards came, with minor modifications, the modern set of five ESP cards which is so widely known.

This was a major advance in method, and I will cite some of its advantages. One is that in general there is neither a strong stimulus preference among the symbols nor any common tendency among subjects for sequence effects. Another is that a batch of five units is not too large to be retained in primary memory. A third, extremely important in Rhine's approach, is that feedback to the subjects about their success will by chance give an intermediate level approximating one positive reinforcement in five trials. This provides enough encouragement to keep the subjects hopeful, and it provides enough failures to make the task stay challenging. A fourth is that the series of 25 is intermediate between a trivially short task and a discouragingly long one. And of course a fifth is that when a long series of the targets is randomly arranged, the obtained success can be judged objectively as falling within or outside of the limits conventionally assigned to chance.

For statistical evaluation of the data, Rhine sought the best advice and continued seeking it; he turned to and continued to depend on two fine mathematicians. Drs. J. A. Greenwood and T. N. E. Greville. He used their formulas to evaluate his data. Although it puts us ahead of our story, it seems appropriate to state here that when their formula showed his results to be extrachance and outsiders criticized his use of statistics, he was on safe ground. He appealed to the Institute for Mathematical Statistics and their president-elect signed and issued publicly a statement which Rhine often delighted to quote: "If the Rhine investigation is to be fairly attacked it must be on other than mathematical grounds."

Here, then, was a first methodological contribution: a simple and appropriate method for forced choices which avoided a whole series of pitfalls in earlier techniques.

You remember that Rhine's primary objective in his first major project was to find gifted subjects who would reliably show high extrachance scores. His dazzling success in finding them would be a pleasure to describe and interesting to examine, but because this is a topic for other papers I will merely mention it in passing. What is noteworthy for my topic of methodology is that while searching for and working with these subjects, he did not blind himself to other possibilities; he did not keep singlemindedly to his first narrow objective. Instead, his keen observations of portions of his data led to two further important methodological advances and to a gallant attempt at a third.

The first of these three related to his decision to test for the gifted subject. This purpose implies a theory: that there is a dichotomy between those capable of prolonged, clear success and others who are incapable of it. It foreshadows Millar's recent provocative hypothesis (1979) that positive findings in psi will come only if the research includes psi stars; that is, only if there are either gifted subjects who are psi stars or else experimenters who are psi stars and can influence their subjects to respond with significant data. The thesis is defensible biologically, because some human characteristics like albinism or some forms of giantism are similarly discontinuous. An ESP ability may thus have a genetic base or some decisive congenital or developmental cause. Rhine's thinking tenatatively followed this line, and one early finding tended to support it. When he asked his subjects whether members of their families showed psychic ability, almost all the star subjects answered affirmatively but the other subjects did not.

A lesser man, having developed this approach and apparently begun to confirm it, would have stayed with it and not looked further. Rhine did not. He had observed well before 1934 that when he gave ESP tests to a largish group and no one individual made an outstanding score, the group mean was still likely to be high — and he did not forget this observation merely because it was irrelevant to his theory. In his second book (Rhine, J. B., 1937) he still wrote that "it seemed entirely safe to estimate that at least one in five of the persons tested showed ESP capacity" (p. 106), but his later work showed that his thinking was changing to fit his data. Tests with unselected subjects gave such interesting results that some twenty years afterward his theory had completely reversed (Rhine, J. B., 1955), and he wrote: "the assumption that certain individuals were endowed with psi ... will have to give way completely to the other extreme: that subjects are *made*, not *born*: that exceptional performance represents a combination of conditions within and around the subject, conditions that favor the functioning of psi to an exceptional degree and may—in fact, usually do—continue for only a limited period of time" (pp. 108–109).

This thesis is important both methodologically and theoretically. It leads to supplementing research on those who are presently gifted by doing research on anyone who is available. It permits a far wider range of investigations than does the earlier theory, and suggests a new set of problems for study.

The second of these three early observations, prominent even in Rhine's first book, describes what he later called "psi-missing." Though Rhine's aim was to find high scores, when he saw consistently low ones he did not neglect or suppress them; he utilized them for new thinking—and new methods. He interpreted them as being a result of tension or of "mental habits and patterns of association that are ... obtrusive to psi" (Rhine, J. B., 1969, p. 17), that is, as resulting from cognitive interference due to stress. (This theory has not yet been adequately tested; the interaction of stress and response bias still deserves more intensive investigation than it has received.) Thereafter, throughout Rhine's career in parapsychology, his methods were enriched by taking psi-missing into account. He recommended ways of avoiding it or of encouraging it; he began to make it predictable. A second methodological innovation, then, was to examine for consistent low scores as well as for consistent high ones. This also expands the area to be investigated.

His attempt at a third methodological advance has not yet been successful. It concerns methods of testing which will elicit psi; and most parapsychologists recognize with regret that we do not yet know how to do this. Even in 1934, however, Rhine's recommendations were so full and seem to me so wise that I consider it astonishing that they failed to be incorporated into a successful method.

They fall into three cateogories. The first relates to conditions conducive to psi in the person being tested. These are, he wrote, a combination of alertness and detachment; in his own phrase, "relaxation of all sensory functions and abstraction from all sense-stimuli"; also effort, striving, motivation for money or for kindness, for play or for display; self-control; capacity for attention; confidence; patient persistence; effort and voluntary attention; easy informality; tendencies to daydreaming, to high imaginativeness, to artistic ability and hypnotizability and sociability.

His second category described conditions that adversely affect psi in the subject: distraction, fatigue, haste, strain, self-consciousness, either an unwelcome change of procedure or any procedure that the percipient expects to be inhibitory, doubt, negativism, monotony, drowsiness.

His third category, prescriptions for an experimenter, include stopping when the subject wants to — or even earlier; giving short runs; expressing no doubt; following the subject's preferences on procedure at first; not giving extravagant praise; showing playful informality and light humor; encouragement; varying the procedures; and, in general, the approach that makes for effective salesmanship in any area.

In spite of this wide range of insightful recommendations, Dr. Rhine was unable to develop a dependable method for eliciting the experimenter–subject relationship that would produce evidence for psi. One of his practical solutions for this difficulty was to observe each experimenter's data, infer that experimenters whose data were consistently null were unable to set up the necessary rapport, and recommend that they refrain from conducting psi research. He argued that failures to produce significant data are not necessarily instructive; and of course this is true. But though the expedient of excluding such experimenters may be useful in the short run, especially when money to support experimenters is limited, Rhine recognized that this policy could sacrifice what might be a useful field of inquiry. He later recommended (Rhine, J. B., 1976) that conditions — including experimenters — expected to produce null results be employed if they were only one aspect of a project and their data were to be compared with data from other conditions expected to yield significant results.

Before I leave this topic, let me add a personal note of appreciation for Dr. Rhine's insights into it. In a recent study comparing experimenters who typically elicit psi with those who typically do not (Schmeidler & Maher, 1981) I compiled a list of adjectives that might discriminate the two groups. Many from Rhine's writings were included because I too thought them appropriate, but I hesitated about "playful" which seemed to me to be inappropriate, and eventually included it only because Rhine had suggested it. And "playful" was one of the adjectives which, as he had anticipated, significantly discriminated the psi-conducive experimenters from the psi-inhibitory.

These last three methodological contributions have all been general ones; it is time to describe some ingenious specifics. Within

ESP, Rhine thought long and hard about the mode in which it appears. Although his earliest research was formally conducted to test the possibility of telepathy, he soon recognized that when the target was both a record or object and also the thought about this in the agent's mind, extrachance data could come from clairvoyance, from telepathy, or from a combination of the two. His earliest methods could not distinguish among them.

Rhine and his staff members soon developed a wide range of testing techniques, from calling down through a concealed deck to screened touch-matching: another set of research contributions. Among these methods were one or two which seemed to exclude even precognitive telepathy, so that their extrachance data established clairvoyance as a mode of ESP.

He then devised an ingenious technique to test for "pure telepathy" with randomized targets. The telepathic agent would translate a random list of digits into ESP symbols by a private code, never spoken or written; the subject would try to respond with the symbols, not the digits. Pure though this seems, Rhine later disavowed its extrachance successes as evidence for telepathy by considering that they might come from clairvoyance of the agent's brain processes, a metaphysical argument which seemed to make the telepathy problem insoluble.

A major contribution to methodology dealt with PK. From the days of his first interest in psychical research Rhine had considered PK an important topic for investigation, and in 1943 he and Mrs. Rhine published an innovative report of a quantitative method for working with it: throwing dice while hoping a particular face would turn up (Rhine, L. E., & Rhine, J. B., 1943). The method was basically parallel to the work with ESP cards. Theoretical expectation for chance success became 1 in 6 instead of 1 in 5; the run unit soon became 24 instead of 25. Justification for using theoretical probabilities even with imperfect dice was achieved by counterbalancing, so that the standard procedure soon demanded that each subject hope an equal number of times for all of the six die faces. This statement of a readily available objective method, sensitive to small effects, inspired attempts at direct replication as well as new ingenious techniques based on the same general principle; it opened up the field.

I have been writing almost as if Rhine's eventual rigorous techniques sprang full-fledged from his brow. This is not only false; it does a disservice both to other parapsychologists and to his own qualities as a man of intellectual integrity and zeal for rigor. What actually happened with both the ESP and the PK research is that Rhine proposed major innovative breakthroughs, tested them in the first heat of enthusiasm, and obtained data too striking to disregard. Critics both within and without parapsychology examined the first work and found, or thought they found, methodological loopholes in it. Rhine welcomed all such criticisms and transformed them into constructive contributions: with the help of his colleagues he invented or utilized new methods which would make the research fully rigorous.

The work on PK is a case in point, for the striking data from his first procedures were provocative but unsatisfying; and indeed by the time the Rhines published their first report (Rhine, L. E., & Rhine, J. B., 1943), more refined methods from his laboratory had been used and were published in the same issue of the *Journal of Parapsychology*. Still later work from his laboratory controlled for motor skill in throwing dice by using mechanical releases; it required subjects to call all faces the same number of times; and it instituted various other controls such as those against optional stopping. It provided some control for recording errors by having two independent records for each outcome. Rhine had earlier insisted on blind recording of all ESP work, and with the advent of Schmidt's random events generator, the recent PK research from Rhine's laboratory has closed this loophole too by using mechanical recording for PK.

Three further methodological contributions need to be described: one which helps toward rigor; one for reliability; and one, not yet fully implemented, which may provide another important breakthrough. The first has already been anticipated. It is in effect a series of caveats, of "Thou shalt not's" — but modified characteristically, by this wise and modest man, to "Thou shalt not at present." Rhine considered that clairvoyance had been established as a mode of ESP and that complicated techniques like Mangan's permitted precognition to be established as another mode, distinct from PK: he also considered PK to be established, as distinct from precognition. He recommended therefore that investigators not befuddle themselves by attempting to work in other, cloudier areas (unless they were able to invent some new technique to make the areas clear). He specifically recommended against attempts to study telepathy, since no method now known could distinguish telepathy from clairvoyant response to agents' brain processes. He recommended against attempts to study retrocognition, because the facts which would establish retrocognitive success might have been available to clairvoyance. He recommended against studying retro-PK, because success here could be interpreted as an experimenter's precognition of the subject's later assignment and then (unconscious) PK upon the targets to make them match the assignment. He recommended against attempts to study either out-of-body experiences or survival because of the possibility of "superpsi" interpretations of all affirmative data in terms of clairvoyance, precognition, or PK in various combinations. But he modestly kept open the possibility that someone might later invent an adequate procedure for any of these; his recommendations were only against unparsimonious attempts to study them with our present inadequate methods.

The second piece of methodological advice was to complete two formal stages of research before publication: to conduct first an exploratory and then a confirmatory project. Most scientists would consider this unconventional. In psychology, for example, it is unusual to state a hypothesis, then test it, and take significant support for the hypothesis as adequate confirmation. If pilot studies are performed they are usually informal, merely preliminary attempts to find a workable procedure. Stating one's hypothesis substitutes for Rhine's first formal exploratory stage.

Rhine's more conservative requirement can be taken as the hallmark of a man who has learned to hold theories lightly; of the empiricist who demands replication of any interesting finding before giving weight to it. Perhaps also it reflects special characteristics of psi research, where an experimenter's initial enthusiasm might, through psi, influence subjects so as to support the hypothesis (even where there is no subtle cuing by verbal suggestions). Since the enthusiasm is likely to diminish after the first series, data which support the hypothesis in a second series will be considered more robust. Replication is in any event appropriate statistically, since even a method which yields a significance value of $p = .01$ will, on average, be due to chance about one time in a hundred. The demand that significant data be labelled exploratory the first time they are obtained, and considered confirmatory only when replicated, may seem unnecessarily onerous to some of us, but surely testifies to Rhine's high standards for research in parapsychology.

The last on my list of Rhine's methodological contributions has as yet been insufficiently utilized and seems likely to prove more important in the future than it has been already. It was stimulated by the discovery of the decline effect in PK. With 24 successive calls for one face of a die, PK successes are likely to be markedly higher at the beginning of the series than at the end. The statistical significance of this decline in success has in general been greater than the significance of all calls, pooled, tested against mean chance expectation. Since decline effects are also common in ESP, they seem to be a characteristic of psi when the subject is required to make a quick succession of forced choices.

Rhine utilized these effects and then generalized from them. He borrowed Ehrenwald's term *tracer* to designate any internal difference within psi data which is observed so often that it seems characteristic of psi (Rhine, J. B., 1975). His basic argument about such tracer effects is that their significant and predictable differences between calls could not occur in the absence of psi. They therefore show that psi has affected the responses. Tracer effects are thus doubly useful. They show that psi has occurred and they also give information about how psi operates, about the nature of psi.

Using tracer effects is potentially so powerful a methodological advance that I will try to spell out some of its implications. The thesis proposes that after a body of data has been obtained in a psi experiment and used to test the experimenter's hypothesis, further searches should routinely be made. One, of course, might be for the decline effect. Others might be for the differential effect; for a relation to the experimenter's (prerecorded) mood or for a correlation between run scores; and there are other possibilities such as sheep–goat differences.

If the search for tracer effects has been prestated as a formal part of the research design, a correction of the probability value for significance of any particular finding must of course be made; but the gain in extracting further information from the data may outweigh the loss from partitioning p. And if the search for tracer effects is considered only pilot work, or perhaps exploratory, even this disadvantage will not be present. By the expenditure of a little extra effort in data analysis, the experimenter may have gained important insights into factors that interact with the original hypothesis, and important leads for later confirmation. Learning through these tracer effects about how psi operates may make it possible to design more fruitful research projects; and Rhine (1975) even speculated that they might be a key to adequate study of the problem of survival.

Have I been neglecting part of my assigned topic: Rhine's contributions to standards of research? Not entirely. They enter in one aspect, through Rhine's demands for rigorous controls and his insistence, long before it was common in psychology, for double-blind experimentation. They explain why he welcomed criticism and then used the criticism to make methodological advances. They enter in another aspect, too, with his rejection of what he considered unparsimonious interpretations of psi data, from telepathy to out-of-body travel.

But there are further ways that they enter his work. I shall cite two examples; there could be many more. Not only did he himself avoid the use of anything resembling deception of the subject in psi testing, but he had so strong a distaste for it that he urged others also against any such attempts. A formal argument against deception is that the subject's ESP might be able to penetrate it, but it seemed clear, as Rhine discussed the topic, that deception per se was so distasteful to him that he felt any experimenter willing to deceive a subject would be incapable of establishing proper rapport and perhaps even felt such an experimenter to be suspect, unworthy to be a parapsychologist.

These high moral standards permeated both his scientific and his popular writing. In his lectures and in all his work from the earliest to the latest, he was careful as he presented his persuasive data or arguments to point out any of their inadequacies which he had privately evaluated. He was cautious in warning his listeners or readers not to overgeneralize from the results. He presented his interpretations in an admirably tentative way, distinguishing carefully between his opinions, which might be strong, and the facts on which the opinions were based.

To a large extent, Dr Rhine's standards were the determinants of his methods. His zeal for rigor in investigations drove him to seek, invent, and encourage methodological advances and refinements.

REFERENCES

MILLAR, B. The distribution of psi. *European Journal of Parapsychology*, 1979, 3, 78–110.

RHINE, J. B. *Extra-sensory perception*. Boston: Branden Press, 1973. (Originally published, 1934.)

RHINE, J. B. *New frontiers of the mind*. New York: Farrar & Rinehart, 1937.

RHINE, J. B. Some present impasses in parapsychology. *Journal of Parapsychology*, 1955, 19, 99–110.

RHINE, J. B. Psi-missing re-examined. *Journal of Parapsychology*, 1969, 33, 1–38.

RHINE, J. B. Psi methods re-examined. *Journal of Parapsychology*, 1975, 39, 38–58.

RHINE, J. B. Publication policy on chance results: Round two. *Journal of Parapsychology*, 1976, 40, 64–68.

RHINE, L. E., & RHINE, J. B. The psychokinetic effect: I. The first experiment. *Journal of Parapsychology*, 1943, 7, 20–43.

SCHMEIDLER, G. R., & MAHER, M. Judge's responses to the nonverbal behavior of psi-conducive and psi-inhibitory experimenters. *Journal of the American Society for Psychical Research*, 1981, 75, 241–257.

Review of
J. B. Rhine's ESP Research

JOHN PALMER

If there is one term in parapsychology that is associated with the name of J. B. Rhine, that term would have to be *extrasensory perception*, or ESP. His contributions to research on this topic were conceptual, theoretical, methodological, and empirical. Although this chapter will focus on his empirical contributions, it must be recognized that the other kinds of contributions cannot be separated from the empirical ones. Likewise, Rhine's empirical contributions cannot be adequately assessed by referring exclusively to the papers on which his name appeared as an author. As director of a major research laboratory for over fifty years, he sponsored much research by other investigators, both at his own laboratory and elsewhere, which represented or extended his thinking. It would be impractical for me to try to cite all the research he sponsored, but I will cite some of it that I consider particularly indicative or representative of Rhinean parapsychology at the time it was conducted.

It is not my primary intention to provide an encyclopedic compendium of the research findings accumulated by Rhine and his coworkers, but rather to highlight the trends which seem to define the evolution of Rhine's approach to ESP research. Thus the perspective here will be somewhat historical. I am speaking as one who is familiar with most of Rhine's published articles throughout his career but whose personal contacts with him date only from 1966, when I began the first of two summers working as a research associate at the Institute for Parapsychology. These various exposures have left me with a personal perspective on his work which I will share with you. It is a perspective which may or may not coincide with that of persons who were associated with him more closely over a longer period of time. Yet I offer my perspective with no apologies.

After all, it is the responsibility of all of us whose lives he touched, however indirectly, to collectively define and evaluate his contribution to parapsychology. Indeed, this conference is a first step toward a discharge of that responsibility.

Rhine's first published research report, ironically enough, was not based on a Duke college student, but on a horse by the name of Lady (Rhine, J.B., 1929). The horse's owner, Mrs. C. D. Fonda, claimed that Lady had telepathic abilities. When Mrs. Fonda would think of a number or letter of the alphabet, Lady would touch her nose to the corresponding block on a table. Lady was excellent at this task when Mrs. Fonda was standing by her side. But Rhine recognized that Mrs. Fonda, who knew the targets, could unconsciously provide Lady with sensory cues. Rhine thus proceeded to institute a series of controls that progressively isolated Mrs. Fonda from Lady. Results became progressively poorer as the controls were tightened, but they remained impressive enough to suggest to Rhine that Lady had genuine psychic abilities. However, sensory isolation was never complete and the statistical tests that later were to become the hallmark of Rhine's research were not applied, rendering the results only suggestive by modern standards. Moreover, a later visit yielded such poor results that Rhine was forced to conclude that Lady had lost whatever abilities she may have earlier possessed (Rhine & Rhine, 1929). Such decline effects were to haunt Rhine throughout his career. *

While the research with Lady was not particularly representative of Rhine's later work, it did contain the rudiments of the forced-choice methodology which he progressively refined during his career. The high point of that career came in the early 1930s. Having been a first-hand witness to the fiasco of the Margery mediumship (Rhine, J. B., 1927), he realized the importance of simple and highly controlled experimental designs in demonstrating the reality of psi. He also had come to appreciate the value of statistics in objectifying the significance of quantifiable outcomes. What he needed was subjects who could produce such significant outcomes under controlled conditions. Unable to find other gifted animal subjects, Rhine pur-

---

*Rhine's other major contact with animal research occurred in 1952 when he undertook an investigation, sponsored by the U.S. military, of the ability of dogs to locate underwater mines by ESP. For each trial, a land-mine case was randomly placed in one of five positions on a linear trail, and the dog indicated his response by sitting down at one of the five locations. Initial results were significantly positive, but a decline effect later set in and the project was abandoned (Rhine, J. B., 1971).

sued his quest for human subjects in a logical fashion by screening classes of college students at Duke using simple card-guessing tests (Rhine, J. B., 1934/1973). The results of these tests were unimpressive on the whole, but they did yield one outstanding subject, A. J. Linzmayer. Soon thereafter, several other outstanding subjects were revealed among the Duke student population, the most notable being Hubert Pearce and Charles Stuart.

Rhine patiently accumulated thousands of trials for card-guessing data from these subjects, all of whom consistently provided scores which, if not always spectacular, were nonetheless above chance to a highly significant degree when statistical tests were applied. In 1934, an account of these tests was published in a monograph entitled, inconspicuously enough, *Extra-Sensory Perception* (Rhine, J. B., 1934/1973.) The furor this monograph created in orthodox academic circles will be discussed by other speakers. It is easy with 20/20 hindsight to criticize the lack of ideal controls which characterized this early work, but one must realize that Rhine was pioneering a relatively new methodology and new methodologies must be refined over time. It is to Rhine's credit that he took to heart the legitimate criticisms of his antagonists and refined his methods accordingly. These advances were reflected in his next major scholarly book, entitled *ESP After Sixty Years*, which was published in 1940 (Rhine, Pratt, Stuart, Smith, & Greenwood, 1940).

The two experiments which Rhine felt provided the strongest evidence for ESP were both conducted with his principal colleague, J. G. Pratt, as the experimenter: the Pearce–Pratt series and the Pratt–Woodruff series. In the former, a BT clairvoyance procedure was utilized, with the subject and experimenter isolated in different buildings on the Duke campus (Rhine & Pratt, 1954). The cumulative results over 74 runs yielded a mean of 7.5 hits per run; the probability of so large a deviation occurring by chance was less than 10^{-22}. Equally impressive were the results of the Pratt–Woodruff experiment, which employed the screened-touch matching (STM) method of clairvoyance testing (Pratt & Woodruff, 1939). A total of 2,400 runs from 32 subjects yielded a mean of 5.20 hits per run, which is associated with a probability of less than 10^{-6}. Neither of these experiments has escaped criticism, but the critics at least were forced to speculate about unusually ingenious fraud on the part of the subjects or fraud by the experimenter(s) to explain away these findings (e.g., Hansel, 1979). A particularly effective defense of the Pratt–Woodruff experiment was recently published by Pratt (1976).

IN SEARCH OF THE LIMITS OF PSI

A strong secondary interest of Rhine at the time these data were being accumulated was the establishment of the physical limits of psi. Large amounts of additional card-guessing data were piling up from testing done at Duke and elsewhere, which allowed for more generalized conclusions along these lines. Rhine repeatedly found himself required to conclude from these data that the physical limits of psi simply did not exist. ESP seemed all-pervasive and, more importantly, it seemed to transcend the laws of classical physics.

Source of Information

Rhine's embrace of the term *extrasensory perception* reflected his premise that ESP is an alternative means of accessing information from the environment. This, of course, had been the model accepted by most parapsychologists up to that time. It also was assumed by most researchers, at least in the English-speaking world, that the paradigmatic form of ESP was telepathy. So pervasive was this assumption in the U.S. that John Coover (1917) insisted upon treating clairvoyance as a non-ESP control condition when presenting the results of his controversial ESP experiments at Stanford.

One of Rhine's most important research contributions was to demonstrate that his subjects could score as well on clairvoyance tests (i.e., when no one knew the target order at the time the subject made his responses) as they could on telepathy or GESP tests (Rhine, J. B., 1934/1973). Although particular individuals would score better with one procedure than another, these trends were never consistent across individuals, suggesting that they were attributable to psychological factors such as preferences. It is perhaps debatable whether the alternative hypothesis of precognitive telepathy had been ruled out in the clairvoyance tests to quite the extent that Rhine (1945) supposed, but he nonetheless drove home the important point that one could no longer blithely assume that only another mind could be the source of ESP impressions. Clairvoyance had dethroned telepathy as the major subspecies of ESP.

Space and Distance

If ESP is not limited by the source of the information, what about the location of the information? Because ESP was implicitly conceptualized as an analog to normal sensory perception, much of the early research had the subject in close physical proximity to the targets. However, even the monograph *Extra-Sensory Perception* included reports of experiments conducted with the targets in a different room, a different building, or even a different city from the subject (Rhine, J. B., 1934/1973). In some cases there did seem to be a decline with distance. In the Cooper–Ownbey "pure telepathy" (PT) series, for example, Cooper averaged 9.2 hits per run when he and Ownbey were in the same room and only 5.8 hits per run when they were one room apart. However, the decline would readily be attributed to psychological factors, as the participants were not blind to their partner's location. Moreover, in the Zirkle–Ownbey experiment, for example, which also used the PT procedure, Zirkle's scores increased from an average of 14 to 16 hits per run as he moved from the same room with the agent to two rooms apart. Neither did distance seem to be a factor in the better controlled Pearce–Pratt series. Although the mean number of hits declined as the distance was increased from 100 to 250 yards, some individual run scores at the longer distance matched the more consistently high run scores at the shorter distance.

Rhine (1937) later summarized the results of all available work over longer distances ranging from 70 to 3,000 miles. The mean for 4,083 runs was 5.11, which was significantly above chance (CR = 3.4).

In the 1940s and 1950s, Rhine and his colleagues, most notably Elizabeth McMahan, reported a series of long-distance tests with a physician from Yugoslavia named Carlo Marchesi, who had reported dramatic success testing himself with cards (McMahan & Bates, 1954; McMahan & Rhine, 1947; Rhine, J. B., & Humphrey, 1942). Several clairvoyance and precognition tests were conducted over a period of approximately 14 years, with the targets in Durham and Marchesi in Yugoslavia. The results were hardly spectacular, but the total of 1,352 runs did manage to reach statistical significance (CR = 2.77). There also were significant internal position effects in the early tests. I will discuss these later in the chapter.

In summary, it appeared that ESP was independent of space and distance. Later research, including studies designed to control for psychological factors (e.g., Osis & Turner, 1968) had done little to alter this conclusion in the opinion of most parapsychologists, although the possibility remains that more reliable data or more refined analysis techniques may yet provide evidence of a dependency of ESP upon distance.

Time

If ESP is not limited by space, perhaps it also is not limited by time. Specifically, can ESP extend into the future?

Rhine initially tackled this problem through a simple modification of his standard card-guessing procedure: instead of shuffling the deck of cards before the subject makes his responses, shuffle it *after* he makes his responses. In 1938, Rhine reported the results of 15 series involving 11 experimenters and 49 subjects utilizing DT and matching procedures (Rhine, J. B., 1938b). The mean number of hits per run over 4,523 runs was 5.14, which was highly significant statistically (CR = 4.5). Moreover, the level of scoring was comparable to that obtained in clairvoyance series using the same test procedures. It appeared that precognition could now be added to the catalog of demonstrated psi effects.

Unfortunately, there was a hitch. Was it possible that whoever shuffled the cards could shuffle them in such a way as to match the subject's guesses, for example, by using ESP to know when to stop shuffling? Rhine was not inclined to favor this "ESP-shuffle" hypothesis, because the precognition results were so similar in pattern to the clairvoyance results and because the results for each experimenter (or shuffler) varied depending upon the particular subject he or she was testing. Nevertheless, it deserved a test. In conjunction with Burke Smith and Joseph Woodruff, Rhine tested the ESP-shuffle hypothesis directly by having subject and experimenter each shuffle decks of cards and match the corresponding sequences (Rhine, Smith, & Woodruff, 1938). A total of 203 subjects and 13 experimenters at both Duke and Tarkio College participated. The results from 8,461 runs yielded a highly significant mean of 5.20 hits per run (CR = 10.4), a mean slightly higher than the 5.14 obtained in the original precognition work. The ESP-shuffle hypothesis was a matter to be reckoned with after all.

A new series of precognition tests now had to be undertaken to rule out the ESP-shuffle hypothesis. This was attempted in the first series of tests by utilizing a matching procedure in which the key cards were selected either by mechanical shuffling or by mechanical dice throws (Rhine, J. B., 1941a). Twenty-four subjects completed 1,608 runs, but the mean was almost exactly at chance. However, there was a strong difference in scoring between the 19 adult and 5 child subjects. The adults scored significantly below chance ($\bar{X}$ = 4.78; CR = 3.59), while the children scored significantly above chance ($\bar{X}$ = 5.25; CR = 2.75), with the difference being highly significant (CR_d = 4.29). Although each of the previous precognition studies also involved both adult and child subjects, this was the first time such a difference was significant in precognition work (although it had appeared in some clairvoyance experiments). Nevertheless, this post hoc effect seemed strong enough and sensible enough to confirm the precognition hypothesis in the context of previous research.

However, even this series proved inadequate methodologically. Could not the mechanical target selection have been influenced by PK? This new counterhypothesis was dealt with in a subsequent report of 2,302 precognition runs completed by 22 children and 19 adults using a DT procedure (Rhine, J. B., 1942). Target orders were determined with reference to the maximum and minimum temperatures of the preceding day from the Durham newspaper, a process seemingly less influenceable by PK. The overall deviations were nonsignificant for both adults and children, but some significant evidence of ESP was obtained post hoc through examination of position effects. These effects, which appeared in a number of other studies, will be discussed later.

Precognition became a standard test procedure at Rhine's laboratory from then on, and numerous studies obtained significant results using this method. Rhine's name generally was not attached to these studies, but one notable exception was a rather ambitious undertaking in which *Maclean's Magazine* and the Canadian Broadcasting Company collaborated with Rhine in a mass precognition test (Rhine, J. B., 1962). An article on ESP appeared in one issue of *Maclean's* along with a postcard on which readers could record a sequence of ten digits (0–9) that later would be matched to a target order generated by computer. A separate target sequence was generated for each of the 29,706 cards received. It was a reflection of the times, perhaps (both in parapsychology and the real world), that the results were significant in the psi-missing direction (CR = 2.53).

Rhine also never found any convincing evidence that precognition scores declined as the time interval between responses and target generation increased (e.g., Humphrey & Rhine, 1942; Rhine, J. B., 1942). ESP really did seem to be independent of time as well as of space, although again we must allow for the possibility that further refinements may someday alter the picture.

THE DISSECTION OF ESP

I noted earlier that Rhine was haunted throughout his career by the decline effect. This was true, not only of particular subjects, but also of the research in general. The consistent success of the early 1930s was not to be duplicated in subsequent decades. There never again appeared a group of star subjects that rivaled Pearce, Linzmayer, et al., although occasionally a few stars appeared on the horizon only to quickly fade away. Perhaps the brightest of these stars was the schoolgirl Lillian, who once achieved a perfect score of 25 hits (Reeves & Rhine, 1942; Rhine, J. B., 1964). More typical of the new trend was the performance of a teenage boy identified as P. H., whose promising psi-hitting when tested informally reverted to significant psi-missing when better controls were applied (Russell & Rhine, 1942).

On rare occasions Rhine would venture out to test more established stars. A two-year card-guessing study with the noted medium Eileen Garrett produced significant results the first year (especially on GESP), but results in the second year declined to nonsignificance (Birge & Rhine, 1942). Psi-missing intruded again into a field study of the dowsing abilities of Henry Gross (Rhine, J. B., 1950). This psi-missing, which received only passing mention in the monograph *Extra-Sensory Perception*, became an increasingly prominent feature of psi results as the decades passed.

Motivation

What was responsible for this decline of fortunes? One finds only oblique references to the problem in the literature (e.g., Rhine, J. B., 1946), but I think it is safe to say that the decline was attributed at least in part to the dwindling enthusiasm of the staff as the novelty wore off, as the battles with the critics became more intense, and as the battles of World War II became everyone's primary preoccupation. Rhine always felt that strong motivation on the part of subjects was essential for success and that this motivation had to be incited and maintained by the experimenters, who must have this same motivation themselves.

There were indications from the early research reported in *Extra-Sensory Perception* that supported such an interpretation. Scores of the star subjects tended to decline to chance when testing sessions became too long and motivation waned. Shifts to novel procedures tended to rejuvenate dwindling critical ratios. In the two cases where scoring fell below chance (Frick and Linzmayer), Rhine attributed the psi-missing to unconscious negativism engendered by the length of the testing. Fatigue, illness, and the depressant drug sodium amytal were found to dramatically reduce scoring rates, whereas the stimulant caffeine caused them to partly recover.

Given the importance Rhine placed upon motivation, it is ironic how little systematic research has been done to explore its effects on ESP scoring. Subjects were often offered small rewards for high scores (e.g., Rhine, J. B., 1941a), but such rewards were never manipulated systematically. Rhine suggested that the children scored more positively than the adults in the 1942 precognition study because they were more highly motivated (Rhine, J. B., 1942), but this lead was never followed up. It was not until 1953 that Remi Cadoret (1953) confirmed the effects of depressant and stiumlant drugs on ESP in a controlled study. Later I will suggest a reason why the motivation hypothesis was not pursued more directly.

The one motivational factor that was systematically explored, at least in terms of retrospective analyses of data, was the effect of delaying feedback of their ESP scores to the subjects. It was found with both clairvoyance and precognition procedures that scores were above chance when subjects received feedback after each run and below chance when feedback was delayed several days (Rhine, J. B., 1938a; 1941a). These latter runs often were conducted at other locations, with the record sheets being scored at Duke and then mailed back to the test site. Thus the sets of runs being compared may have differed in other respects besides delay of feedback. Nonetheless, such delays remain the most likely interpretation of these findings.

Separating Hitters and Missers

The lack of star subjects caused the research emphasis to shift to studies amassing data from relatively unselected volunteers, often high school and college students. Rhine quickly realized that the overall chance deviations frequently obtained in these studies could be attributed to a cancellation of psi-hitting and psi-missing. Thus a major research strategy at his laboratory from the 1940s through the 1960s was to identify factors that might discriminate hitting and missing. In the 1940s and 1950s, emphasis was placed on individual differences or personality variables as the discriminators. The persons primarily responsible for this emphasis was Betty Humphrey, one of the most prolific of Rhine's colleagues. The most widely used and successful of these predictors were certain personality inventories, especially the Bernreuter (e.g., Humphrey, 1945); the Stuart Interest Inventory (Humphrey, 1949, 1950a); and freehand drawings rated for expansiveness and compressiveness of form (Humphrey, 1946a, 1946b). These variables were combined as predictors in retrospective analyses to demonstrate greater separation of hitters and missers (e.g., Humphrey, 1950b).

In the 1960s, Ramakrishna Rao (1965) introduced the concept of the differential effect. This concept caused more emphasis to be placed on experimental manipulations, especially with regard to the nature of the targets as discriminators of hitting and missing (e.g., Rao, 1962, 1963). The concept of run-score variance provided a mechanism for evaluating changes in the direction of ESP scoring within a session and stimulated much research in the late 1960s (e.g., Carpenter, 1968; Rogers, 1966).

Position Effects

The contrast of psi-hitting and psi-missing was also manifested through the study of position effects within the run. As we all know, Rhine was a strong advocate of forced-choice as opposed to free-response methods of testing ESP. The only significant amount of free-response work ever to crack the *Journal of Parapsychology* were the drawing studies of Charles Stuart in the 1940s (e.g., Stuart, 1946, 1947). The relative virtues of the two kinds of tests have been debated vigorously (Honorton, 1975; Kennedy, 1979), and it seems that free-response methods are slowly winning the day. However, an important advantage of forced-choice tests, which Rhine fully exploited, was their conduciveness to the examination of internal scoring patterns in ESP data.

As early as the 1930s, Rhine noticed such scoring patterns in the runs of his star subjects (Rhine, J. B., 1934/1973). Some of these were decline effects, but the most striking were the salience effects, or U-curves, which seemed restricted to the DT test procedures. Specifically, he noticed with most of his star subjects that the psi-hitting tended to be concentrated in the first and last five-trial segments of the run. He attributed this effect to greater motivation on the part of the subject at these points in the run.

In the early 1940s, a series of research reports appeared that examined the salience effect more systematically. In the first and most elaborate of these studies (Rhine, J. B., 1941b), 1,114 DT clairvoyance runs were completed by 30 adult and child subjects. Experimental manipulations were introduced in an effort to vary the likelihood of the salience effect. Reasoning that salience would be most likely if the segmentation of the run was made identifiable to the subject, Rhine introduced brief interpolated tasks after each segment in some of the runs. Specifically, subjects were asked to either draw a picture or guess a number at these points. The uninterrupted runs were divided into those where subjects wrote down their responses and those where they called them out. Rhine reasoned that salience should be most apparent on the written runs because the record sheets used at Duke highlighted the segmentation.

This segmentation allowed Rhine to extend the concept of salience from the run to the segment; that is, greater ESP deviations would be expected on the first and fifth trials of each segment. Thus there was segment salience as well as run salience, and both were evaluated in the study I am describing.

As expected, the salience effects were significant only for the interrupted runs, and they appeared with both the adult and child subjects. Segment salience also was evidenced in the uninterrupted runs, but only by adults when they wrote their responses. This seemed reasonable, since adults would be more likely than children to pay attention to the structuring of the record sheet. It is also noteworthy that the adults, who scored below chance overall, revealed an inverted-U type of salience effect; that is, the extreme psi-missing occurred in the first and fifth segments.

Finally, Rhine noticed that the patterns of run salience and segment salience seemed to coincide in the data. This led to the development of a new test statistic to measure this "covariance of the salience ratios," and application of this statistical test demonstrated that the covariance was indeed significant.

Although Rhine's salience analyses, especially the salience ratio, have been criticized as an abuse of the principles of probability pyramiding through post hoc analysis (e.g., Hilgard & Atkinson, 1967), it should be noted that the salience effects were replicated in a number of the early card-guessing experiments. The covariance effect was significantly confirmed in the early precognition work (Humphrey & Rhine, 1942; Rhine, J.B., 1942), in the preliminary sheep–goat research of Schmeidler (1944; Humphrey & Rhine, 1944), and in the first of the long-distance experiments with Marchesi (Rhine, J. B., & Humphrey, 1942).

On the other hand, replication by no means has been universal. Salience analyses tended to fall into disuse after the 1940s at the Duke laboratory and they never really caught on anywhere else. A brief renewal of interest in position effects occurred at Rhine's laboratory in the late 1960s, highlighted by the introduction of the concept of the cancellation effect. This concept, which spawned a couple of exploratory experiments before expiring (Rogers, 1967; Stanford, 1966), states that psi-missing in one half of the run cancels out psi-hitting in the other half. It was devised as an attempt to explain significantly low run-score variance in some ESP data.

The tradition of internal analyses of forced-choice ESP data survives most conspicuously in the response-bias research pioneered by Rex Stanford, which Rhine enthusiastically supported in the 1960s (e.g., Stanford, 1967).

RHINE THE EMPIRICIST

Many of the studies discussed in the previous section provided much potentially valuable information about the psychological processes underlying ESP. Although these theoretical issues were doubtlessly of considerable interest to at least some of Rhine's colleagues, it is my impression that they were never really of primary concern to Rhine. One reason for this might be that he was trained as a botanist rather than as a psychologist. A more important reason may be that his principle objective throughout his career was not to understand psi theoretically but to provide evidence for its existence that would be sufficiently conclusive to the scientific community to annihilate the skeptical position. I do not think this reflected so much a lack of interest in the psi process (which, after all, he did discuss in many of his writings) as a sense that priority must be given to the evidentiality question.

So then why did Rhine support so much research at his laboratory which seemed to address theoretical and psychological issues about the nature of the psi process? I suspect that this was because he saw this research as a new way to demonstrate the existence of psi effects in data that seemed on the surface to be nonevidential. If the overall deviation was nonsignificant, one could still demonstrate psi by showing that the deviations of predefined subgroups were significant and that these deviations differed significantly from each other.

Perhaps the best illustration of the empiricistic nature of this research were the studies involving the Stuart Interest Inventory. This relatively successful predictor of ESP scoring was developed, validated, and cross-validated without any regard to the relevance of the items to any explicit or, as far as I can tell, implicit theory of the psychology of psi. The same could be said for the scoring scheme. Only briefly in the discussion section of one article could I find any mention of how the Stuart inventory profiles of hitters and missers might be interpreted, and was never followed up (Humphrey, 1950a).

There are other indications of Rhine's empiricism that could be cited, only a few of which I will mention here. I found it revealing that, in his 1969 article on psi-missing, he hailed the differential effect, not as suggesting anything about the psychology of psi, but as a way to create conditions for demonstrating statistical significance (Rhine, J. B., 1969). I think his empiricism explains why he never saw any reason to abandon the critical ratio as the principle method of analyzing psi data statistically. If one is interested only in whether there is evidence of psi in the data, the *CR* is quite adequate. Finally, his empiricism explains why so many suggestive effects about the psychology of psi were never followed up, including the many intriguing patterns uncovered by Louisa Rhine in her analyses of spontaneous cases (e.g., Rhine, L. E., 1956, 1962).

Although my own approach to parapsychology has been considerably more theoretical than Rhine's, my purpose in dwelling upon his empiricism is not to criticize it. I dwell on it because I think it is the fundamental cornerstone of what might be called the Rhinean paradigm, and its central place in his thinking must be acknowledged if one is to come to grips with the nature of his research contribution. His professional life, in my view, was a single-minded quest for conclusive evidence of psi. The fact that it could not be achieved in his lifetime is the challenge he has left to those of us seated in this room — a challenge to follow through. He laid for us a firm foundation, and in the final analysis that was his most important contribution to psi research.

REFERENCES

BIRGE, W. R., & RHINE, J. B. Unusual types of persons tested for ESP: I. A professional medium. *Journal of Parapsychology*, 1942, 6, 85–94.

CADORET, R. J. The effect of amytal and dexadrine on ESP performance. *Journal of Parapsychology*, 1953, **17**, 259–274.

CARPENTER, J. C. Two related studies on mood and precognition run-score variance. *Journal of Parapsychology*, 1968, **32**, 75–89.

COOVER, J. E. Experiments in psychical research. *Psychical Research Monograph No. 1*. Stanford: Stanford University, 1917.

HANSEL, C. E. M. *ESP and parapsychology: A critical reevaluation.* Buffalo: Prometheus Press, 1979.

HILGARD, E. R., & ATKINSON, R. C. *Introduction to psychology* (4th ed.). New York: Harcourt-Brace, 1967.

HONORTON, C. Receiver-optimization and information rate in ESP. Paper presented at the 141st annual meeting of the American Association for the Advancement of Science, New York City, January, 1975.

HUMPHREY, B. M. An exploratory correlation study of personality measures and ESP scores. *Journal of Parapsychology*, 1945, **9**, 116–123.

HUMPHREY, B. M. Success in ESP as related to form of response drawings: I. Clairvoyance experiments. *Journal of Parapsychology*, 1946a, **10**, 78–106.

HUMPHREY, B. M. Success in ESP as related to form of response drawings: II. GESP experiments. *Journal of Parapsychology*, 1946b, **10**, 181–196.

HUMPHREY, B. M. Further work of Dr. Stuart on interest test ratings and ESP. *Journal of Parapsychology*, 1949, **13**, 151–165.

HUMPHREY, B. M. A new scale for separating high- and low-scoring subjects in ESP tests. *Journal of Parapsychology*, 1950a, **14**, 9–23.

HUMPHREY, B. M. ESP score level predicted by a combination of measures of personality. *Journal of Parapsychology*, 1950b, **14**, 193–206.

HUMPHREY, B. M., & RHINE, J. B. A confirmatory study of salience in precognition tests. *Journal of Parapsychology*, 1942, **6**, 190–219.

HUMPHREY, B. M., & RHINE, J. B. The evaluation of salience in Dr. Schmeidler's ESP data. *Journal of Parapsychology*, 1944, **8**, 124–126.

KENNEDY, J. E. Methodological problems in free-response ESP experiments. *Journal of the American Society for Psychical Research*, 1979, **73**, 1–15.

McMAHAN, E. A., & BATES, E. K. Report of further Marchesi experiments. *Journal of Parapsychology*, 1954, **18**, 82–92.

McMAHAN, E. A., & RHINE, J. B. A second Zagreb–Durham ESP experiment. *Journal of Parapsychology*, 1947, **11**, 244–253.

OSIS, K., & TURNER, M. E. Distance and ESP: A transcontinental experiment. *Proceedings of the American Society for Psychical Research*, 1968, **27**, 1–48. (Monograph)

PRATT, J. G. New evidence supporting the ESP interpretation of the Pratt-Woodruff experiment. *Journal of Parapsychology*, 1976, **40**, 217–227.

PRATT, J. G., & WOODRUFF, J. L. Size of stimulus symbols in extra-sensory perception. *Journal of Parapsychology*, 1939, **3**, 121–158.

RAO, K. R. The preferential effect in ESP. *Journal of Parapsychology*, 1962, **26**, 252–259.

RAO, K. R. Studies in the preferential effect. I. Target preference with types of targets unknown. *Journal of Parapsychology*, 1963, **27**, 23–32.

RAO, K. R. The bidirectionality of psi. *Journal of Parapsychology*, 1965, **29**, 230–250.

REEVES, M. P., & RHINE, J. B. Exceptional scores in ESP tests and the conditions: I. The case of Lillian. *Journal of Parapsychology*, 1942, **6**, 164–173.

RHINE, J. B. One evening's observation on the Margery mediumship. *Journal of Abnormal and Social Psychology*, 1927, **21**, 401–421.

RHINE, J. B. The investigation of a mind-reading horse. *Journal of Abnormal and Social Psychology*, 1929, **23**, 449–466.

RHINE, J. B. The effect of distance in ESP tests. *Journal of Parapsychology*, 1937, **1**, 172–184.

RHINE, J. B. ESP tests with enclosed cards. *Journal of Parapsychology*, 1938a, **2**, 199–216.

RHINE, J. B. Experiments bearing on the precognition hypothesis. *Journal of Parapsychology*, 1938b, **2**, 38–54.

RHINE, J. B. Experiments bearing upon the precognition hypothesis: III. Mechanically selected cards. *Journal of Parapsychology*, 1941a, **5**, 1–57.

RHINE, J. B. Terminal salience in ESP performance. *Journal of Parapsychology*, 1941b, **5**, 183–244.

RHINE, J. B. Evidence of precognition in the covariance of salience ratios. *Journal of Parapsychology*, 1942, **6**, 111–143.

RHINE, J. B. Telepathy and clairvoyance reconsidered. *Journal of Parapsychology*, 1945, **9**, 176–193.

RHINE, J. B. The source of the difficulties in parapsychology. *Journal of Parapsychology*, 1946, **10**, 162–168.

RHINE, J. B. Some exploratory tests in dowsing. *Journal of Parapsychology*, 1950, **14**, 278–286.

RHINE, J. B. The precognition of computer numbers in a public test. *Journal of Parapsychology*, 1962, **26**, 244–251.

RHINE, J. B. Special motivation in some exceptional ESP performances. *Journal of Parapsychology*, 1964, **28**, 41–50.

RHINE, J. B. Psi-missing re-examined. *Journal of Parapsychology*, 1969, **33**, 136–157.

RHINE, J. B. Location of hidden objects by a man–dog team. *Journal of Parapsychology*, 1971, **35**, 18–33.

RHINE, J. B. *Extra-sensory perception*. Boston: Branden Press, 1973. (Originally published, 1934.)

RHINE, J. B., & HUMPHREY, B. A. A transoceanic ESP experiment. *Journal of Parapsychology*, 1942, **6**, 52–74.

RHINE, J. B., & PRATT, J. G. A review of the Pearce–Pratt distance series of ESP tests. *Journal of Parapsychology*, 1954, **18**, 165–177.

RHINE, J. B.; PRATT, J. G.; STUART, C. E.; SMITH, B. M.; & GREENWOOD, J. A. *Extrasensory perception after sixty years*. New York: Henry Holt, 1940.

RHINE, J. B., & RHINE, L. E. Second report on Lady, the "mind-reading" horse. *Journal of Abnormal and Social Psychology*, 1929, **24**, 287–292.

RHINE, J. B., SMITH, B. M., & WOODRUFF, J. L. Experiments bearing on the precognition hypothesis: II. The role of ESP in the shuffling of cards. *Journal of Parapsychology*, 1938, **2**, 119–131.

RHINE, L. E. The relation of agent and percipient in spontaneous telepathy. *Journal of Parapsychology*, 1956, **20**, 1–32.

RHINE, L. E. Psychological processes in ESP experiences. Part I. Waking experiences. *Journal of Parapsychology*, 1962, **26**, 88–111.

ROGERS, D. P. Negative and positive affect and ESP run-score variance. *Journal of Parapsychology*, 1966, **30**, 151–159.

ROGERS, D. P. An analysis for internal cancellation effects on some low-variance ESP runs. *Journal of Parapsychology*, 1967, **31**, 192–197.

RUSSELL, W., & RHINE, J. B. A single subject in a variety of ESP test conditions. *Journal of Parapsychology*, 1942, **6**, 284–311.

SCHMEIDLER, G. R. Position effects as psychological phenomena. *Journal of Parapsychology*, 1944, **8**, 110–123.

STANFORD, R. G. A study of the cause of low run-score variance. *Journal of Parapsychology*, 1966, **30**, 236–242.

STANFORD, R. G. Response bias and the correctness of ESP test responses. *Journal of Parapsychology*, 1967, **31**, 280–289.

STUART, C. E. GESP experiments with the free response method. *Journal of Parapsychology*, 1946, **10**, 21–35.

STUART, C. E. A second classroom ESP experiment with the free response method. *Journal of Parapsychology*, 1947, **11**, 14–25.

J. B. Rhine and the
Study of Psychokinesis

Diana Robinson

The Beginning

What if...? How very many "what ifs" there are, particularly when one thinks of someone as influential as J. B. Rhine in the field of parapsychology, and in psychokinesis (PK) most especially. What if Rhine had not been thinking about the possibility of PK, and so had not been receptive to the visit of that legendary gambler in January 1934? What if he had been feeling out of sorts and had given the man short shrift? That, of course, was not his way. He was open, courteous, encouraging to everyone, known and unknown, who knocked on his door or mailed him requests for information and advice (as I well know!). What if he had been different? How many people now active in parapsychology would have felt rejected or lost interest in the field, without the encouragement of his unfailingly constructive responses?

But Rhine was open to the superficially ridiculous idea that this gambler might somehow be able to affect the way the dice fell, and so psychokinesis became a valid area of study for parapsychologists.

The term *psychokinesis* itself was coined by Rhine and his wife, Dr. Louisa Rhine, who explained in a footnote to their first paper on PK (1943) that they did not like the term *telekinesis* that had been used until then:

> "to those who are familiar with this word, it connotes 'ectoplasm,' mediums, dark room seances, and other associations which it has accumulated and which we do not deal with in these experiments. We believe we are legitimately avoiding unnecessary difficulties by not adopting the name, telekinesis."

But I should start at the beginning. For PK the beginning was that day when the gambler crystallized ideas already developing as a result of Rhine's work with ESP. Since the gambler was used to throwing the dice two at a time, and to aiming for high scores, the first experiments that resulted from his visit were run that way. Two dice were thrown 12 times for each run, with the aim being to set as many scores of eight or above as possible. After 562 runs a very significantly high number of hits had been obtained (Rhine & Rhine, 1943). Obviously further research was warranted.

All concerned realized that this experiment, and those which followed it, were not tightly controlled. Rhine and his colleagues at the Parapsychology Laboratory were simply riding the crest of an exciting new wave to see where it might lead, knowing that tighter controls could be introduced later (Rhine, L. E., 1970). At that time there were no immediate plans to publish the reports of the experiments that were being carried out.

For a while the experimenters continued to follow the gambler's bent, with subjects aiming for "high dice." Then, still using two dice per throw, came the "sevens" and "low dice" experiments. In "sevens" the aim was to get a score of exactly seven for each throw, while "low dice" experiments aimed for six or lower. These experiments were designed to check on whether the above-chance scores being obtained in the high dice experiments could be accounted for by the dice being biased. Since the dice were "excavated," that is, the dots were slightly hollowed out, the high faces were minutely lighter than the low faces, and so would tend to fall uppermost more often. The fact that scores were significantly above chance in the "sevens" experiment, using the same dice as in the "high dice" experiment, seemed to vindicate the dice. However, in the "low dice" experiment subjects were less successful. The unexpected result they obtained was an above chance number of sevens (Rhine, 1945). This may have been related to die bias, but it may also have indicated that the subjects found it difficult to adjust their aim to low dice, which are generally considered to be undesirable in die-throwing games (Robinson, 1981).

The question of die bias continued to be a problem, but was largely dealt with when "round the die" throwing was introduced (Gibson, Gibson & Rhine, 1943). Since this technique involved throwing for all the die faces in turn, any bias toward one side would automatically be cancelled out by an equal bias away from the opposite side. Rhine was still not satisfied. He did not feel that reports of the PK work should be published until more and better evidence had been accumulated. In the meantime, other methodological problems needed attention.

In addition to the biased dice explanation, the possibility had been raised that the significant results could be due to skilled throwing. For this reason, hand-throwing was one of the first early techniques to be discarded. Work at the Parapsychology Laboratory moved from cup-throwing to semi-mechanical throwing, and, in 1936, to the rotating wire cage which was to become the standard for dice work for many years (Gibson, Gibson & Rhine, 1943; Rhine, 1943).

The Quarter Distribution Effect

World War II affected the Parapsychology Laboratory in a most unexpected way. Few workers were available to run new experiments and Rhine decided to use the time available for a re-analysis of all the PK data that had been accumulated up to that time. The analysis showed a totally unexpected pattern of declines across each of the 18 experiments (Rhine & Humphrey, 1944a; Rhine & Humphrey, 1944c; Rhine & Pratt, 1945). Records of these 18 experiments (out of the 24 run up to that time) had been kept in such a way that the trials which made up each individual run were listed in columns down the page, one column per run. The decline that appeared extended both across and down the page, indicating that scores went down within each run and over the course of several runs. If a page was divided into quarters, the scores recorded in the top left quarter were higher than those in the bottom right quarter. So strong was this effect that it became known as the *Quarter Distribution*, or QD effect.

A general decline in the scoring of individual subjects had been observed previously, and had in fact been a source of major concern in ESP work because it meant that few subjects could continue to score well over an extended period of time. When, then, did Rhine herald the QD with such enthusiasm that it, together with some other circumstances to be discussed later, resulted in the publication of reports on the PK experiments in the *JP* in spite of his earlier resistance to such publication?

In the first place, the decline had appeared in all 18 of the experiments analyzed. (The other six experiments had not been analyzed only because their records had not been set out in such a way as to make this analysis possible.) There did not seem to be any logical "normal" reason why such a decline should have occurred so regularly; there had been no changes in the experimental conditions that would have caused it. Therefore, the finding seemed to point quite strongly to some kind of lawful behavior connected with psi, something that parapsychologists had been seeking for many years.

In addition, the QD seemed to answer a number of criticisms of the earlier PK work. Although no reports had been formally published, word of the PK experiments had spread throughout the parapsychological community and somewhat beyond. Inevitably, the experiments had been subject to some of the same criticisms that had concerned Rhine and caused him to delay publication of any PK reports. There were three major possibilities as far as normal explanations for the significant results were concerned: (a) biased dice, (b) skilled throwing, and (c) inaccurate recording, either through carelessness or deliberate fraud. When considered in the context of these criticisms, it can be seen that the QD actually answered all three of them. For example, if dice bias was responsible (in spite of the introduction of round-the-die throwing), then that bias would have to exist throughout each experiment, for the same dice were used from start to finish. The biased dice explanation could not account for the fact that scores dropped significantly, for the bias would always have been the same.

Similarly, the introduction of mechanical throwing techniques in later experiments had not entirely silenced those who believed that some form of skilled throwing had to explain the results of at least the earliest experiments. However, skill comes with practice. It would therefore be expected that scores would increase as subjects moved from run to run, with each run serving as an opportunity to practice for the next. The fact that the reverse of this actually occurred seemed to answer this criticism.

Finally, both carelessness and fraud seemed unlikely candidates to explain the QD. Had scores increased over runs, it might have seemed legitimate to suggest that the experimenters could have started recording the results of each experiment carefully, but became careless and accidentally recorded more hits as time went by and boredom or fatigue set in. However, to suggest that they were careless to start with and became more careful over time is to go against most of what is known about human task performance. Lastly, could the scores be the result of deliberate fraud? The 18 experiments had been carried out by several experimenters. None of them had suggested the possibility of the QD during the experimental period. To suggest that they planned such an unlikely distribution of hits, doctored their records accordingly, and then put the records aside (in many cases going on to careers far away from the Parapsychology Laboratory), leaving the finding of the effect entirely to chance, seems unlikely, to say the least.

Publication Pressures

Not surprisingly, Rhine's reluctance to publish the PK work began to wane in view of such a discovery. Also he was committed to publishing four issues of the *JP* per year. As more and more scientists joined the war effort, less and less ESP work was reported, and the *JP* was faced with a serious dearth of material. Late in 1942 he made the decision to publish the PK work, and together with his wife, prepared the first report (Rhine & Rhine, 1943).

In it they noted that the work completed at that time had been contributed by "a score of experimenters," and included 24 publication-ready reports and several others awaiting only editorial or statistical work. These were duly published, giving readers some insight into the questions that had been asked about PK over the previous nine years. A tremendous variety of questions had been covered: differences in PK performance in the dark, as opposed to light (Gibson & Rhine, 1943); whether "harrassment" of the subject could affect PK scores (it could) (Price & Rhine, 1944); the effect of caffeine and alcohol on performance (caffeine improved performance, and alcohol lowered it) (Averill & Rhine, 1945; Rhine, Humphrey & Averill, 1945). With hindsight, some of these findings (which were, in any event, labelled exploratory) may be seen as possibly resulting from psychological variables such as the preferential effect, or to subjects' expectations. However, in spite of this, and even though many of these experiments were performed during the days before experimental procedures had been tightened sufficiently for ideal control, they remain a rich lode of hints and inspirations that can be usefully mined by parapsychologists to this day.

Perhaps most important, at least theoretically, was the work on physical effects on PK performance that was carried out in those early days. Did PK work as well when a larger number of dice were being thrown as when just two were in use? Did the size of the dice, or what they were made of, make a difference (Hilton, Baer & Rhine, 1943; Hilton & Rhine, 1943; Humphrey & Rhine, 1945; Rhine & Humphrey, 1944b; Rhine & Humphrey, 1945)? Did it matter whether the subject was within a certain distance of the dice (Nash,

1946; Nash & Richards, 1947)? For the most part the answers were that none of the physical effects studied made any difference unless the subject expected it to.

The apparent imperviousness of the PK effect to variations in the number and size of dice and to distance strengthened Rhine's opinion that PK was not related to physical energies. (An unabashed dualist, he still held to this opinion when, in 1977, I raised the issue of a connection between PK and quantum mechanics with him. He replied that if physicists wanted to annex PK as being within their domain, then it was up to them to demonstrate a physical condition that clearly affects PK — something he did not consider to have been done.)

Placement Tests

Yet even while this work was being done, and in spite of the many questions that could be asked using these techniques, face-tests were clearly limited. As long as investigators had to confine their work to the die's six sides there were many questions that could not be asked experimentally. In 1946 Ed Cox, one of the researchers for whom Rhine had provided a home base at the Parapsychology Laboratory, started to work with "placement tests." In placement work, the aim was not to make the dice fall with a certain face upwards, as had been done in the past, but to make them fall in a certain direction.

The introduction of this concept was a major step, freeing PK researchers from their original confines, and from the constant question of die bias. Although the first placement tests were conducted with dice, it was quickly realized that any object could be used in a PK test. Spheres and discs were the immediate candidates (Rhine, L. E., 1951). Later reports would tell of experiments using water droplets, air bubbles, sodium ions and many more items that might be subject to the influence of PK (for a survey of this work, see L. E. Rhine, 1970).

Another major body of placement work that would be reported later and was directly attributable to Rhine's influence is that done by Forwald (Rhine, 1951; Forwald, 1952), which resulted from Forwald's correspondence with Rhine and which was based on Rhine's advice.

For the moment, though, just as Rhine had chosen to withhold publication of the face tests until a strong case could be made for them, so with placement tests. It was not until satisfactory reports by several experimenters were in hand that they were published (Cox, 1951; Pratt, 1951; Rhine, 1951; Rhine, L. E., 1951).

For a while the interest prompted by the new placement reports led to a further blossoming of PK research. Public interest continued, and Rhine presided over a wide variety of experiments and experimental apparatuses. Before long, however, interest in PK seemed to fade. The pendulum of parapsychological interest was swinging back toward ESP and away from PK. Had Rhine not encouraged Ed Cox's PK experiments through the years that followed, interest in PK might, as Honorton has observed (1976), have faded completely away.

But Rhine was there, and Cox was there, and PK experimentation continued. In the meantime, technological progress was being made that would revolutionize the methodology of PK experiments. Around 1970 the first computer was installed in the Parapsychology Laboratory. Before long most of the experimental work relating to PK was being run with the aid of the computer and the random event generators developed by Helmut Schmidt. PK experiments acquired a character that Rhine could hardly have anticipated in 1934. Large numbers of trials could be run at much faster speeds than had been possible using dice. This, together with the instantaneous feedback now possible, made running experiments more interesting and less time-consuming. In addition, automation of record-keeping lessened the likelihood that recording errors could be blamed for apparently significant scores.

However, despite all the advantages of automation, it was such an automated PK experiment that made possible the Levy fraud (Rhine, 1974). (The same type of automation now helps to ensure that the incident will not be repeated.) It was characteristic of Rhine that even though the fraud concerned one of his most trusted assistants he did not hesitate to inform the parapsychological world. It was his courageous decision to suggest that not only the experiment involved but all experiments with which Levy had been in any way associated must be held suspect (Rhine, 1975). That this decision invalidated at least twenty major experiments run at the Parapsychology Laboratory did not seem to influence him. It was the right thing to do, and he did it. After that he established procedures to ensure that the situation could not be repeated, and, though deeply wounded by the betrayal, he put the unpleasantness firmly behind him.

A bibliography of Rhine's work appears at the back of this book. What is truly astonishing is not only the size and range of his interest and reported work, although this is wide enough. The greater astonishment comes when one considers the immense volume of work that does not bear his name, and yet was guided and inspired by him. Rhine's influence as a mentor in parapsychology was apparent even in his first PK report, which referred to "a score of experimenters" who had already been involved in PK research, mostly following advice given by Rhine (Rhine and Rhine, 1943). In the years to come this training and guiding function was expanded and the Parapsychology Laboratory became a major training ground for the field. Today it would be impossible to attempt to name those experimenters in PK who have worked with and been influenced by Rhine. Almost two generations of researchers have at some time in their careers worked under his wing, found a home for their work under his auspices, and guidance for their ideas under his tutelage. Without the researchers he guided, current research in PK would be very different, if it existed at all. The fact that many have since branched out in directions within parapsychology that might not be described as precisely Rhinean does not negate Rhine's influence. As John Palmer has said so well, Rhine's greatest achievement is the foundation that he laid down for future parapsychologists (Palmer, 1981). What we build on that foundation is our own responsibility, but we should always be aware that the elegance of our edifices is only made possible because they are built on the foundation so painstakingly created and made firm for us by J. B. Rhine.

REFERENCES

AVERILL, R. L., & RHINE, J. B. The effect of alcohol upon performance in PK tests. *Journal of Parapsychology*, 1945, 9, 32–41.

COX, W. E. The effect of PK on the placement of falling objects. *Journal of Parapsychology*, 1951, 15, 40–48.

FORWALD, H. A continuation of the experiments in placement PK. *Journal of Parapsychology*, 1952, 16, 273–283.

GIBSON, E. P., GIBSON, L. H., & RHINE, J. B. A large series of PK tests. *Journal of Parapsychology*, 1943, 7, 228–37.

GIBSON, E. P., GIBSON, L. H., & RHINE, J. B. The PK effect: Mechanical throwing of the dice. *Journal of Parapsychology*, 1944, 8, 95–109.

GIBSON, E. P., & RHINE, J. B. The PK effect: III. Some introductory series. *Journal of Parapsychology*, 1943, 7, 118–134.

HILTON, H., JR., BAER, G., & RHINE, J. B. A comparison of three sizes of dice in PK tests. *Journal of Parapsychology*, 1943, 7, 172–190.

HILTON, H., JR., & RHINE, J. B. A second comparison of three sizes of dice in PK tests. *Journal of Parapsychology*, 143, 7, 191–206.

HONORTON, C. Has science developed the competence to confront claims of the paranormal? *Research in Parapsychology 1975*, J. D. Morris, W. G. Roll and R. L. Morris (eds.) Metuchen, N.J.: Scarecrow Press, 1976, 199–223.

HUMPHREY, B. M. Help-hinder comparison in PK tests. *Journal of Parapsychology*, 1945, 11, 4–13.

HUMPHREY, B. M., & RHINE, J. B. PK tests with two sizes of dice mechanically thrown. *Journal of Parapsychology*, 1945, 9, 124–132.

McMAHAN, E. PK experiments with two-sided objects. *Journal of Parapsychology*, 1945, 9, 249–63.

NASH, C. B. Position effects in PK tests with twenty-four dice. *Journal of Parapsychology*, 1946, 10, 51–57.

NASH, C. B., & RICHARDS, A. Comparison of two distances in PK tests. *Journal of Parapsychology*, 1947, 11, 269–82.

PALMER, J. Review of J. B. Rhine's research findings: I Extrasensory perception. *Journal of Parapsychology*, 1981, 45, 25–40.

PRATT, J. G. The Cormack placement PK experiments. *Journal of Parapsychology*, 1951, 15, 57–73.

PRICE, M. M., & RHINE, J. B. The subject–experimenter relation in the PK test. *Journal of Parapsychology*, 1944, 8, 177–86.

RHINE, J. B. Dice thrown by cup and machine in PK tests. *Journal of Parapsychology*, 1943, 7, 207–217.

RHINE, J. B. Early PK tests: Sevens and low-dice series. *Journal of Parapsychology*, 1945, 9, 106–115.

RHINE, J. B. The Forwald experiments with placement PK. *Journal of Parapsychology*, 1951, 15, 49–56.

RHINE, J. B. A new case of experiment unreliability. *Journal of Parapsychology*, 1974, 38, 215–25.

RHINE, J. B. Comments: Second report on a case of experimenter fraud. *Journal of Parapsychology*, 1975, 39, 306–325.

RHINE, J. B., & HUMPHREY, B. M. The PK effect: Special evidence from hits patterns. I. Quarter distribution of the page. *Journal of Parapsychology*, 1944a, 8, 18–60.

RHINE, J. B., & HUMPHREY, B. M. PK tests with six, twelve and twenty-four dice per throw. *Journal of Parapsychology*, 1944b, 8, 139–57.

RHINE, J. B., & HUMPHREY, B. M. The PK effect: Special evidence from hit patterns. II. Quarter distribution of the set. *Journal of Parapsychology*, 1944c, 8, 254–71.

RHINE, J. B., & HUMPHREY, B. M. The PK effect with sixty dice per throw. *Journal of Parapsychology*, 1945, 9, 203–18.

RHINE, J. B., HUMPHREY, B. M., & AVERILL, R. L. An exploratory experiment on the effect of caffeine upon performance in PK tests. *Journal of Parapsychology*, 1945, 9, 80–91.

RHINE, J. B., & PRATT, J. G. The PK effect: Special evidence from hit patterns. III. Quarter distribution of the half-set. *Journal of Parapsychology*, 1945, 9, 150–68.

RHINE, L. E. Placement PK tests with three types of objects. *Journal of Parapsychology*, 1951, 15, 132–38.
RHINE, L. E. *Mind over matter*. New York: Macmillan Co., 1970.
RHINE, L. E., & RHINE, J. B. The psychokinetic effect: I. The first experiment. *Journal of Parapsychology*, 1943, 7, 20–24.
ROBINSON, D. *To stretch a plank: A survey of psychokinesis*. Chicago: Nelson–Hall, 1981.

J. B. Rhine and Psi-Missing

H. KANTHAMANI

Today psi-missing is an integral and important aspect of the psi phenomenon, and most experimental efforts at studying psi are aimed at catching or controlling missing. In the early days of experimental research, however, very little attention was given to negative deviations, as the emphasis then was on obtaining a strong proof of positive scoring. When the field itself was so new it was understandable that negative deviations were more of a headache than a welcome occurrence.

Dr. Rhine noticed signs of missing in one of his star subjects as early as in 1932, but waited 20 years to publish his first paper on the subject of psi-missing (Rhine, 1952). Seventeen years later, he reexamined the issue in another paper (1969).

Rhine said that psi-missing is a merely descriptive term which covers the tendency of some subjects under certain conditions to give significantly negative deviations; that is, to average below mean chance expectation. As long as MCE is taken as the criterion to determine if the obtained results are significant, then the same logic governs the evaluation of hitting as well as missing. Although Dr. Rhine was not the first to observe negative deviation, he was the first to label it and explain it as an indication of psi in its own right.

Estabrooks, in his work at Harvard during 1926, came across a case of "puzzling negative deviation." He reported that in the last series the subjects reversed their earlier high scoring trend, dropping significantly below MCE. These subjects had participated in four series of tests; the low scores were found only in the fourth series. Estabrooks gave two reasons for this apparent psi-missing. The subjects were at a greater distance from the targets in this series, and they "needed urging" to complete the task. Estabrooks proposed what he called "adverse autosuggestion" to explain the outcome. Jephson reported (1928) a similar drop in the scoring rate even in the short runs of five trials. Commenting on these early studies, Dr. Rhine wondered whether such a decline in scoring rate may not be caused by a mere falling off of the amount of ESP, or whether it is a genuine psi effect.

In his own work, Rhine noticed missing trends with one of his star subjects. In one session the subject, AJL, was made to stay longer than usual to complete certain runs. Such a delay was unexpected. The outcome of these runs, Rhine noted, was that the subject's scores abruptly dropped to a level below chance. Intrigued by this sudden change in the scoring direction, Rhine kept track of future sessions whenever similar situations arose. Also, he purposely introduced certain simple conditions to create stress without the subjects' knowledge. A total of 1650 trials were gathered as distinctly different from his normal procedure. The scoring on these trials was significantly below chance. Thus, an incidental observation of below chance scoring in one session led to the discovery of this unexpected kind of psi — the tendency to miss. The concept of psi-missing eventually became as significant for researchers as his highly successful experiments in which hitting occurred.

Based on this work, Rhine proposed the idea of "negative motivation" as responsible for producing psi-missing. Referring to the case of AJL, he pointed out that in some half-conscious way the subject was perhaps trying to use ESP to avoid the targets. Any sort of stress or strain during the testing may be sufficient to produce negative motivation in the subjects.

The idea of "negative motivation" is, however, inconsistent with Rhine's assumption that the subjects would want to do well in each run and to obtain more hits. So, the role of motivation is more complex than it appeared at first. Experimenters realized that even with a highly motivated individual, it is not easy to obtain good results. More importantly, the idea that the same subject could produce both above chance and below chance scoring at different times formed the seeds of future research using subject variables.

Considering AJL's case as a pilot study, Rhine proceeded to look for similar missing effects in other subjects with whom he was working. He formulated a hypothesis, *will-to-miss*, which suggested that subjects could deliberately try to miss the targets and succeed in obtaining negative deviations. This led to the idea of dirigibility, which means that the subjects can direct their psi ability towards either hitting or missing, at will. He carried out a series of tests with his two other high-scoring subjects, HP and CES, who consciously tried to miss the targets. The results showed a significant number of misses. Further, the negative deviation was as strong as their normal positive deviation. Thus, this study not only provided a confirmation of the missing effect found in AJL's work, but also formed the basis of later "low-aim" and "high-aim" tests.

With these two cases of significant negative deviation, Rhine could no longer ignore the phenomenon. By 1934, psi-missing was identified, labeled, and explained as recognizable evidence of psi. The confirming statistical evaluation was exactly the same kind as in the case of extra-chance hits. Psi-missing was described as not the mere lack of success or chance missing. It is the actual avoidance of targets when hitting is intended. To be psi-missing, missing has to be not only strong enough to be significant, but it should occur when the subject is actually aiming at hitting. The only theory of psi-missing proposed at that time was negative motivation, that the subjects were somehow motivated to miss.

The negative motivation hypothesis was helpful to explain the earlier results of Estabrooks. Rhine felt that Estabrooks' subjects might have perceived the task as "harder" because of the greater physical distance from the targets, and therefore, possibly were resistant to the idea that they could succeed. This might have produced missing.

While the negative motivation hypothesis was perhaps sufficient to account for Estabrooks' and Rhine's early results, a challenge to it came from another Duke subject, HLF, who was involved in a self-testing project. He carried out one long run of 100 trials per day trying to identify the suits of playing cards in a clairvoyance task. He did this for nine days. The total results were nonsignificant. Then, for some reason, Rhine broke each run into five equal units of 20 trials each. The results looked interesting when the segments were analyzed. Taking the first 20 trials from each day, the second 20, the third 20, and so on, each segment had 180 trials. The scoring trend showed that the first 20 trials of the day produced the highest positive deviation, followed by a scoring decline, ending with the last 20 having the highest negative deviation. This pattern came to be recognized as the decline effect. The difference between the first two segments and the last two were statistically significant. Furthermore, the hitting and missing of the end two segments were approximately equal. This encouraged Rhine to feel that ESP performance is shown in both hitting and missing. But Rhine's negative motivation hypothesis fails as an explanation; it is difficult to imagine positive motivation in the beginning of a run gradually becoming negative during each run. Similarly, the negative motivation hypothesis does not seem sufficient to account for Jephson's observation of decline in scoring across the five trial runs.

In another experiment of the clairvoyance type AJL did there were 50 trials in each run. Each target card was enclosed in a sealed opaque envelope and the experimenter had to record both the subject's guess and the envelope number. Thus, it was rather a slow procedure. The total score was close to chance. When five segments with 10 trials in each were looked at separately, again there was maximum positive deviation in the first segment declining to maximum negative in the last. The difference between the first two and the last two segments was statistically significant. Rhine did not have any explanation for this form of psi-missing at the time. Only in 1952 did he develop his second hypothesis, *systematic cognitive error*.

The cancelling effects of the two types of scoring directions within a run, and across a set of runs was alarming to the experimenter of that period. It was bringing down the total score, which was still the main basis of test significance. Dr. Rhine called this a case of "pitting psi against itself." In one way it was very disappointing to him because of its cancelling effects; but in another way, highly intriguing since the "missing" in each case was as strong as the hitting was. His main struggle with the ESP issue, however, allowed little time for speculating about negative deviations. The first monograph had been published; the controversy and attacks were pouring in. At this stage it was not easy for Rhine to propagate the importance of negative deviations and at the same time sell ESP to critical scientists. The demand was for better evidence for ESP. These cancelling effects of negative and positive deviations were considered little more than irritating.

As a way out from such a dilemma, Rhine took certain practical steps and proposed that the experimenters avoid conditions in testing which would cause negative deviation. A simple and safe rule was "to discontinue working with a subject if the trend of his scoring shifted downward below MCE." His next step was to make negative deviations "work for the research program instead of against it." This resulted in the development of several new ideas which flooded the experimental parapsychology scene.

Psi-Missing Associated with Position Effects

Position effects or PEs, like psi-missing, were observed in Rhine's work from the beginning. We have already seen how AJL and HLF showed steep declines in their scoring across the five segments of a run. Psi-hitting was strongest in the first segment and psi-missing was equally strong in the last, with a significant difference between the two segments. This came to be known as the decline effect. The decline effect can be said to be due to psi-missing in certain parts of the run.

An interesting decline effect was noticed in a PK experiment conducted to study the effects of caffeine on PK performance (Rhine, Humphrey & Averill, 1945). The test involved releasing 96 dice at each trial. Since the recording was complicated the trials progressed at a very slow rate. The results showed a significant drop (from hitting to missing) in the scoring rate across the trials done in precaffeine condition. However, in the postcaffeine condition, although there was a drop in the scoring, it did not fall below MCE. Commenting on these results, Rhine said,

> Whatever was responsible for the negative deviation of the pre-caffeine series was either overcome or obscured in the post-caffeine. Such a decline cannot be identified as the result of psi-missing, but it could well have been due to that [Rhine, 1952, p. 99].

In the same way, those studies which show a decline effect without apparent psi-missing are hard to interpret as evidence of psi-missing. Rhine conjectured that there could be other types of missing occurring in such studies which go undetected.

In contrast to declines, Rhine identified *inclines*, where the scoring rate would gradually increase from initial psi-missing to psi-hitting towards the end of the run. While inclines are rare, Rhine commented that inclines may occur in situations where the subject overcomes a condition of temporary stress.

In addition to inclines and declines, another form of PE came to be recognized as very prominent in many research works. Subjects who took standard ESP tests with 25 trials began to show U-curves of hit distribution within the run when the runs were broken down into segments of five trials.

The scoring rate showed above chance scoring in the beginning and end segments and below chance in the middle three segments;

thus, a graph of the scoring rate follows a U-pattern. The U-curves became a very popular finding. The heightened scoring on the first and last segments came to be called the *salience* effect.

Rhine came to see increasingly the importance of the structure of the record sheet as salience effects seemed to reflect the way the record sheets were printed. The evidence obtained in the ESP work of the thirties was followed by similar and much stronger evidence of PK work in the forties. Declines occurred in different forms and took different names: decline in scoring across the page from left to right, down the column, from top to bottom, and diagonally. Similarly, U-curves also acquired various descriptions depending upon the unit of analyses of the record sheet: U-curve within a set, within a run, and within a segment. Interestingly, in some studies the same type of U-curve reflected in all analyses. Rhine suggested the use of PE as an answer to the question that habit pattern interferes with psi process.

He suggested ways of increasing spontaneity, such as introducing competitive games, and dual task experiments. He commended Forwald's work where, as planned, he took only the first of the five throws in a run, to test his idea of spontaneity.

Although it is thought that PEs are in some way the result of the subject's reaction to a structured record page, it is not clear how this effect is actually produced.

According to Rhine, PE and psi-missing are produced by different factors. While PE is attributed to the structure of the record sheet, the test conditions tend to determine whether a particular trial would be a hit or a miss. While such a notion leads to an understanding that the two are independent effects, Rhine felt that it would be difficult to eliminate psi-missing with confidence as a possible contributor to PEs in some instances.

Psychokinesis studies support the notion that position effects and psi-missing are independent. While early PK studies are replete with PEs, few instances of psi-missing are observed in them. The reason, according to Rhine, is to be found with the practice of providing feedback after each trial in the PK set up. Such feedback is rarely given in the traditional ESP experiments. Thus, feedback appears to reverse psi-missing, but does not alter PEs.

Commenting on the interaction of PE and overall scoring rate, Rhine felt that no relation exists between them. PEs have shown up in the data with overall significance, with psi-hitting and psi-missing, and also in chance data.

Position effects are one type of internal evidence of psi. Rhine believed that PEs provide evidence that may be considered in a significant sense fraudproof because the experimenters in many cases had no knowledge of these effects and, therefore, could not be expected to fake them.

Psi-Missing Associated with Dual-Aspect Experiments

"Dual aspect" refers to any two conditions which are inherently present in a testing procedure. This could be two types of targets that the subject is required to respond to, or two types of testing procedures, and so on. Although Rhine himself did not carry out any experiments of this nature, several others both in his laboratory and outside encountered the psi-differential effect. The differential effect is the tendency of the subjects to obtain above chance scores in one condition of the experiment and below chance on the other condition. Rao (1965) provides an extensive review of the literature and points out the various ways in which psi-hitting and psi-missing could occur together. He advocates the notion that psi is essentially bi-directional in nature.

The term preferential effect is also used in place of "differential effect" in those cases where subjects' conscious preference on one set of conditions is reflected in their scoring rate. However, Rhine prefers to use "differential effect" as it is more a neutral term. He pointed out that by providing an avenue for psi-missing to operate, the research methodology is able to take advantage of the negative deviations instead of cancelling the overall effect. Thus he encouraged a great number of research projects to provide a built-in system of two conditions in the experiment so that the missing trends could be captured more beneficially.

One of the early studies on differential effect was carried out by Skibinsky (1950) who used family names and ESP symbols as targets. The subjects showed above chance scoring on symbols and below chance on names. West and Fisk (1953) have reported the first study in which the dual-experimenter effect was observed. The subjects, although unaware that two experimenters prepared the targets, showed hitting on the targets prepared by one and missing on the other. This example suggests that the differential effect could occur even when the subjects are not informed of the two conditions present.

Chauvin (1961), using different size targets in an experiment, found positive scoring on the normal size symbols and negative on microfilmed symbols. Rao has carried out a series of experiments using choice cards and ESP symbols (1962) and words in two languages as targets (1963). In all these and numerous other studies, there were significant differences between the two sets of conditions.

In differential effect studies, the negative deviation found in one condition is as important as the positive deviation in producing the overall effect. In many cases neither of these deviations is significant by itself, but only by contrasting the two can evidence of psi be noticed. It appears that it is easier to capture psi under conditions that permit registering of hitting and missing. Maybe because of this, even in the present day, differential effect research is still in the foreground.

Psi-Missing Associated with Conditions of Stress and Frustration

Stress or strain leading to psi-missing was noticed, as pointed out earlier, when AJL was made to stay late to complete a number of runs. Rhine found a confirmation of this effect in other sessions where he purposely introduced some form of stress. Since then a number of experiments have been carried out to study "stress" effects on psi performance.

Stress or strain could be experienced in different forms in a testing situation. Schmeidler's skeptical goats are said to have felt a form of intellectual conflict, because they were participating in a test that purported to measure ESP, an effect they did not accept. Such conflict might have led to negative motivation, which resulted in psi-missing. In a precognition experiment Rhine (1941) observed that his adult subjects significantly psi-missed while the children who were subjects produced an equally significant positive deviation. Rhine explained this finding as due to intellectual conflict experienced by adults who while participating in a test to measure it believed that precognition was not possible. On the other hand, the children who were subjects did not experience any such doubt and therefore acted spontaneously, free of stress.

Extending the stress hypothesis to encompass personality studies, one could formulate that introverted, highly anxious and insecure subjects generally would experience some sort of tension in a testing situation. Most of the testing set-ups are made more congenial to extroverts, and therefore, when an opposite type is tested, he naturally tends to be ill at ease. Thus scoring of introverts tends to be negative.

The effect of stress is not only noted on stable characteristics like attitude and personality traits, it is also seen on more transient states like mood. The work of Humphrey (1946) using drawings to indicate mood began studies in this direction. She observed that those subjects rated as expansive showed psi-hitting, while those subjects rated as compressive gave evidence of missing. Kanthamani and Rao (1973), using a more objective criterion to determine expansive-compressive ratings, found the same trend among a large sample of subjects. Carpenter (1968, 1969) and Rogers (1966, 1967) used other methods to separate positive and negative mood and found differences between them. Other forms of transient states have also been explored.

Yet another source of tension leading to psi-missing has been identified as frustration. Using a picture-frustration test, Schmeidler (1954) was able to separate those subjects rated as extrapunitive, who tend to express their aggression on external things. Among these subjects, those who were also annoyed to a moderate degree by the ESP task showed a negative correlation with ESP scores. The others who were not aggressive, although moderately annoyed by the testing, still produced a positive correlation with ESP scores. Rhine (1964) in his interesting article on "Special Motivation in Some Exceptional ESP Performances" points out that strong drive is necessary for high-level performance. However, it is well-known that many high scoring subjects tend to get easily frustrated in a laboratory setting, but perform their best under informal conditions. In these cases, internal tension in the subjects tends to inhibit their performance.

The above-mentioned studies have one aspect in common. The methodology utilizes the psi-missing effect to its advantage by separating the type of subjects who are likely to miss from those who tend to hit, and by understanding the conditions that might lead to missing. By this approach the investigator attempts to exercise certain controls over the phenomenon.

After reviewing these three types of conditions that produce psi-missing, Rhine (1969) concludes as follows:

> The chief distinction of this third section on conditions is that in all cases a more-or-less obvious strain or stress seems reasonably inferable. On the other hand, in position-effect cases of psi-missing, as well as in most of the two-aspect examples, the shift back and forth from hitting to missing generally on a trial-by-trial basis would appear to work too fast for changes of mood or affect to account for the differential effect. The other types of psi-missing seem to call for something other than a state of tension [p. 14].

Although it is difficult to postulate how much stress is necessary to produce psi-missing, in many cases even a slight degree of it is sufficient. Gibson and Rhine (1943) observed that PK tests done in darkness produced significant negative deviation. Rhine commented that the recording procedure which required a flashlight undoubtedly was slow, tedious and probably frustrating although it might have acted as a novelty in the beginning.

In another PK test McMahan (1947) studied the effects of light and dark conditions. She observed that the subjects were enjoying their trials in darkness which utilized discs with luminous faces. Accordingly, the total scores done in darkness showed positive deviation, while those done in the light showed greater negative deviation.

Bevan (1947) observed that the subjects scored negatively when the subjects were tested alone in a dark room. Woodruff (1943) also found a similar effect when the subject was placed in an aviation chamber. Rhine points out that in these two studies physical limitation might have caused a psychological strain which led to missing. From this angle, those studies where delayed checking was done becomes more meaningful. When the subjects have to wait to know how well they have done in a test, they may experience frustration and be more likely to produce psi-missing.

Significance of Psi-Missing

The discovery of psi-missing and the possibility that it may be controlled is very important for the advancement of parapsychology. The idea that psi could be measured effectively on either side of MCE turned out to be conceptually useful and very productive in generating research.

Although the operation of psi is still considered to be unconscious, studies showed that subjects could voluntarily aim for high scores or low scores. Thus, concepts like "dirigibility" and "will-to-miss" came into usage. Again, psi-missing studies suggest that psi does not work on an all-or-none basis. Rhine felt that the test methods should be sensitive enough to capture such an "unconscious delicate process" in its attempt to register at the conscious level. This had important consequences in terms of later attempts to study the relationship of ESP and subliminal perception.

Another line of research, opened up by the possibility that hitting and missing may occur in the same testing situation, involved testing for variance effects. Variance tests take into consideration the deviation from chance irrespective of the sign and, therefore, appear to be more sensitive. In a series of studies Rogers (1966, 1967) and Carpenter (1968, 1969) report interesting interactions between mood variables and variance scores of the subjects.

Many experimental efforts in the forties and fifties were directed towards separating those subjects who tend to psi-miss from those who psi-hit. These studies assumed that people tend to be psi-missers or psi-hitters consistently, and that they can be identified as such by other external criteria. Schmeidler's attitude variable was a front runner in this direction. Humphrey and many other investigators extended this line of research to encompass many personality variables.

Rhine tried to integrate the findings of these tests and find similarities in conditions that produce psi-missing. In his 1952 paper he associated psi-missing with position effects, two-aspect or dual-task experiments, and conditions of stress. When he re-examined psi-missing in 1967, he found the same categories still true, even with new research.

Rhine offered two hypotheses to explain the psi-missing phenomenon. They are negative motivation, and systematic cognitive error. Negative motivation insofar as it is related to psi scoring seems to be a consequence of stress, strain, conflict or frustration felt during the experimental situation. In such a case, psi-missing seems to occur.

Cognitive error hypothesis implies a certain similarity of ESP process with sensory perception. Rhine gives the analogy of a rifleman with a specific visual problem who repeatedly misses the target. Similarly with psi, the subject is aware of the target, but distorts it in a systematic way before making a conscious response. Instances of consistent missing such as those observed by Cadoret and Pratt (1950) support this view.

Although several examples can be explained by either of the two hypotheses, neither is sufficient in all cases. Also, the process by which psi-missing operates is still unknown. However, one thing is clear. Psi-missing is central to psi process. Without such a concept, it would be difficult to make any sense of personality-ESP research, variance studies, differential effects and a host of other research findings in parapsychology.

It may be interesting to speculate about the impact of the reality of psi-missing on other sciences, especially psychology. First of all, the idea that psi is a bi-directional phenomenon was unique.

Unlike most of the other human potentials which are one directional, psi phenomenon can operate in two directions, hitting and missing. Questions arise: Are other human potentials like this? Is there something like negative memory when a person fails to recall? Does something akin to psi-missing operate in all aspects of cognitive functions? Does psi-missing play a role in subliminal perception? Rhine, by raising such questions attempted to integrate psi into the total picture of human nature.

REFERENCES

BEVAN, J. M. The relation of attitude to success in ESP scoring. *Journal of Parapsychology*, 1947, 11, 296–309.

CADORET, R. J., & PRATT, J. B. The consistent missing effect in ESP. *Journal of Parapsychology*, 1950, 14, 244–256.

CARPENTER, J. C. Two related studies on mood and precognition run-score variance. *Journal of Parapsychology*, 1968, 32, 75–89.

CARPENTER, J. C. Further study in a mood adjective check list and ESP run-score variance. *Journal of Parapsychology*, 1969, 33, 48–56.

CHAUVIN, R. ESP and size of target symbols. *Journal of Parapsychology*, 1961, 25, 185–189.

ESTABROOKS, G. H. A contribution to experimental telepathy. *Boston Society for Psychical Research* (Bulletin No. 5), 1927, 1–30.

GIBSON, E. P., & RHINE, J. B. The PK effect: III. Some introductory series. *Journal of Parapsychology*, 1943, 7, 118–34.

JEPHSON, I. Evidence for clairvoyance in card-guessing. *Proceedings of the Society for Psychical Research*, 1928, 38, 223–71.

HUMPHREY, B. M. Success in ESP as related to form of response drawings: II. GESP experiments. *Journal of Parapsychology*, 1946, 10, 181–196.

KANTHAMANI, B. K., & RAO, K. R. Personality characteristics of ESP subjects: V. Graphic expansiveness and ESP. *Journal of Parapsychology*, 1973, 37, 110–129.

MCMAHAN, E. A PK experiment under light and dark conditions. *Journal of Parapsychology*, 1947, 11, 46–54.

RAO, K. R. The preferential effect in ESP. *Journal of Parapsychology*, 1962, 26, 252–259.

RAO, K. R. Studies in the preferential effect II. A language ESP test involving precognition and "intervention." *Journal of Parapsychology*, 1963, 27, 147–160.

RAO, K. R. The bidirectionality of psi. *Journal of Parapsychology*, 1965, 29, 230–250.

RHINE, J. B. Terminal salience in ESP performance. *Journal of Parapsychology*, 1941, 5, 183–244.

RHINE, J. B., HUMPHREY, B.M., & AVERILL, R. L. An exploratory experiment on the effect of caffeine upon performance in PK tests. *Journal of Parapsychology*, 1945, 9, 80–91.

RHINE, J. B. The problem of psi-missing. *Journal of Parapsychology*, 1952, 16, 90–129.

RHINE, J. B. Special motivation in some exceptional ESP performances. *Journal of Parapsychology*, 1964, 28, 41–50.

RHINE, J. B. Psi-missing re-examined. *Journal of Parapsychology*, 1969, 33, 1–38.

ROGERS, D. P. Negative and positive affect and ESP run-score variance. *Journal of Parapsychology*, 1966, 30, 151–159.

ROGERS, D. P. Negative and positive affect and ESP run-score variance: Study II. *Journal of Parapsychology*, 1967, 31, 290–296.

SCHMEIDLER, G. R. Picture-frustration ratings and ESP scores for subjects who showed moderate annoyance at the ESP task. *Journal of Parapsychology*, 1954, 18, 137–152.

SKIBINSKY, M. A comparison of names and symbols in a distance ESP test. *Journal of Parapsychology*, 1950, 14, 140–56.

WEST, D. J. & FISK, G. W. A dual ESP experiment with clock cards. *Journal of the Society for Psychical Research*, 1953, 37, 185–197.

WOODRUFF, J. L. ESP tests under various physiological conditions. *Journal of Parapsychology*, 1943, 7, 264–71.

Extra-Sensory Perception and the
Research Tradition of Parapsychology

S. H. Mauskopf and M. R. McVaugh

In an article written several years ago, which argued for the paradigmatic status of J. B. Rhine's *Extra-Sensory Perception*, our focus was principally on the relationship of this book to earlier work in experimental psychical research. As we put our thesis there: "*Extra-Sensory Perception* is in fact a synthetic exposition, based upon new research, of previous conclusions going back half a century, and its power over parapsychologists must surely have lain in part in the fact that it incorporated in coherent fashion all the truths of psychical research that two generations of students had laboriously uncovered but had not yet properly drawn together" (McVaugh & Mauskopf, 1976, p. 163).

Since writing that article, we have gone on to explore the antecedents to *Extra-Sensory Perception* much more thoroughly; furthermore, we have examined developments in the decade following the publication of Rhine's book in some detail: its reception by the psychical research and the general scientific communities, and the articulation of the research it set forth. Our sense of *Extra-Sensory Perception* as a paradigm for psychical research now takes into account its import for the subsequent psychical research in the field, as well as its import as a synthesis of the earlier research. Our understanding has also been affected by the fact that the concept of "paradigm" has not remained static, either in Kuhn's own writings or in that of his critics and colleagues.

An especially fruitful development of Kuhn's ideas has been given by Larry Laudan in his book, *Progress and Its Problems* (1978). Lauden modifies Kuhn's concept of "paradigm" by using a more flexible and dynamic term: *research tradition*. We propose to outline Laudan's idea of the research tradition, using it as the basis for examining *Extra-Sensory Perception*, and to discuss the question of what might constitute a Rhinean research tradition.

By *research tradition* Laudan means "a set of general assumptions about the entities and processes in a domain of study, and about the appropriate methods to be used for investigating the problems and constructing the theories in that domain" (p. 81). With respect to the specific entities that comprise the research tradition, Lauden takes a more fluid position than Kuhn: "Research traditions do not entail their component theories; nor do those theories, taken either singly or jointly, entail their parent research traditions.... A research tradition, at best, specifies a general ontology for nature and a *general* method for solving natural problems within a given natural domain. A theory, on the other hand, articulates a very specific ontology and a number of specific and testable laws about nature" (p. 84).

Indeed, in Laudan's formulation, the same research tradition can comprise contradictory (and competitive) theories: thus both the wave and corpuscular theorists studying optical periodicity in the early nineteenth century were part of the same research tradition. The term is also more dynamic, allowing for the evolution or even transformation of various aspects of the research tradition: the theories, the techniques, and even core elements, values and metaphysics. In achieving this greater degree of flexibility and dynamism, however, Laudan obscures the relatively neat and clear divisions of Kuhn's definition of scientific development: paradigms, normal science, crisis, revolution. Laudan might argue that his developmental view of scientific activity gives a truer picture of how science actually operates.

Laudan's research tradition is quite close to Kuhn's *paradigm* in that both emphasize the high value placed on "open-endedness" (Kuhn's term) or "problem-solving effectiveness" (Laudan's) by the receiving scientific community. Here, too, Laudan goes beyond Kuhn (adopting Imre Lakatos' notion of "progressive" research traditions), attempting to define criteria of rational choice among competing research traditions in terms of the amount of problem-solving progress afforded (or more precisely the *rate* of progress).

We propose to examine the book *Extra-Sensory Perception* in terms of its impact on the development of the field of parapsychology, using Laudan's notion of an evolving research tradition, in which all of the component concepts might undergo transformation without destroying the continuity of the tradition. We also wish to raise some questions concerning the status both of some of the general implications and narrower research prescriptions to be found in Rhine's epochal monograph.

There are three particularly broad implications which emerge from *Extra-Sensory Perception*: the disciplinary location in which Rhine believed the field should be placed, the methodological style of Rhine's research program, and the metaphysical position Rhine upheld regarding psychical phenomena and abilities.

Disciplinary Location

Rhine's adoption of the term *parapsychology* (from the German, meaning "beside" psychology) reflected his own professional situation in 1934 as a member of an academic psychology department; it also reflected an important set of traditions within psychical research, including the instances of institutionalization of parapsychology in academia prior to Rhine at Duke. Furthermore, Rhine's choice of the term *extrasensory perception* (his first thought had been the equally telling *extrasensory cognition*) reflected his concern that psychical phenomena be subsumed under disciplinary categories familiar to psychologists. Finally, much of the experimental work displayed in Rhine's book exhibited a psychological orientation: the concern for "decline curves," the inclusion of personality profiles of his subjects, and the description of his subjects' mental states all indicate this orientation. Much of the research in this period also grew out of a psychological orientation; the personality correlations of Humphrey and the "sheep–goat" work of Schmeidler in the 1940s are examples. Yet not all the ideas concerning parapsychology enunciated in *Extra-Sensory Perception* were psychological, nor have all subsequent researchers been psychologists. We would raise the following question: how central to the well-being of parapsychology is an emphasis upon association with psychology, as opposed to physics, or even engineering or some other discipline?

Methodological Style

In *Extra-Sensory Perception* Rhine focused on one strand of what had been a complex, disparate set of interests in previous psychical research: the quantitative, experimental strand, through his famous "examplar" of statistically evaluated ESP card-guessing experiments for GESP, clairvoyance and telepathy. Ordinary college students were substituted for colorful mediums; the psychological laboratory took the place of the seance parlor; quantification supplanted the dramatic anecdote. Writing in 1964, Rhine (1934/1964) could still say: "In the main, however, the [our] methods have been built on or around the skeleton of test structure used throughout this book" (p. xxxix, *Extra-Sensory Perception*).

Yet even within the domain of experimental psychical research, there had been other traditions of research, less quantitative and more comprehensive and subtle in their concern for the psychological context of psychic manifestations; for example the research of Rene Warcollier and, to a degree, Whately Carington and later, Gardner Murphy. These traditions (and researchers) continued to be influential after the publication of *Extra-Sensory Perception*. In addition, by the mid-1940s, after perhaps a decade of dominance by experimentally oriented research, the field began to open up again to some of the more traditional interests of the pre-Rhinean era, and by the mid-1960s, the age of the spectacular psychic subject had returned. Part of this change, or so it seems to us, involved a revision of one of Rhine's basic assumptions about psychical ability, that it was common, and easily discoverable in human subjects. We wonder: is it possible currently to identify a dominant research tradition in parapsychological research? and, if so, what is the place of the Rhinean tradition in that research?

Metaphysical Position

Two aspects of *Extra-Sensory Perception* are important here. The first was explicit in Rhine's monograph: his commitment to an antiphysicalist position on the nature of ESP. As he put it: "Of first importance, perhaps, are the facts pointing to the absence of any yet known energy principle in ESP" (Rhine, 1934/1964, p. 157). Rhine, along with many of his predecessors and contemporaries in psychical research, did not believe that any known mode of energy transfer could offer a mechanism for clairvoyance, telepathy, and other psychical abilities. To our knowledge Rhine never denied categorically that such a mechanism *might* be discovered, but the emphasis of his public and private statements was that through the elucidation of psychic abilities and phenomena, the materialistic interpretation of man's place in nature would be stemmed and the existence of mind as an independent entity existing beyond the confines of space, time, and matter would be confirmed.

Antiphysicalism seemed to be buttressed by the recognition of precognition and psychokinesis, which seemed to undercut the very basis of physical causation as traditionally understood. Still, the quantum revolution of the 1920s notwithstanding, the espousal of an antiphysicalist viewpoint has undoubtedly hindered the serious consideration of parapsychological claims by other scientists. The endeavor continues today to "reduce" parapsychology by explaining it in terms of the physical sciences (usually quantum theory). Yet others deny the possibility of reductionism, and urge abandoning an explanation in terms of Western science for a completely different type of explanation, usually using an Oriental religious model. We wonder: is there any consensus on this issue? Is Rhine's original position still sound?

We spoke of a second metaphysical aspect of psychical research, conspicuous by its absence from *ESP*: the survival hypothesis. The question of survival after death has always been a primary underlying impulse for interest in parapsychology, yet in *Extra-Sensory Perception*, this issue receives no consideration, nor does it in the Duke Laboratory's other major monograph geared toward scientific persuasion, *ESP After 60 Years*. The reason for this omission in *Extra-Sensory Perception* is clear: Rhine was trying to bring the subject matter of psychical research under experimental control, and this involved focusing on those aspects of psychical research which might be amenable to such a method. There was also no question that any emphasis on the survival question would have weakened the consideration of parapsychology by the scientific community. Yet, in his correspondence of the period, Rhine showed interest in the survival question; he even termed it the ultimate goal of his own researches in extrasensory perception. With the broadening of interests in the mid-1940s, in the writings of Rhine, and in the writings and research of others, this question returned to some prominence. We would ask, to what degree has the survival hypothesis become a significant part of parapsychological theory and experimentation today?

Having looked briefly at some of the general implications of Rhine's book, let us now consider the narrower prescriptions for a research program which can be found there. In either Kuhn's or Laudan's formulation, the research promise, problem solving effectiveness is what leads to the dominance of a particular research tradition over its predecessors and competitors. What were the research programs set forth in *Extra-Sensory Perception*? Let us consider three overlapping components.

The Research Strategy

The basic exemplar of Rhine's research was the card-guessing experiment using the familiar 25 card, five symbol deck. This particular set of targets was selected for two reasons: simplicity in statistical analysis over the conventional playing-card deck and the psychological neutrality of its symbols. Various strategies were devised to isolate the different types of psychic abilities (such as the DT method for clairvoyance) and to prevent chicanery. The basic method was extended to precognition experiments; an analogous method (using dice) was used in PK testing. Two problems which continued to concern researchers were how to insure complete elimination of any cues from the test material to the percipient, and how to insure the complete randomness of the test material. Extension of the research methods of Rhine's early work included not only the devising of new types of controls and varied test situations, but also the apprehension in Soal's work that the correlation between target and guess does not necessarily need to be temporal.

As we have noted, the card-guessing method was one of a variety of experimental methods used before Rhine's research, and some other methods continued to be used even after the publication of Rhine's book, for example the picture-guessing method favored by Whately Carington. Furthermore, some of the alternative approaches to experimentation — approaches which may have been submerged but never died out — returned after the mid-1940s. At Duke, Louisa Rhine's analysis of anecdotal material in the late 1940s represents such an expansion of methodology beyond the purely experimental. It has, of course, always been a point of controversy within the field as to whether an experimental laboratory approach was really the best manner of eliciting and studying psychical abilities; this is an issue that still has not been resolved by parapsychologists. Experimental methods have been extended into new domains: animal experimentation and experiments in altered mental states. We ask: in what ways can the approach taken by *ESP* still be seen as an exemplar?

Enhancing the Phenomena

By enhancing we mean determining the conditions under which psychical abilities were manifested or inhibited. In *Extra-Sensory Perception*, the focus was on psychological and physiological conditions. The former set of conditions most closely reflected earlier views: conditions of abstraction, with a minimum of distraction from outsiders were most conducive to success. In subsequent publications, other conditions were added to these: a relaxed, playful setting; the absence of boredom with the experimental tasks; and perhaps most important, the role of the experimenter in encouraging success. Given the severe difficulties researchers have faced (and continue to face) in establishing experimental control over psychic phenomena, it would be interesting to know which of these conditions are currently generally accepted as necessary and which are not.

Correlating the Phenomena

Correlating phenomena obviously overlaps considerably with enhancing them. Rhine considered many, principally psychological correlates: between personality types of individual subjects, their family backgrounds, and their psychic abilities. He also studied patterns within the experiment, such as the decline pattern already so prominently displayed in *Extra-Sensory Perception*. Especially in the 1940s, these areas of correlation became dominant in the published research in this country: Rhine's on salience and QD, Humphrey's on personality correlation, and, a novel extension, Schmeidler's on percipient attitude. Do the same sorts of psychological correlations continue to be so prominent in current parapsychological research?

We have touched on some of the broader assumptions as well as the narrower strategies of Rhine's monograph of 1934 in an effort to reflect upon their relationship to the researcher of the present day. It may well be that the relatively inflexible word "paradigm" can no longer capture that relationship; but speaking of a Rhinean "research tradition" allows us to emphasize the continuity of research in this field, even as some of the fundamental concepts and techniques have inevitably been modified or even discarded.

References

Laudan, Larry. *Progress and its problems: Toward a theory of scientific growth*. Berkeley: University of California Press, 1978.

McVaugh, J., & Mauskopf, S. H. J. B. Rhine's *Extra-Sensory Perception* and its background in psychical research. *Isis*, 1976, 67, 161–189.

Rhine, J. B. *Extra-sensory perception*. Boston: Branden Press, 1964. (Originally published, 1934.)

J. B. Rhine and
Post-Mortem Survival:
A Reappraisal and Vindication

C. T. K. CHARI

I felt greatly honored when Professor Ramakrishna Rao invited me to contribute an article on Rhine's views concerning post-mortem survival (PMS) to this volume. During the quarter of a century in which J. B. Rhine gave me much friendly encouragement for research through correspondence, we discussed various complex theoretical aspects of ESP and PK. The survival question was seldom brought up. The more I read his pronouncements on the question (J. B. Rhine, 1947, 1951, 1953, 1960, 1974) and the more he came to know about my published work on the issue (Chari, 1962a, 1962b, 1976a, 1977, 1978), a deepening unspoken understanding grew between us. We seemed to know how we would both deal with several facets of this extremely complex problem.

Should the Survival Question Survive?

The phrasing of the question is Rhine's, not mine. He wrote (1951) that "the survival question is a very, very, difficult one" because "it is not even easy to state the problem clearly.... Different persons read different meanings into this issue, even when they use the same terms." The survival question is not a privileged issue awaiting its resolution by a few sequestered parapsychological groups and associations. The problem is tied up with the whole gamut of scientific knowledge and all the imperfectly expressed aspirations of religion. Even when we think we have dissected out the empirical issues that, we imagine, concern parapsychology alone, the question throws long metaphysical shadows. Unobtrusive nonempirical meanings fringe the empirical problems.

As a pioneer of ESP and PK research, J. B. Rhine realized only too well that experimental inquiry came after a century and more of spiritual and survival studies in revolt against the *fin de siècle* materialism of the West. Almost the first task William McDougall assigned to his new assistants at Duke, J. B. and L. E. Rhine, was an assessment of the records drawn up by J. F. Thomas, a Detroit educator, of his work with mediums in England and America. The records seemed to disclose a subtle "psychic trail" left by Ethel, the deceased wife of Thomas. The Rhines, therefore, confronted the PMS problem on the very threshold of their parapsychological careers, which, I believe, few other researchers have done. Thomas (Gibson, 1954) became a convinced survivalist. The Rhines (L. E. Rhine, 1975) realized the magnitude of the problem.

The penultimate answer to the PMS question, for J. B. Rhine, is not a bare negative, a frigid *non possumus*. Negatives, he knew, are difficult to prove. Receptivity to new formulations of PMS will open up interdisciplinary perspectives for the research. Rhine warned parapsychologists that their scruples and inhibitions about PMS, however understandable and excusable, should not blunt their handling of new techniques of PMS research and new assessments of PMS evidence. We must combine the utmost open-mindedness to the problem with extreme reserve and caution in considering the solutions.

New Strategies of PMS Research and New Academic Quandaries

J. B. Rhine (1960) grouped the PMS events into three broad classes: spontaneous events, semispontaneous and recurrent events, and mediumistic occurrences. Many approaches added new sophistication to PMS investigation: L. E. Rhine's memorable classification of the huge Duke collection of spontaneous cases with a search for motivation, the novel traps set for poltergeists, better evaluations of mediumistic material (Saltmarsh, Pratt-Birge), combination lock tests and ciphers (Thouless, Pratt, Stevenson), Hereward Carrington's word-association tests applied to mediums, Whately Carington's analysis of variance used to separate the "controls" of mediums from the more baffling "communicators," the study of uninvited "communicators," reincarnation field studies from Asia and elsewhere — all these and more provided for J. B. Rhine an ever-broadening framework for viewing the PMS problem, but no *experimentum crucis* of survival.

Along with fashioning new investigative designs, sharp declines in research occurred everywhere. These declines could not simply be attributed to lack of funds and investigators. There seemed to be a growing, uneasy realization that the strategies evolved in PMS research fell woefully short of solving the real problem. Discomfort was caused too by the continued incredulity and skepticism of orthodox biology, neurophysiology, and psychology, which stressed more and more mind's dependence on intricate bodily mechanisms. Recent "bissected brain" experiments (Chari, 1976c) have robbed the time-honored paradigms of "mental unity" and "mental dissociation" of their plausibility. Writers like R. H. Thouless (1979) and Michael Grosso (1979) who speculate freely on survival in terms of "consciousness" have regrettably little to say about the nature, the contents, and the texture of the "surviving consciousness." Their "nay" takes away much of the cold comfort of their "yea." Heated contemporary debate over PMS involves questioning what survives: the private self, the public self, or quasipublic quasispatial clusters of images. Such debates are highlighted by the new cybernetic and psychopharmacological models for "altered states of consciousness." Recent thinking seems to imply the possibility of a system with a nonlinear transformation function calling for a multivalued logic rather than traditional "true-false" logic (Fisher, 1969). The most sanguine spiritualists and reincarnationists can no longer nestle in their comfortable rival tabernacles.

Early PMS Research

Surveys of spontaneous psi phenomena, used for the light they may throw on psi in the laboratory (L. E. Rhine, 1961, 1967, 1975), will always be needed. But PMS researchers have to engage in more daring and speculative flights, manipulating unwieldy masses of spontaneous phenomena to extrapolate tentative hypotheses about post-mortem consciousness. Such a venture landed early researchers in the difficulty of separating ante-mortem appearances from the authentic post-mortem appearances. An arbitrary line had to be drawn at an awkward and wholly presumed "telepathic lag" (Tyrrell, 1938). As the Rhines noted on several occasions, telepathy was almost the only alternative to survival considered by the early SPR and ASPR investigators. It occurred to few at that time that "telepathic lag" might be retrocognitive ESP of unknown range, depth and potency.

To take only one instance (the illustration is mine): On September 24, 1905, at one o'clock, in England, Miss Ramsden (a well-known figure in the annals of telepathy) conducted a prearranged "telepathic" experiment with a Danish friend in Copenhagen. Allowance was made for the difference in times. The friend seemed to be cooperating in the experiment; for Miss Ramsden *mentally* heard him say in an amused voice *in Danish*: "Are you there? I cannot hear...your living wires." It transpired later that he had not sat at all for the experiment. But *earlier* in the day he had conversed in Danish with a friend about Miss Ramsden's letter arranging the sitting and used the expression "living wires." The episode is classed as one of "unintentional telepathic transmission" and "intentional perception" by Anna Hude (1913).

To the modern PMS researcher who has reaped the rich harvest of J. B. Rhine's psi research, the small episode opens up vistas. What perhaps operated in the 1905 experiment might have been retrocognitive ESP; or more likely a GESP of the "psychometric" or "psychoscopic" variety, using Miss Ramsden's letter as a "link." There is also a possibility that the *Danish* remarks apparently mentally addressed to Miss Ramsden were not addressed to her at all in the objective situation in Copenhagen. The percipient's activity cannot always be fathomed in terms of obvious motivation. In an early article (Chari, 1952), I have shown that "telepathy" in the life-situation may have retrocognitive and precognitive stretches, often long. Making a few amiable and perfunctory gestures to telepathy, clairvoyance, and precognition regarded as *separate* alternatives to survival will not suffice in PMS theory-building. It is to the credit of the Rhines that they demonstrated this point.

Is the Logic of Inference Used in Survival Research Foolproof?

It seems to me that the logic used in much PMS research centered on spontaneous psi opens the door dangerously to the inductive fallacy. Heaping an empirical Pelion on an empirical Ossa will not somehow generate inductive probabilities without clearly defined hypotheses. For PMS research, J. B. Rhine asked, where are the clearly conceived hypotheses?

In contemporary philosophy of science (Suppe, 1977), the confirmation of general hypotheses has become a battleground for sharply divergent views. The survivalist can no longer suppose he can ignore the problem by claiming to be a specialist, the caretaker of a century of much maligned research. Karl Popper in particular has challenged the notion that a general hypothesis can receive non-zero probability. He maintains that the acceptance and rejection of proposed general theories must be done on *nonprobabilistic* grounds. In contradistinction to those who claim that a finite number of cases, say C, relevant to a hypothesis H, can admit of a theoretical probabilistic assessment $p(C,H)$, Popper argues that the *content relationships* of empirical theories (can survival be regarded as an empirical theory or not?) are not reducible to the probabilities of their components, (a), (b):

$$p\,(a) > p\,(a,b) < p\,(b).$$

This will hardly suit many survivalists, industriously piling up case material without clear-cut hypotheses. I contend, however, that neither survival nor reincarnation can be defined by inductive approximations supposedly extracted from case material.

Abner Shimony has suggested that at least seriously proposed hypotheses in an inquiry can be assigned nonzero probabilities, while the nonseriously proposed hypotheses receive zero probability. In PMS research, which are seriously proposed and which nonseriously proposed hypotheses?

Is a nonsurvivalist hypothesis *necessarily* nonserious in PMS research? Arthur Burks has developed an inductive logic which uses suitably defined "subjective probabilities" and "presuppositions" which are neither *a priori* nor *a posteriori*. I do not know how many PMS researchers would care to follow him. Swinburne (1973) defends "probabilistic confirmation" of general hypotheses against Popper, but makes the damaging admission (apparently to appease the importunate followers of T. S. Kuhn) that the criteria of confirmation are *not* necessarily transcultural. If the point is admitted at all, it should be of great importance in evaluating the *logic* of reincarnationist research conducted in the East as well as in the West. In the welter of contemporary opinions, I confess that I find it attractive to follow the lead of Lakatos and think of PMS research in terms of "programs" and "problem shifts." I greatly fear that to talk of "paradigm shifts" in the sense of Kuhn (as some invite us to do) may take away altogether whatever objectivity and continuity scientific knowledge may have. Few parapsychologists who gratefully accept Kuhn's "revolutions" seem to be aware of the pitfalls of doing so. One may end up denying that survival research is scientific. Supposing we adopt the modest approach of Lakatos, what problem shifts would be significant in PMS research? Is there any consensus at present?

In any case, whatever approach we take, our survival and reincarnation hypotheses *must* have reasonable *alternatives*. Otherwise they may not admit of "confirmation" or "falsification" in any sense of the term. It is J. B. Rhine's signal merit to have shown that the whole enterprise of framing "alternative hypotheses" in PMS research is fraught with unprecedented difficulties. The process of theory building in PMS research must be examined in depth and detail.

PMS and Superpsi

J. B. Rhine (1951) hypothesized an "omnibus" type of psi as an alternative to survival. This omnibus psi or "superpsi" has met with varying responses from survivalists. Some would accept the demonstrated forms of psi in the laboratory and in life but call the concept of superpsi far too sweeping and gratuitous. Superpsi explains any and every piece of survival evidence and admits of no falsification at all. What would J. B. Rhine say about this? I submit that, apart from a few tested but very limited hypotheses about psi (Rao, 1966) (and perhaps a few suggested interesting "psychological parallels"), we know next to nothing about the *intrinsic nature* of psi and its ranges and limits in life (Chari, 1977). It seems to me that *all* psi is "super" because it departs radically from the framework of contemporary science. I would consider (Chari, 1974, 1975, 1976b) GESP operating in its "psychometric" or "psychoscopic" form (occasionally along with GPK), extracting paranormal knowledge about deceased persons, as a valid alternative to proposed survival and reincarnation hypotheses.

I do not have to depend on any other research in staking so stupendous a claim. My own Indian survival studies incline me in this direction. A very casually encountered and scarcely remembered item (not only a person, name, or incident, but in India even a horoscope, temple, or idol) can serve as an unsuspected psychometric link with deceased persons. I quite realize that a hypothesis of this range has to be developed in some detail to explain both mediumistic communications and reincarnations. I have advanced some suggestions elsewhere (1962a, 1962b). The rest of my theorizing can wait; J. B. Rhine's argument goes much deeper than superpsi regarded as an alternative to survival. He argued repeatedly that superpsi is presupposed in all forms of the survival hypothesis. The deceased person has lost completely his anchorage in the neuromuscular system with its exosomatic and endosomatic information processing of received "signals." His props in space and time have all been knocked away. How can the deceased person achieve mediumistic return or reincarnation without a very extensive psi; not to trifle, a superpsi?

Is ESP–PK Not the Alternative but the Sole Basis of Alleged "Discarnate Memories"?

To sharpen Rhine's argument, I focus attention on the problem of memory, so crucial for PMS research. So far as contemporary scientific research goes, long-term memory involves a highly complex array of molecular DNA and RNA factors. How are we to conceive of the concatenation of factors explaining discarnate memory? Even holographic models of memory do not obviate *this* difficulty. Reincarnation, hypothesizing re-embodiment of discarnate minds, is apt to end up as a thinly disguised neo-Lamarckism (Chari, 1977, 1977–1978). According to reincarnation's premises, the memories, habits, and even physical features, like scars, *acquired* by individuals of one generation are transmitted to individuals of another generation by their surviving minds being reborn. Biological information, so far as established science knows, flows from the DNA of one generation to the DNA of another. Pattee (1968) has extrapolated quantum-mechanical analogues of genetic coding theorems to preserve the asymmetrical flow of information so essential to the stability of the species and the individual. Frölich has invoked long-range correlations akin to those of quantum-mechanical superfluidity and superconductivity to account for coherent phylogenetic and ontogenetic information-patterns. In the neo-Lamarckian interpretation of reincarnation it appears that information flows from the RNA and protein of the deceased individual (via "astral bodies" and "psi-components?") to the DNA of a newly-born individual in another generation.

Perhaps I should add (to anticipate some survivalists who are fond of all kinds of bizarre pseudoscientific speculation) that the recent experiments in cloning and genetic engineering (Chari, 1977–1978) are only attempts to transfer *primary* DNA information to other *primary* systems. In the more controverted experiments of Ungar and others, the attempt is to transfer, at least for a short while, some of the secondary protein information of individuals (such as rats which have learned a task) to the secondary systems of similar, uninformed individuals (rats which have *not* learned the task). In the most recondite experiments, there is not the remotest analogue to reincarnation, to the highly selective transfer of *secondary* protein information from one specified individual in one generation to the *primary* information system of another individual. "Mediumistic memories," too, have no analogue, unless "discarnate intervention" in the brain is biochemical. There should be evidence for so weird a supposition.

So far as I can see, there is only one way out of the impasse. Memory for the discarnate mind must be a highly specialized form of *paranormal retrocognition*, bypassing the formidable biochemical array postulated for normal long-term memories. Reincarnation can neatly evade Crick's "central dogma of molecular biology," since it involves prodigious ESP and PK. The PK could act directly on the human fetus. No specific Lamarckian fallacy would then be involved, only a glaring departure from all the known laws of biology.

I hope I have now underlined the kind of predicament that, according to J. B. Rhine, survival speculation involves. Since survival in any form *must* use a very comprehensive psi (in any coherent theory), superpsi can be an *alternative* to any survival hypothesis. What reliable criterion have we for distinguishing superpsi from survival? Theory-building in PMS research has hardly begun.

Superpsi Is Not "Ptolemaic" and Survival Is Not "Copernican"

Superpsi has no Ptolemaic complexity, and the survival hypothesis has no overwhelming Copernican simplicity. There are several *kinds* of simplicity (and complexity) appropriate to scientific theories. Just what *kind* is needed for theory-building depends on the particular context and the ongoing epistemic enterprise. Cyril Burt used to say that for the socio-psychological disciplines, simplicity is no desideratum at all. Popper has attempted to explain "degrees of simplicity" in terms of "degrees of falsification." I hope I have shown that this helps PMS research not at all. Superpsi and survival are neither confirmable nor falsifiable at present. The only hopeful approach to survival is to take superpsi and look for some clues to survival. Superpsi can never be repudiated as a presupposition of the survival hypothesis. Some survivalists might stop with superpsi, considering it a big enough step without going on to survival. I suspect that a majority of parapsychologists who are not PMS researchers at all may reject *both* superpsi and survival as unwarranted in the present stage of investigation. J. B. Rhine wanted to keep the survival problem *open*. One cannot keep it open unless the superpsi question is *also* kept open; for superpsi is the *basis* of all survival speculation.

Animal Psi and Survival

I turn to yet another facet of the PMS problem as J. B. Rhine viewed it. He was interested in animal psi (anpsi) right from the beginning of his career and even tried to replicate a few neo-Lamarckian experiments of McDougall. All his life Rhine was launching new anpsi programs. Anpsi has a bearing on the survival problem viewed in a larger biological context. Some might object to survival by reminding us of the long and arduous evolution of man. The bissected brain and self-consciousness came after much evolutionary fumbling.

There are three general theoretical possibilities in anpsi research. First, anpsi might be a rudimentary and vestigial function, an anachronistic survival of a primeval adaptation. Second, anpsi might promote biological adaptation, and thus have gained an increasing foothold in higher organisms. A third possibility has been mooted by the Kreitlers (1974): Psi is a static function. It is neither retrogressive nor progressive. It might have lost its exosomatic range in order to establish an endosomatic range in memory retrieval and other cognitive functions. In order words, psi may be an aspect of internal information processing in organisms. The time for a choice between theories has not come. Anpsi research, after taking several wrong turns, is coming of age (Davis, 1979). The possible effects produced by human experimenters, however, have to be eliminated convincingly.

I am inclined to suppose that some compromise between the second and third approaches to anpsi might promote research. Psi by itself may indeed be a static possibility, yet it might have contributed indirectly to organismic adaptation. I wonder whether a hypothesis along these lines would account for the striking difference between the positive and effective adaptation of Graham Watkins' lizard and the shockingly maladapted "psi-missing" of Helmut Schmidt's cockroaches. The latter received more shocks than they should have if their responses had been random; and the experiments seem to have been replicated. (However, we must consider experimenter effects: Schmidt had a thorough dislike of cockroaches and perhaps unconsciously wanted them punished by electric shocks.) Could there be unsuspected mediation by the ganglion nerve system of the cockroach? The olfactory receptors in the antennae of the cockroach respond anomalously to many stimuli (Yamada, 1969) and there would seem to be a curious dual sensitivity in the compound eye of the cockroach (Carthy & Newell, 1968). In the woodlice which figured in some early and inconclusive experiments of Randall (1972), there are curious oscillations between photo-positive and photo-negative responses based on a primary humidity response (Chari, 1970, postscript).

The whole question of survival, J. B. Rhine believed, must be revised in the light of a new "psi biology." To do so may change the approaches of both anti- and prosurvivalists. Professor C. W. K. Mundle (1973) remarked that "Sidgwick and Myers would not have wished to ascribe immortal souls to insects and unhatched eggs." Perhaps not. Yet many Asian survivalists who believe in transmigration might wish to extend their "search for proof" to the humblest denizens of the animal kingdom. Rhine would counsel us to go beyond both metaphysical stances for some significant reformulation of the survival question. It may be that only when self-consciousness has emerged that psi can "reach out" (an oft-disputed expression used by J. B. Rhine) into the network connecting objects, organisms, and persons. There may be some unorthodox linking up of consciousness; the network may survive the dissolution of the brain. Anpsi may not have quite this "reach." When Rhine talked of the "non-physical" ranges of mind (1974), he was not asking us to abandon physics. He was inviting us to look beyond the known ranges of physics. Surely physics has not said its last word. Neutrino physics, quantum physics and relativistic physics have all been used by psi-theorists. There will be more to come.

Out-of-the-Body Experience and Its Import for Survival

It need hardly be pointed out that J. B. Rhine was interested in the "self-projection" experiments of Hornell Hart (1954, 1959). They yielded no certitude of survival for Rhine, however. He feared that it was too premature to claim that the "exteriorized I" in the experiments gathered *more* information than ESP could furnish, produced more paranormal physical effects than PK could account for, and behaved in quasispatial ways alien to mere "telepathic hallucinations." I have remarked that the "post-mortem appearances" which prompted early survivalist conjectures were also often highly debatable.

A new era of experiments in out-of-body experience (Osis, 1974; Osis & McCormack, 1980; Rogo, 1978) seems to have begun. Is J. B. Rhine's guarded stand still justifiable? I believe so. Since most modern cases are more fragmentary and less startling than the classical cases, I prefer to use a classical case, that of Vincent Turvey (1909) in making my theoretical points.

I agree with John Palmer that we must use the hypothesis of dislocated body images induced by experimental insecurity, stress, and threats to the ego. Teitelbaum induced by hypnosis striking deformations of body image paralleled only by the dislocations produced by cerebral lesions. During an "out-of-the-body excursion," a few miles away from home, Turvey claimed to have "possessed" a Mr. Blake. During the trance, he cried out, "Cat, cat." It turned out that a Persian cat had followed Mrs. Turvey to her home and clamored for attention. The suggestion here is not of disembodied ESP-PK. Between what Turvey called "it," "me," and "I" there would seem to be a shared *coenesthetic* core, possibly even a few sensory cues. The hypothesis of "two bodies" which my friend Dr. R. Crookall uses for analyzing his huge collection of OBE cases may be an undue simplification of a very complex situation.

Hart referred to the alleged fact that the out-of-the-body traveller perceives both persons and objects in appropriate surroundings and even meets occasionally other out-of-the-body travellers. But does this mean that we can affirm an unambiguous geography for either the location of the traveller or the environment he apparently perceives? Turvey reported that while "out-of-the-body" he could perceive persons and details of objects, but sometimes he failed to perceive large objects (for example, a bookcase) directly in the line of vision if one were perceiving normally. Occasionally he diagnosed the diseased condition of a person's body which (he claimed) he could not have done normally. Besides, he precognized earthquakes and floods while out-of-the-body. Extrasensory perception and PK form the core of some striking OBEs.

The "spirits" encountered occasionally during OBEs are no more evidential than the "spirits" manifesting through mediums. Extrasensory perception and PK together with the OBE would constitute a serious alternative to mediumistic communication.

Lastly, while the deformation of the body image in OBEs may convey hints of death, it may be very different from the far more serious wrench occurring at bodily death. Out-of-body experiences cannot be safely used for theory-building in PMS research as of now.

Conclusion

I conclude by submitting that J. B. Rhine was justified in arguing that the survival problem must be "laid on the shelf" for the present while survival research is vigorously pursued. Our most hopeful clues come from "enlarged" forms of ESP and PK such as "superpsi." The horizons of parapsychology are far-reaching. J. B. Rhine was honest enough to admit that it *may* be that in parapsychology we have put a little image on a high pedestal. Yet, the chances are, as L. E. Rhine reminds us (1975), that we are like Columbus when he reached San Salvador. With one important difference, however; we seem to be glimpsing the mainland beyond.

REFERENCES

CARTHY, J. D., & NEWELL, G. E. (EDS.). *Invertebrate receptors* (Symposium of the London Zoological Society). New York: Academic Press, 1968.

CHARI, C. T. K. A note on precognition. *Journal of the American Society for Psychical Research*, 1952, 46, 85–95.

CHARI, C. T. K. Paranormal cognition, survival and reincarnation. *Journal of the American Society for Psychical Research*, 1962a, 56, 158–83.

CHARI, C. T. K. Paramnesia and reincarnation. *Proceedings of the Society for Psychical Research*, 1962b, 53, 264–86.

CHARI, C. T. K. Psychophysiological issues about EEG alpha activity and ESP. *Journal of the American Society for Psychical Research*, 1970, 64, 411–20.

CHARI, C. T. K. Ein systemtheoretischer Zugang zur paranormalen Kognition. *Zeitschrift für Parapsychologie und Grenzgebiete der Psychologie*, 1974, 16, 158–66.

CHARI, C. T. K. Siamo forse parte di una straordinaria "rete"? *ESP: Parapsicologia e Fenomeni dell'Insolito*, 1975, 1, 44–52.

CHARI, C. T. K. The challenge of psi: New horizons of scientific research. In White, R. A. (ed.), *Surveys in parapsychology*. Metuchen, N.J.: Scarecrow Press, 1976a.

CHARI, C. T. K. Prolegomena to some theories of "psi information." *Journal of Research in Psi Phenomena*, 1976b, 1, 5–23.

CHARI, C. T. K. Letter on the two halves of the brain. *Journal of the Society for Psychical Research*, 1976c, 48, 285–87.

CHARI, C. T. K. Some generalized theories and models of psi: A critical evaluation. In Wolman, B. (ed.), *Handbook of parapsychology*. New York: Van Nostrand Reinhold, 1977.

CHARI, C. T. K. Radhakrishnan's interpretation of rebirth. *The Indian philosophical annual* (Dr. S. Radhakrishnan Center for Advanced Study in Philosophy, University of Madras), 1977–8, 12, 131–40.

CHARI, C. T. K. Reincarnation research: Method and interpretation. In Ebon, M. (ed.), *The Signet handbook of parapsychology.* New York: New American Library, 1978.

DAVIS, J. W. Psi in animals: A review of laboratory experiments. *Parapsychology Review,* 1979, **10**, 2–9.

GIBSON, E. P. The Ethel Thomas case. *Tomorrow,* 1954, **2**(4), 59–72.

FISHER, R. On creative, psychotic and ecstatic states. In Jakab, I. (ed.), *Psychiatry and art,* 2 (International Colloquium of the Society for Psychopathology of Expression). New York: Karger, Basel, 1969.

GROSSO, M. The survival problem in a mind-dependent world. *Journal of the American Society for Psychical Research,* 1979, **73**, 367–80.

HART, H. Man outside his body? *Tomorrow,* 1954, **2**(2), 81–9.

HART, H. *The enigma of survival.* Springfield, Ill.: C. C. Thomas, 1959.

HUDE, A. *The evidence for communication with the dead.* London: T. Fisher Unwin, 1913.

KREITLER, H., & KREITLER, S. ESP and cognition. *Journal of Parapsychology,* 1974, **38**, 267–85.

MUNDLE, C. W. K. Strange facts in search of a theory. *Proceedings of the Society for Psychical Research,* 1973, **56**, 1–20.

OSIS, K. Out of the body research at the A.S.P.R. *ASPR Newsletter,* 1974, Summer, 1–3.

OSIS, K., & MCCORMACK, D. Location of an out-of-the-body projection during perceptual testing. *Journal of the American Society for Psychical Research,* 1980, **74**, 319–29.

PATTEE, H. H. The physical basis of coding and reliability in biological evolution. In Waddington, C. H. (ed.), *Towards a theoretical biology: Prolegomena.* Edinburgh: Edinburgh University Press, 1968, 69–93.

RANDALL, J. L. Recent experiments in animal parapsychology. *Journal of the Society for Psychical Research,* 1972, **46**, 124–135.

RAO, K. R. *Experimental parapsychology: A review and interpretation.* Springfield, Ill.: C. C. Thomas, 1966.

RHINE, J. B. *The reach of the mind.* New York: William Sloane, 1947.

RHINE, J. B. *Telepathy and human personality* (Tenth Frederic W. H. Myers memorial lecture, 1950). London: Society for Psychical Research, 1951. *See* pp. 28–31.

RHINE, J. B. *New world of the mind.* New York: William Sloane, 1953. *See* pp. 302–18.

RHINE, J. B. Incorporeal personal agency (IPA): The prospect of a scientific solution. *Journal of Parapsychology,* 1960, **24**, 279–309.

RHINE, J. B. Man's nonphysical nature. In Cullen, J. W. (ed.), *The legacies in the study of behavior.* Springfield, Ill.: C. C. Thomas, 1974.

RHINE, L. E. *Hidden channels of the mind.* New York: William Sloane, 1961. *See* Ch. 15.

RHINE, L. E. *ESP in life and lab: Tracing hidden channels.* New York: Macmillan, 1967. *See* pp. 27–28; 206–9.

RHINE, L. E. *Psi: What is it? The story of ESP and PK.* New York: Harper & Row, 1975. *See* Chapters 24–25.

Rogo, D. Scott (ed.). *Mind beyond the body? The mystery of ESP projection*. New York: Penguin Books, 1979.

Suppe, F. (ed.). *The structure of scientific thought*. Urbana: University of Illinois Press, 1977.

Swinburne, R. *An introduction to confirmation theory*. London: Methuen, 1973.

Thouless, R. H. Theories about survival. *Journal of the Society for Psychical Research*, 1979, **50**, 1–8.

Turvey, V. *The beginnings of seership*. London: Stead's Publishing House, 1909.

Tyrrell, G. N. M. *Science and psychical phenomena*. London: Methuen, 1938.

Yamada, M. Extracellular recordings from single neurones in the olfactory centre of the cockroach, *Nature*, 1968, **217**, 778–79 (Letter).

J. B. Rhine on
the Nature of Psi

JOHN BELOFF

Throughout his long career Rhine was the acknowledged spokesman and representative of parapsychology, not only for the general public, but even more for the scientific community. As such he wrote and lectured extensively on every aspect of parapsychology, its aims, its achievements and the challenge which it presented to received ideas.

In attempting to expound Rhine's teachings on the nature of psi, the first thing one has to realize is that Rhine was primarily a practical man, a scientist and administrator, and that his two main objectives were (a) to make sure that research should proceed along the most productive and effective lines and not lose itself in futile projects, and (b) to justify parapsychology to the world at large as a pursuit of preëminent importance for mankind and to dispel the occult associations that it had inherited. Rhine was an enthusiast but he was not a philosopher. He was passionately committed to his views, but he had no interest in abstract ideas for their own sake. We may look in vain for any systematic exposition of his theories or for any concerted attempt to defend his position against its critics or for any profound analyses of the concepts that he uses so freely. These have to be disengaged from a general survey of his pronouncements.

What I propose to discuss in this paper is his conception of psi and how he thought it fitted into the scheme of things. Since one must perforce be selective, I shall confine the discussion to four themes to which, in his writings, he constantly returned. Naturally, they by no means exhaust the many topics on which he had something important to say but they illustrate, I think, as well as anything what is most characteristic of the Rhinean conception of psi. They are, in the order in which I shall discuss them: (1) the nonphysicality of psi, (2) the unconscious nature of psi, (3) the problem of survival, and (4) the universality of the psi faculty.

The Nonphysicality of Psi

Undoubtedly, the most central tenet of Rhinean doctrine is that psi is nonphysical. Like his predecessors who founded the Society for Psychical Research, Rhine was convinced that parapsychology, and parapsychology alone, could provide the scientific answer to materialism. This is how he puts it in one of the many passages in which he makes the point:

> It is now fairly clear that psi phenomena are identified by the fact that they defy physical explanation and require a psychological one. They always happen to people (or animals) or involve some associated or at least suspected agency or experience; but ... they do not follow conventional physical principles [Rhine, 1953, p. 150].

In short, psi is mental but not physical. And the reason for calling it nonphysical was, so far as Rhine was concerned, quite straightforward; namely, that neither the physical properties of the ESP target nor its positioning relative to the subject seemed to have any effect on that subject's scores. Neither distance nor intervening material barriers were relevant variables in the psi experiment. Moreover, although this claim has periodically been challenged, I think it safe to say that so far no serious evidence has been produced that contradicts it. There may well be deeper, philosophical reasons for regarding psi as nonphysical, but these were the primary considerations that weighed with Rhine, coupled, of course, with the facts of precognition. For, even if we could conceive of some mechanism, some hypothetical radiation, that could bridge the space gap in ESP, we would still be left with no physical explanation of the time gap. Indeed, I think this accounts for Rhine's well-known predilection for the precognitive mode in ESP testing; at one stroke it disposed of any hypothetical mechanism of transmission.

In the passage I have quoted, Rhine advisedly uses the words "conventional physical principles," for by then he was aware that quantum theory had opened up a whole new world of subatomic particles whose behavior was as much at variance with the laws of classical physics as psi itself. The concept of "nonlocality" or of "space-time independence" is today entertained by quantum theorists without any sense of their having thereby repudiated physicality. However, "nonphysicality" is, as Rhine insists, only the negative criterion of psi; its positive criterion, as I have said, is its mentalistic attributes. "Nothing but a psi phenomenon..., appears to defy all these criteria of physical operation and at the same time displays intelligent purpose in the process" (Rhine, 1953, p. 164).

The critical question that arises in connection with the mind–brain relationship is whether, as the materialist holds, the brain conceived as a purely physical system is alone responsible, in the last resort, for the whole of our behavior and experience, in which case mental phenomena may be regarded as mere "epiphenomena" of their underlying brain processes, or whether, as the mentalist holds, mental events can be causally efficacious. In plain language, are our thoughts, feelings, and strivings no more than the subjective reflection in consciousness of what is going on in our brain; or do they, as our intuitions would suggest, make a difference to what we actually do? Rhine keenly appreciated what was at issue and rightly, in my opinion, argued that, if psi is a reality, the materialist thesis collapses, since no one has been able to suggest how the brain, conceived purely as a physical system, could produce a psi effect.

It is, perhaps, not always realized by the layman how widely the materialist thesis is currently held by psychologists, brain physiologists, philosophers, and other authorities. Many of them simply take their materialism for granted; but the more perspicacious among them, like the philosopher David Armstrong, would agree with Rhine that parapsychology *does* pose a threat to the materialist thesis. They differ from him only in refusing to acknowledge that the case for psi has been made. The ramifications of materialism are, truly, very far-reaching. For, if it is the case that all our decisions in life are made for us by the state of our brain at the moment, in accordance with impersonal electrochemical forces, then the notion of free will—that is, of man as a responsible moral agent—that is at the heart of so much that we have come to accept in ethics, in jurisprudence, in religion, and so on, is radically undermined. Rhine was right, therefore, to place so much emphasis on the nonphysicality of psi if he wanted to show that the importance of parapsychology went far beyond its purely scientific implications. At the same time it was, Rhine insisted, by virtue of its attachment to scientific methodology and criteria of evidence that parapsychology could hope to exert its influence in the modern world. His faith in the power of science is nicely illustrated by his repeated plea that parapsychology was the best defense the free world had against totalitarian communism, as the materialist foundations of communist doctrine would crumble once the facts of psi were more widely known.

In the context of the traditional mind-body problem, Rhine would qualify as a dualist-interactionist. Yet he persistently disavowed the designation of dualist or, rather, confessed to being at most a relative or provisional dualist. This has always struck me as a curious idiosyncrasy for one who so clearly envisaged psi phenomena as representing a mind-matter interaction, but I think I can discern the reasons that led him to adopt this position. In the first place he was always concerned to dissociate himself from any kind of supernaturalist or transcendentalist view of psi. He clung firmly to the view that psi was as much part of nature as life itself, that there was nothing other-worldly about it, that it had its own set of laws and could be studied as a natural phenomenon like any other. Secondly, as a scientist, he preferred to leave the door open to the possibility of some ultimate cosmology that would embrace both mind and matter and derive the properties of each from some more fundamental set of principles. In one place we find him saying: "It seems justifiable to expect to find underneath the surface of our somewhat arbitrary academic distinctions ... a less definable but more basic reality than has been known hitherto in natural science" (Rhine, 1953, p. 164); and elsewhere, he is even more explicit in qualifying his postulate of nonphysicality, as when he says: "This distinction of nonphysicality is reasonably certain to prove to be a transient, even though a temporarily very important, point. It is important now as the essential negative boundary in the definition of parapsychology; it is necessary in order to call the attention of science to the existence of another domain of nature that is now measurably and experimentally demonstrable as a distinctive territory"; and then adds: "At least one inquirer has been urging exploration also of the positive or *common ground of nature that makes a psychophysical border necessary*; this should in due time become a principal object of scientific study for those in the field of parapsychology" (Rhine, 1960, pp. 75–76).

Perhaps Rhine's position could not unfairly be described as that of a would-be monist. In a letter he wrote to me in February 1964, after reading my book, *The Existence of the Mind*, written from a dualist standpoint, he explains why he is reluctant to go all the way with the dualists and more or less admits that it is partly a matter of policy. "The main difference it will make," he writes, "is on our getting together with our modern scientists in the United States and those in the U.S.S.R. They will much more quickly add a new *energetic element* than they would admit another order of nature. I am trying them out in Russia and, I think, making headway" (my italics). The fact that he speaks so frequently of psi as some new form of energy is surely revealing. Strictly, to speak of a "nonphysical energy" is as much a contradiction in terms as it would be to speak of an "unextended space." But Rhine, in his desire to promote parapsychology, wanted to have it both ways. Psi was at once the spiritual, immaterial component of the human personality and, at the same time, a new "energetic element" in nature. The confusion can also be traced, I believe, to certain common misconceptions about dualism that have been prevalent ever since Descartes himself first attempted to define the distinction between mind and matter. "One cannot even conceive the possibility" Rhine (1953) says at one point, "of two completely different systems interacting and, yet, at the same time, constituting so manifestly unified a whole as the personality of man — without having something fundamental in common" (p. 161). It was this very point that worried Descartes and, even more, his disciples, some of whom tried to meet the objection by inventing fantastic models of parallel worlds that ran in synchrony but never interacted.

In fact, however, the objection had no force. Descartes and his followers had simply taken over a principle of scholastic philosophy according to which an effect must be of the same nature as its cause. But there is no reason in logic why this must be so. There is nothing contradictory in supposing that an immaterial entity, if that is what the mind is, could produce physical effects. There is, moreover, nothing to stop the mind creating mental representations of the external world in consciousness (what else do we mean by perception?) nor is there any reason why the material brain should not be made to conform to the will or intentions of the immaterial mind (what else do we mean by voluntary action?). The idea, still being purveyed by so many modern philosophers, that there is something absurd or incoherent about dualist interactionism is without foundation. Rhine was quite right to insist that mind and matter must have "something fundamental in common" but that something is, precisely, the power to influence one another; nothing more than that is required.

The Unconscious Nature of Psi

Rhine points out (1953) that, while psychiatry gave to psychology the concept of the unconscious, "the experimental tools by which to deal quantitatively with unconscious processes have been and are being developed through the psi investigations" (p. 203). Moreover psi, Rhine believed, was unconscious in a stronger sense than the unconscious with which psychiatrists are concerned; "the operation of psi is *really* unconscious. It is unconscious in a different degree or way from experiences that are merely forgotten or repressed.... The operation of psi is, so far as the researches can indicate to date, irrecoverably unconscious" (pp. 203–204. italics in original). This somewhat cryptic passage calls for elucidation. What did Rhine mean by psi being "really" or "irrecoverably" unconscious?

The word *unconscious* is used by psychologists in a variety of different senses, not all of them pertinent to the case of psi. Let us consider some of these. Perhaps the simplest meaning of the term is: not accessible to introspection. It is in this sense that a large proportion of all our cognitive processes, perceiving, thinking, remembering, etc., are unconscious inasmuch as we cannot know by introspection the information processing that must go on in the brain to make these possible. What we are conscious of is only the outcome or end product of such processing, the percepts, the thoughts and ideas, the memory images, etc. Now the psi process, whatever we may understand by that, is certainly unconscious in this sense. What differentiates it from normal sensory awareness is, as Rhine has pointed out, that there is no specific modality of consciousness through which it is manifested. The psi signal is recognized as such only by the circumstances in which it occurs and the veridical information it conveys. It may be received in the form of an image but, equally, as Rhine mentions, as "an outburst of emotion or a compulsion to act." In a typical routine card-guessing test there may be no intimation of any sort, nothing beyond the guessing behavior itself. In the so-called physiological approach to psi, the unconscious aspect is taken a step further by cutting out the verbal call altogether and relying on some physiological index, a fluctuation in the subject's EEG record or GSR record, to serve as the response. By this means the subject does not even need to attend to what is happening and can let his mind wander. But perhaps the ultimate development of this approach is the "disguised" psi experiment that has become widely popular with investigators in recent years. For this, the subjects need never know that they are being tested for psi; they are told that the task is one of perception, memory, subliminal perception, or whatever, while in fact the situation is so contrived that success is made dependent on their utilizing their ESP or PK in some way to achieve their conscious aim. Stanford's concept of the psi mediated instrumental response is a recognition of this idea that the entire psi process can if need be operate at a completely unconscious level.

Thus, recent parapsychology has done much to vindicate Rhine's insistence on the unconscious nature of psi. And this idea has profound philosophical implications because it provides an answer to a question that has persisted in the philosophy of mind since Descartes; namely, can an event be both mental and yet unconscious? Normal cognition could never provide an unambiguous answer to this question, for it could always have been said that whatever was not conscious, in this instance, belonged, not to the mind, but to the physical processes of the brain and nervous system. "Unconscious cerebration" was how it was described in the 19th century. In the case of psi, however, we cannot attribute the effect to cerebral activity, but neither can we doubt that we are dealing with a mental activity inasmuch as it is intelligent, purposeful, and is concerned with communication and control. Thus, we have here an example of something that is, at once, mental and unconscious. It would seem, therefore, that the empiricists were wrong to make mind coextensive with consciousness.

The meaning of *unconscious* that we associate with Freud is very different. In this case what concerns us are the hidden motives or reasons for our actions which, because they are so discreditable, we dare not admit to consciousness or acknowledge even to ourselves. Therapy then consists in overcoming this initial resistance. The Freudian unconscious, we may note, is an abstract theoretical construct in psychology and hence is not, in principle, incompatible with a physicalistic account of our mental processes. Now, is there any analogy in parapsychology to this meaning of *unconscious*? I think that there is and it is to be found most clearly in the phenomenon of psi-missing about which Rhine had plenty to say (Rhine, 1952, 1969). Psi-missing has been variously interpreted as due to an unconscious wish to avoid the target, whether because we are skeptics and so are anxious lest we add to the positive evidence for psi, or because we are secretly fearful lest we ourselves possess occult powers, or because we want to spite an experimenter who has bullied us into doing a task that we find irksome, or for any other such hidden reason. The closest analogy to psi-missing in sensory psychology is the phenomenon of "perceptual defense" in subliminal perception. Thus it has been shown that the threshold for recognition of emotionally charged words using tachistoscopic presentation is higher than for emotionally neutral words. Now the interesting point about perceptual defense is that, in the logic of the situation, there must be an unconscious recognition of the word prior to our capacity to articulate this: otherwise we could not know that it was a threatening stimulus. Likewise, in psi-missing, we must postulate unconscious recognition of the target; otherwise target avoidance would not be possible.

A third and final meaning of *unconscious* that I wish to discuss is that which devolves on our control over our sensorimotor skills. It cannot be too strongly emphasized that all the skilled activities of our daily life depend on a vast amount of "tacit knowledge" which never enters conscious awareness at all. It is sometimes said to be "preconscious." Moreover, as our skills become more fluent and proficient, so they become more automated and hence unconscious. As beginners, we are all too painfully conscious of each movement we make, but with practice this awareness fades away and, although we can, by an effort of attention, bring some particular component of the skill back into the focus of consciousness, this normally involves disrupting its smooth operation. Nevertheless, an essential feature of any normal skill that we have acquired is that it always remains under voluntary control so that we can at all times deploy it as and when we require. This stands in marked contrast with the case of psi. So much so, indeed, that many philosophers have questioned whether it is proper to call our potentiality for using psi a skill or ability in any meaningful sense. Perhaps it would be less contentious if we called it simply a "gift." Now a gift can be cultivated, but whether it can be acquired or trained like any normal ability is more doubtful.

At the present time there is much discussion among research workers as to whether a psi ability can be trained or developed using the well-tried procedure of practice combined with instantaneous feedback. The evidence would suggest to me, at least, that the wrong analogy is being used. It could be that a closer analogy would be some such process as falling asleep. Thus we cannot, alas, will ourselves to fall asleep; it is something that happens to us rather than something that we do. Nevertheless, we are not completely helpless in this regard. We can discover by trial and error what are for us the most favorable conditions to facilitate the onset of sleep, what diet or exercise to pursue, or how best to compose our minds so that we may become sleepy. Psi-hitting seems to be as little under conscious control as falling asleep. When it comes off, it does so spontaneously. This, however, need not discourage us from searching for effective psi-conducive conditions or for techniques and disciplines both mental and physical that might enhance the probability of hitting. Even the possibility of finding a psi-conducive drug comparable to the existing sleep-conducive drugs need not be ruled out. The point is, however, that if Rhine is right when he warns us that psi is irrevocably unconscious in its manifestations, then we can at best resort to these oblique methods in our attempts to gain some degree of mastery over it.

The Problem of Survival

It is now common knowledge that Rhine set his course firmly against research on post mortem survival. It is therefore ironical to discover that it was the survival problem that first brought him to Duke University. Thus we read (Rhine & Associates, 1965), "The special mission which brought the Rhines to Duke, although it did not measure the entire range of their interest in psychical matters, had to do with the claims of mediumistic communication with discarnate personalities, the question of spirit survival" (p. 6). And yet, by the time Rhine (1951) came to deliver his Myers Memorial Lecture to the Society for Psychical Research in London on "Telepathy and Human Personality" in May 1950 — one of the most definitive statements of his career — he had reached the conclusion, which he never subsequently saw fit to modify, that the problem of survival, along with the problem of pure telepathy, must, as things stand, be reckoned among the insoluble problems of parapsychology on which no wise parapsychologist would henceforth waste any further time or effort. Here, by way of illustration, are a few characteristic passages:

> A hundred years of more or less scientific consideration of the survival question has left the scientific professions more unconvinced and more indifferent to the claims today than ever [p. 25].

and

> The question of whether the spirit survives bodily death depends first on whether there *is* anything like a spirit in man at all, or whether the belief that there is stands entirely without foundation in fact [p. 26].

and

> So long as we are ignorant as to whether there is a distinctive spiritual component in the living individual, what sort of a sub-

> division it is if there is one, how independent and possibly separable
> such an element may be within the total personality, and what its
> properties are, we cannot expect to be able to design a *crucial ex-
> periment* to test the hypothesis that such a spiritual portion of
> personality survives the destruction of the body [pp. 26–27; my
> italics].

What had brought Rhine to this negative conclusion? The logic
of his reasoning becomes plain enough if we view the matter historically. Myers, who coined the term *telepathy*, argued that, if we
could demonstrate telepathy between the living, we would then be
in a position to say that there was at any rate a known process that
could, in principle, serve as a vehicle of communication between the
living and the dead. Accordingly, the supposition that mediumistic
communications might be inspired by discarnate agencies, using
telepathy, would no longer seem absurd. As it turned out, however,
experimental parapsychology demonstrated that we had to reckon,
not just with telepathy but equally with clairvoyance, with a very
general ESP faculty in effect. Even more disconcerting, while there
was some evidence for pure clairvoyance, untainted by telepathy,
the attempt to demonstrate pure telepathy untainted by clairvoyance
ran up against certain insuperable methodological difficulties. At all
events, once we grant that the medium in question could have obtained all the veridical information found in her communications by
virtue solely of her own ESP powers, recourse to a discarnate intelli-
gence is no longer warranted.

Rhine (1956) never denied that survival was a theoretical possibility; privately he may well have believed that it was true. Indeed,
the gist of what he is saying is that, by demonstrating this nonphysical component in personality, parapsychology had made more
plausible the hypothesis that we survive the dissolution of our brains
and body. Nor did he regard the problem as unimportant. "Everyone," he writes, "no matter what nor how extreme his position, will
recognize that, for most of the critical thinkers in the world, it will
be highly important to find out, on the basis of incontestable evidence, just what the post mortem destiny of personality really is"
(p. 30). But, as he here insists, it must be "incontestable evidence";
he saw no value whatever in continuing along the lines developed by
the spiritualist movement.

I share Rhine's agnosticism as to whether we do in fact survive
but I must question the validity of the arguments that he brings forward to dismiss the existing evidence that purports to demonstrate

survival. He was, it seems to me, the victim of a false notion of scientific method. He uses, repeatedly, expressions such as "crucial experiment," "incontrovertible evidence," "conclusive proof," and so on. Yet, in point of fact, as Karl Popper has been at such pains to stress, in science there can be no finalities. At each step it is always a question of deciding on the most reasonable interpretation of the data, and it is only in the more favorable situations that anything approaching a general consensus of informed opinion can be expected. In parapsychology one is virtually never in this happy position. Once this is understood, Rhine's rejection of the survivalist claims is as arbitrary as his rejection of telepathy. Thus, if, in a given case of ESP, there is reason to think that the agent plays a critical role, this in itself is justification for invoking the concept of telepathy. Likewise, in the case of mediumistic communications, if it looks as if the initiative came from the discarnate agent — as, for example, in the case of the famous cross-correspondences scripts of the Society for Psychical Research — that would be justification for retaining the concept of post mortem ESP or, to use Roll's neater expression, "theta psi." There will, no doubt, always be those who would prefer to posit a "super-ESP" on the part of the living medium than posit theta psi on the part of the deceased entity just as, no doubt, there will always be those who would prefer the clairvoyant interpretation to the telepathic one and vice versa. However, once we are no longer beguiled by the false quest for certainty this need no longer worry us.

Rhine may well have been justified in thinking that survival research was not a good investment for parapsychology at the present time, but the theoretical reasons he gave for this were misconceived. As a result he failed to appreciate the very real advances in survival research that were being made during the '60s and '70s, most notably, of course, the scholarly studies of cases of the reincarnation type by Stevenson, but also the phenomenon of "near-death experiences" to which Moody drew attention, or the accounts of deathbed visions assembled by Osis and Haraldsson. Rhine, no doubt, would have pointed out that we are dealing here with spontaneous phenomena where we are necessarily dependent on the veracity of human testimony with all its uncertainties. For, although he often mentions the spontaneous case studies of his wife, Louisa Rhine, he was emphatic that such evidence has no scientific status in its own right; its value consists in the hypotheses it suggests for experimental research. But dare we any longer assume that a laboratory investigation automatically takes precedence over the study of some real-life phenomenon? Consider the following passage in which Rhine (1953) comments on the investigation by the English parapsychologist, S. G. Soal, of his special subject, Basil Shackleton:

> It is difficult to do justice to so extensive an experiment as this. Only those who have laboured for years under the strain of equally complex precautions can come anywhere near appreciating the evidential quality of these results. Such a person surely is entitled to wonder why anyone asks for further evidence. After all, what more could further evidence add to the assurance that under certain conditions ESP does occur? [p. 68]

I quote this passage not, heaven knows, to mock Rhine, for I have said as much myself on this topic, but to drive home the point that, no matter how impressive the precautions, no investigation considered in isolation is any more secure evidentially than the integrity of those who were responsible for it. We now know, alas, thanks to Betty Markwick, that this historic investigation was in fact worthless. The superiority of experimental evidence arises only when one has a clearly repeatable experiment that no longer rests on the trustworthiness of individuals. Until such a time a well-attested spontaneous case has as much claim on our credence as a laboratory report.

The Universality of the Psi Faculty

Rhine was unsure as to how far back in evolution to assign the origins of psi; but he believed that it was most probably something that we shared with much of the animal kingdom and almost certainly a common possession of humankind. It might, indeed, be more salient in certain individuals, with certain personalities, with certain groups or societies; but he was convinced (1947) it was there potentially in every one of us. "Most experienced investigators...," he writes, "have come more and more to accept the view that while individuals differ greatly in their potentialities, most people—probably all—possess some of these parapsychical abilities to some degree" (p. 138). He was particularly insistent that psi should not be regarded as any sort of freakish abnormality. What gave him his confidence? I think he was impressed, in the first place, by the fact that, in so many of the experiments he discusses, psi shows the same sensitivity to psychological conditions as we would expect to find in testing for any normal skill or ability. Thus, the inhibitory effects of stress, distraction, boredom, frustration, etc., seem to operate as much with respect to psi performance as they do with respect to any more or less delicate psychological task. And the same holds good of such positive influences as encouragement, excitement, challenge, and so forth.

In the second place, Rhine took full cognizance of the important findings of Gertrude Schmeidler which showed a relationship between the pattern of scoring, psi-hitting versus psi-missing, and the beliefs and attitudes of the subjects involved. Her so-called "sheep–goat effect" has, in fact, stood up to replication as well as anything in the parapsychological field. Third, he draws our attention to the kind of salience effects, the U-shaped curves and suchlike, that crop up alike in ESP testing as they do in tests of recall. There are, of course, some striking contrasts. Most normal abilities show learning; psi notoriously, shows decline effects. But there was, Rhine argued, sufficient lawfulness in the manifestations of psi to justify us in looking on it as a universal function or faculty.

Can we say that he has now finally been vindicated on this point? Alas, like almost every issue in this perplexing field it remains unresolved, as can be seen by the fact that at the 1980 Parapsychological Association convention a special roundtable was held to discuss the "distribution of psi" at which widely differing views were voiced. On the one side there are those currently working on the relationship between psi and personality who assume the validity of the universalist position and see their work as lending it further support. On the opposite side are those who rarely if ever obtain positive results and are acutely aware of the fact that certain experimenters consistently do so. They have raised the specter of the "psi experimenter effect" and ask whether these successful experimenters might not represent the self-selected few who use their own psi to achieve the results which they then attribute to their unselected volunteer subjects. Perhaps, they suggest, Rhine was misled by his sheer good luck in having among his early entourage a number of these psi-positive experimenters? Rhine, himself (1947, pp. 137–138), did indeed recognize early on that some of his experimenters, like Margaret Price or Margaret Pegram, could obtain positive results where others failed but, at the time, he naturally attributed this to their social skills rather than to anything as extraordinary as their own psychic powers.

For my part I am still unsure where I stand on this issue. My own lack of success makes me sympathize with those who see psi as something very rare and exceptional. On the other hand, it is important to keep in view the distinction between psi performance and the potentiality for psi. There may be good reasons why we refrain from using psi except on very special occasions. For most purposes it pays us to rely on our sensorimotor system both for extracting information from the environment and for executing our intentions with respect to that environment. Most of us, I suspect, are so comfortably integrated with our brain and nervous system that we can no longer dispense with their aid. The crux of the problem when it comes to psi, as I see it, is how to induce your subject to forego these psychological crutches.

This completes my brief examination of Rhine's philosophy of psi. It is, as I have tried to suggest, a working philosophy for parapsychologists, not a finished or integrated theoretical doctrine that must be accepted or rejected *in toto*. Ever since its inception, there have, one can say, been two main views as to what parapsychology is really about. According to one school of thought parapsychology is a science with no subject matter of its own; it takes as its field of inquiry those puzzles and anomalies that have been disowned by the other sciences. According to the other school of thought parapsychology is an integral part of psychology, perhaps its most fundamental part — at any rate that part that deals with the mind–matter interface. I would say that Rhine's most important contribution to the philosophy of parapsychology is the impetus he gave to this latter point of view.

REFERENCES

RHINE, J. B. *The reach of the mind.* New York: William Sloane, 1947.
RHINE, J. B. Telepathy and human personality (Tenth Myers Memorial Lecture). *Journal of Parapsychology,* 1951, 15, 6–39.
RHINE, J. B. The problem of psi-missing. *Journal of Parapsychology,* 1952, 16, 90–129.
RHINE, J. B. *New world of the mind.* New York: William Sloane, 1953.
RHINE, J. B. Research on spirit survival re-examined. *Journal of Parapsychology,* 1956, 20, 121–131.
RHINE, J. B. On parapsychology and the nature of man. In S. Hook (ed.), *Dimensions of mind.* New York: New York University Press, 1960.
RHINE, J. B. Psi-missing re-examined. *Journal of Parapsychology,* 1969, 33, 1–38.
RHINE, J. B., & ASSOCIATES. *Parapsychology from Duke to FRNM.* Durham, N.C.: Parapsychology Press, 1965.

J. B. Rhine and
the History of Ideas

BRIAN INGLIS

Although J. B. Rhine's place in history cannot yet be assessed with any certainty, one thing is clear; he began the process by which parapsychology has gradually, in the face of rancorous opposition, begun to achieve academic respectability. And this poses a question: Why did the results of some research conducted by an unknown young man at a little-known university succeed where far more striking results obtained elsewhere had failed?

The fact that they did is all the more surprising in view of the climate of opinion at the time. Orthodox science had obtained an ascendancy among sane, intelligent people to a degree few religions have enjoyed. Its temple appeared securely founded on three solid-looking piles, driven deep into the human mind: mechanism (the doctrine that the universe functions like a machine), materialism, and neo-Darwinianism.

To understand how Rhine came to create a small but widening fissure in the foundations, it is necessary to examine the process by which these foundations had been laid. Until the Renaissance, vitalism had reigned virtually unchallenged. Vitalists assumed the existence of a force capable of transcending those encountered in everyday life—the force (or forces) now embraced in the term *psi*. Psi could be exploited by gods, demons, spirits, shamans, and sorcerers; classical literature from Homer to Apuleius abounds in the evidence for it. There were skeptics, like Cicero, but they were chiefly concerned with exposing spurious imitations: conjuring tricks masquerading as divine intervention, coincidences interpreted as omens. Skepticism about the existence of psi rarely surfaced before the 16th century; it was only then, in fact, that the term *supernatural* came into use to distinguish between phenomena at-

111

tributable to psi and those which could be attributed to "natural" forces.

In the 17th century the rapid development of science began to encourage the belief that in time, the supernatural would wither away. When phenomena formerly regarded as supernatural, like magnetism, were naturalized, the idea that all forces would eventually be shown to be part of a giant machine was adopted with relish by mechanists, like Voltaire and Hume, who were doing battle with vitalism's residuary legatees, the churches. Miracles — breaches of the laws of nature — were impossible and Hume claimed that because "a firm and unalterable experience has established these laws, the proof against a miracle, from the very nature of the fact, is as entire as any argument from experience can possibly be imagined."

It is often argued by skeptics, who still cite Hume as their authority, that the only reason parapsychologists believe in the existence of psi is their need to believe. How much more true this is of the skeptics' devotion to Hume! The fallacy in his reasoning is obvious: historically speaking, experience of the laws of nature at that time was very far from "firm and unalterable," as, indeed, Hume admitted. The evidence of the miracles — and by his reckoning they would have qualified as miracles — wrought a few years before at the tomb of the Jansenist François de Paris at St. Medard had been "immediately proved upon the spot before judges of unquestioned integrity" (as he had to concede) and were "attested by witnesses of credit and distinction." Yet he felt compelled to reject this testimony because of the "absolute impossibility of the miraculous nature of the events."

Hume was saying, in effect, that skeptics need not accept any evidence which they do not want to accept, a proposition which has served them ever since. From time to time, however, they have been forced to agree that their definition of what is natural, and therefore "real," has been mistaken, as with meteorites early in the 19th century, and hypnotic trance state towards the end of the century. In both these cases, however, acceptance came as something of a relief, because both could be accounted for without having to accept a "supernatural" explanation. There had simply been a mistake about space: stones *do* float around in it. As for the hypnotic trance, it was reclassified as "induced hystero-epilepsy," a mental disorder. This diagnosis was quickly shown to be incorrect, but no matter: the hypnotic trance had been kidnapped from the "occult" camp, and could henceforth be categorized as "natural."

What were coming to be called "psychical manifestations," however, remained occult, partly because they could not be fitted into the accepted code of natural law, but chiefly because they were identified with spirits. It is fascinating, if futile, to speculate on what might have happened had table-turning arrived in mid-century as a parlor game without spiritist trappings. All over the United States, Britain and Europe eminent people took part in it and vouched for the fact that tables did turn, move, and perform strange antics in ways which could not conceivably be accounted for "naturally," but it was the spiritist link which appalled Faraday, leading him to set up the bogus experiment by which he could pretend to have solved the mystery in natural terms. And by this time, people were happy to believe him. Nearly all educated men, Lecky wrote in his *History of Rationalism* in 1865, received accounts of miracles "with an absolute and even derisive incredulity." Those who had played the table-turning game could not deny the evidence of their senses; but many of them could, and did, thankfully receive the news that Faraday had shown how their senses had deceived them.

That scientists should mistrust the intrusion of a faith into their domain was understandable. The mechanist principle had been powerfully reinforced by Darwin's theory of evolution and was now being fused with the new materialism. What the scientists did not realize, however, was the extent to which their beliefs had also become a faith. When Oliver Lodge, describing the Royal Institution, remarked that the physicist Tyndall had been "in a manner the officiating priest, with Faraday a sort of deity," he was not just being flippant: Tyndall in his articles (and in his celebrated Presidential Address to the British Association at its 1874 Belfast meeting) not merely used biblical language, denouncing spiritualism as "intellectual whoredom," but also urged scientists and their supporters to go out and propagate the materialist creed for the benefit of the public.

As a result, psychical phenomena never received the detached attention which scientists boasted they would give to anything they investigated. Faraday declined to examine the claims made for Daniel Dunglas Home unless Home repudiated spiritualism. Tyndall attended a few séances — but only, he later boasted, to disrupt them. Huxley attended one séance and presented his speculation about how the phenomena might have been obtained by sleight-of-hand, as if that must have been what actually happened. And although the great majority of the scientists who actually investigated Home, and later Eusapia Palladino, were convinced that the phenomena were genuine, David Hume's contention about "the absolute impossibility of the miraculous nature of the events" sufficed to invalidate their testimony. When Palladino was apparently discredited by the trials in the United States in 1910, demonstrably rigged though they were, psychical research sank out of sight.

This, then, was the climate of opinion at the time Rhine reached Duke. Not that the psychical researchers ceased to provide impressive evidence: Crawford in Belfast, Murray with his family telepathy game, Schrenck-Notzing and others on the Continent. So far as the general public were concerned, however, psychical phenomena were again identified with Spiritualism — by this time a religion, with a capital S — which the casualty rate in the trenches had levitated back into the leading role on the psychic stage. Significantly, when *An Experiment with Time* was published in 1927, J. W. Dunne was at pains to dissociate himself from any connection with "occultism," as he thought of it: one of the seminal works for parapsychology was presented as straight science.

There was another force at work which I suspect was more important in influencing public opinion than has been realized. In medicine, vitalism had taken longer to succumb to the assaults of the mechanists — notably Huxley, with his contention (worthy of B. F. Skinner) that consciousness is as completely without the power to modify the workings of the body as a steam whistle is to modify the workings of a locomotive. Here, at least, common sense and common experience rebelled. But when, a century ago, Pasteur, Koch and the rest demonstrated the connection between microbes and infectious diseases, materialism soon swept in. Diseases, the belief was, are divided into two categories: organic and functional. Organic diseases have specific physiochemical causes; functional diseases do not. Inexorably, the trend was toward the assumption that only organic diseases are "real"; a patient with a functional disorder is not really ill, but simply neurotic or hysterical.

How completely his grotesque idea captured the medical profession can be seen from the writings of the maverick F. G. Crookshank, who was forever reminding his colleagues that as people sweat from embarrassment and have bowel movements from nervous tension, it is absurd to reject out of hand the possibility that the emotions may precipitate skin disorders or colitis. "I often wonder," he remarked sadly in 1930 — when Rhine was beginning his researches at Duke — "why some hard-boiled and orthodox clinician does not describe emotional weeping as a 'new disease,' call it paroxysmal lachrymation, and suggest treatment by belladonna, astringent local application, avoidance of sexual excess, and a salt-free diet with restriction of fluid intake; proceeding, in the event of failure, to early removal of the tear-glands." "Ludicrous though it might sound," Crookshank observed, "a good deal of contemporary medicine and surgery seems to me to be on much the same level."

What this shows is that psychical research, in order to stage a comeback, had to break through *two* layers of doubt. When people were being assured that their minds could in no way be responsible for the behavior of their bodies, how much more diﬁcult it had become to accept the possibility that their minds might be able to transcend the barriers of space and time and still more that their minds might influence *other* bodies psychokinetically.

That Rhine's work made an impression right from the start (at least from the publication of *Extra-Sensory Perception*) is consequently an even more striking tribute to its importance than most of us have realized. Why did it have such an impact?

There were two contributory factors. One was the development of the radio. Most people, even many skeptics, have had experiences of a kind which, given the possibility of telepathy, are easier to explain that way than by coincidence or delusion. If wireless waves could transmit an announcer's voice virtually instantaneously all around the globe, telepathy ceased to be such an improbability. Scientists might patiently try to explain that the two were not the same thing at all; but if one set of waves had been discovered, might not a different set be awaiting discovery?

The other factor was that the Duke experiments were free from any link with Spiritualism. They could be tried in the home without any of the mumbo-jumbo that had so often accompanied table-turning. And this put the mechanists/materialists on the defensive. They were able to mount the powerful rearguard action which is still being fought; but they have never, even with the help of smear tactics that would have excited Tyndall's envy, been able to banish the specter that those Duke results conjured up to haunt them.

In the second volume of his autobiography, *The Invisible Writing*, Arthur Koestler describes a meeting with his old friend the German philosopher Reichenbach in 1952. Reichenbach expressed his opinion that Rhine's work was hokum; Koestler replied that no less an authority than R. A. Fisher had checked the statistics. Reichenbach actually turned pale: "If that is true," he said, "it is

terrible, terrible. It would mean that I would have to scrap everything and start again from the beginning." In other words, Koestler
commented, if ESP exists "the whole edifice of materialist philosophy
crumbles." Crumbling it most certainly is; and whatever verdict
may eventually be reached on Rhine's work as a whole, there can be
no question that he was the man who first shook it to its foundations.

J. B. Rhine and Philosophy

Frederick C. Dommeyer

One experience with Dr. Rhine I recall with special vividness. He invited me to "picnic" with him on the large tract of land surrounding his home outside of Durham. Upon my arrival, he appeared in rough clothing, carrying a lunch for both of us. Rhine headed for his Jeep, threw two axes into it and directed me to get into the frontseat with him. It was an unusual ride, over fields with no roads, up and down steep hills and through a brook, while I held on as best I could. The zest and joy that Dr. Rhine had in his Jeep's performance were obvious. Arriving at his objective, he handed me an axe and suggested that we clear the area of its dead trees. As we worked, at one time his axe almost grazed me in its backward swing over his shoulder. Noticing this, Rhine said in some dismay, "I guess I have a streak of recklessness in me."

Reflecting on that comment, I concluded it was fortunate that he had a bit of the reckless in his nature. It probably accounted for his willingness to leave an academic career in the biological sciences for the insecure life of a parapsychologist in the late twenties, when psychical research had little status among scholars and scientists. Added to this trait, however, were his marked abilities in developing the psi field into one that attracted considerable attention among contemporary scholars and scientists. If the growing recognition of parapsychology as a science continues, it is quite possible that J. B. Rhine will eventually rank with Darwin or Pasteur in bringing new insights into the frameworks of science and philosophy.

It would be convenient if a precise definition of philosophy could be provided in initiating a discussion of the philosophical implications of Rhine's discoveries in parapsychology, as he viewed them. Such a definition could be offered, but it would represent only one of many different conceptions of philosophy that are currently entertained by academic philosophers. Rather than introduce such a definitional bias, a more pedestrian approach to philosophy will be attempted here. Have the psi phenomena that J. B. Rhine researched been considered by recognized philosophers? If so, how have Rhine's discoveries influenced philosophy?

Though acquainted casually with philosophy, even having taught it at Duke University for a time, Rhine was not an academically trained philosopher. His Ph.D. was in botany. But because Rhine achieved such a high place among parapsychologists and because he did reflect seriously on some traditional philosophical issues, it is appropriate to see what eventuated from those reflections.

Rhine reported that at an early period in his life he had an inclination to philosophize. He related (Rhine, 1937) that while in high school in a small Ohio town he participated with his wife-to-be in "long, juvenile discussions of religion and our philosophical perplexities, and in the course of them [he and his wife] became attached to each other" (p. 52).

This early tendency to philosophize did not leave Rhine; it continued over many years and throughout his major writings. A strong motive behind Rhine's psi researches was his desire to answer such philosophical questions as the following "As human beings, what are we? What is our place in nature?" (p. 3). It would not be wrong to say that Rhine was motivated by philosophic interests almost as much as he was by scientific ones.

Rhine had however little use for the speculative philosophies of the past. He wrote that "with the development of culture, came the many speculative philosophies, theories concocted by the reason out of the tissues of untested logic" (p. 3). In his evaluation of past philosophies, Rhine was in agreement with most 20th century philosophers; they have made a similar judgment. Rhine did however add something that most of them would not have, namely, that philosophical problems could be dealt with successfully by the "methods of science" (p. 3). Rhine's resolutions of the several philosophical problems with which he dealt were conceived by him to be implied by his scientific discoveries as to the nature of extrasensory perception and psychokinesis. It was in this way that he considered himself to be free from the unverified speculations of past philosophers and their "untested logic."

A theme that runs through all of Rhine's philosophizing is that his discoveries in parapsychology were not compatible with materialism, which he viewed, correctly, as the generally accepted metaphysical theory of orthodox science. Nor has this metaphysics disappeared from science even today. In October, 1980, the well-known Cornell University astronomer, Carl Sagan (1980) asserted it. He said: "I am a collection of water, calcium and organic molecules called Carl Sagan. But is that all? Is there nothing in here but molecules? For myself, I find it elevating that our universe permits the evolution of molecular machines as intricate and subtle as we."

What is it in psi phenomena that is incompatible with materialism? Rhine (1966) held that "we can say a phenomenon is parapsychical when it is beyond physical principles of explanation" (p. 84).

Telepathy, clairvoyance, precognition and psychokinesis in their empirical manifestations all testify to the truth of this assertion. Rhine said (1947) "if thought can be transferred directly from one mind to another without the use of the senses, man must possess mental powers transcending brain mechanics" (p. 13). The same independence of mind from the material world is shown in clairvoyance, which revealed "that the mind could enter into an active cognitive relation with matter without the use of any known sensori-mechanical means" (p. 108). And, regarding precognition, Rhine wrote: "No better experiment could have been found to put the hypothesis of the nonphysical character of psi to test than one designed to see whether the ability could be used to respond to events beyond the present" (Rhine & Pratt, 1957).

In discussing psychokinesis, Rhine (1947b) held to the same general thesis. He wrote: "The mind, then, has a force that can act on matter. Whatever PK is ... it does something to matter that is statistically measurable. It produces results in the physical environment that are unexplainable by any factor or energy known to physics" (pp. 107-8). Moreover, "Psychokinesis is ... produced by no mere blind and purposeless force ... PK reacts with the physical object according to intelligent design and direction" (p. 117). PK is so closely related to ESP that both of these interactions can be considered as one "basic parapsychological process" (p. 130).

Rhine also maintained that no special organ of the body is involved in ESP, that percipients are not passive, that they show volitional control despite the fact that ESP is mainly unconscious, that psi phenomena occur despite any physical variations in the target, whether or not, say, the card is exposed to light, at the bottom of the deck, or inverted. Nor does the number of symbols on the card, whether the symbols are distorted or the card held at an angle to the percipient, or even physical barriers between the experimenter and the percipient or their distance in space or time make any difference to the phenomena.

The above summary of some of Rhine's conclusions about ESP and PK constitutes his reasons for opposition to a metaphysics of materialism. There is force to what Rhine believed about psi phenomena, and one is left to wonder how Carl Sagan, or any other materialist, could explain them away solely on the basis of molecular brain activity.

It is then clearly the experimental data of psi that forced Rhine to oppose a metaphysics of materialism. To assert, however, the existence of both body and mind, as Rhine did, is no definitive answer to the classical body–mind problem, which runs through a good deal of modern and contemporary philosophy. After all, there is the question of interaction, of causal dependency. Is mind dependent upon body or the other way around? Are they independent of each other? Or is there a reciprocal mode of interaction? Or are body and mind both causally dependent on some underlying substance which gives rise to them? In order to see Rhine's answer to these sorts of questions in proper perspective, it is well to state very briefly several of the philosophical solutions given to the body–mind problem. Rhine was aware of these different answers to this classical philosophical issue and therefore did not choose his own in a philosophical vacuum.

There is, of course, the materialism that Rhine opposed. This view holds essentially that such mental events as sensing, imaging, imagining, feeling, thinking, remembering, and so on are nothing but other names for material occurrences, such as molecular activities that go on within the brain. Rhine saw that this view would not explain events that simply did not obey the laws of physics in regard to space, time, and mass. Moreover, as C. J. Ducasse has affirmed (1961), the identity of body and mind that the materialist believes to exist is based on a semantic confusion: the terms 'image,' for example, and 'a molecular brain activity' do not denote the same thing at all. It is only by a perversion of language that they seem to do so. By thus perverting language, the materialist does not assert a falsity but an absurdity.

A view of the body–mind relation in direct opposition to materialism is that of idealism. George Berkeley, an adherent of this position, held that *the object perceived* was identical with *the perceiving of an object*, that is, to be is to be perceived. Here again, the same sort of semantic confusion exists in assuming there is only one denotatum for these two terms, when there are in fact two. Whatever the relation of the object perceived to the perceiving of an object, it is not that of identity.

There is also the view of psychophysical parallelism, which was held by the brilliant philosopher, Leibniz — a view which is today mainly of historical interest. He held that body and mind are related as two clocks can be. The two clocks can consistently "tell" the same time, but that is *not* because they are causally connected; they function quite independently of each other. Neither do body and mind, Leibniz asserted, have any causal connection with one another. Yet, the series of bodily and mental events parallel each other. If a pin is stuck into a finger, there is pain. But the pin-sticking does not cause the pain, nor the pain the pin-sticking; each is causally independent of the other. What accounts for this wondrous relationship? Leibniz attributed it to "a pre-established harmony" instituted by God. The limitations of his assumptions are too obvious to need discussion.

A body–mind theory of considerable popularity and plausibility is that of epiphenomenalism. Here, priority is given to the body, but mental phenomena are conceived to exist; they are causal byproducts of the brain's activity. But whereas bodily events can cause mental events, mental events cannot cause bodily ones. The causal relation operates only in one direction. There is in this view, however, a recognition that mental events *do* exist though they have only a dependent status. If the mental events did not occur at all, the body would go on acting in the same manner as if they did. Injuries to, or diseases of, the brain are usually offered as evidence for this view in that they bring about changes sometimes in the mental life of the individual. But this view seems patently false in its denial of the influence of mental events on the body.

There is a converse view to that of epiphenomenalism, sometimes called hypophenomenalism. In this view, the physical realm of bodies is a byproduct of mind. It differs from Berkeley's idealism in that it does not presuppose an identity of body and mind. Body is the "epiphenomenon" in this instance, the byproduct of mind, which can have no causal influence on mind. It has, of course, an analogous defect to that found in epiphenomenalism in its one-directional line of causation. The philosophy of Plotinus can be conceived as a version of this view.

Another view of body-mind is that of dualistic interactionism. In this theory, body and mind are causally related in both directions, that is, a pin-prick can cause pain and a desire to lift one's arm can be a cause of its rising. This view does not preclude bodily events from having effects on mental events or mental events on bodily ones. René Descartes held to a view of this sort. Mind and body were for him each a "substance." Each was wholly self-sufficient in respect of the other, though both were ultimately dependent upon God. Descartes, struggling to account for their interaction, assigned its place to the pineal gland within the brain. Ducasse, in this century, held to a dualistic interactionism also, but without the substance concept of Descartes.

There is also the "double aspect" theory of body–mind, a form of which was maintained by Benedict Spinoza. This view holds that body and mind are two aspects of some underlying factor. Rhine held to a double aspect theory in one of his two hypotheses for the interaction of body and mind, though he referred to it by a different name.

It is not necessary here to make Rhine's double aspect theory of body–mind the subject of controversy or even to judge whether it is the only theory that conforms to the facts of parapsychology. Rhine's mind was a brilliant and penetrating one; it is enough to see what he conceived the philosophic implications of psi to be and to savor his conceptions. To evaluate or criticize his ideas in the market-place of academic philosophy would only be to subject them to the idle crosscurrents of controversy, and to no point.

Rhine recognized in dealing with the body-mind problem that he had "definitely crossed the borders of academic philosophy" (Rhine & Pratt, 1957, p. 122). He did not, in crossing this border, fall back on the "untested logic" of traditional philosophers, or rather he did not intend to; at least he hoped to base his philosophic theorizing on conclusions flowing from his researches in parapsychology, especially on the one central insight of the nonmateriality of psi phenomena.

Rhine believed an "absolute dualism" to be false and defended what he called a "relative dualism." (He called his theory "relative monism" or simply "relativism" as well. See Rhine, 1945.) He said that the interaction that exists between body and mind is such that it "unifies" the two. As he wrote (1947b):

> The mistake lies ... in thinking that ESP and PK lead to dualism. The evidence for psychophysical interaction contributed by parapsychology logically opposes any basic duality in the nature of man. The very act in which the two systems of mind and body

operate upon each other necessarily unifies them to some degree into a single process, much as the reaction of two substances in a chemical beaker makes a single functional whole out of the two [p. 178].

He then added, significantly, immediately after: "no one can conceive of the interaction of two systems, except by supposing that there are properties common to both. ... We know of no other way to understand causal change of any kind." The dualism seen in parapsychological phenomena must therefore be 'relative' and "the facts of parapsychology not only do not require one to be a[n absolute] dualist — they do not *allow* one to be" (p. 179).

Rhine of course thought here of the living man in all of his complexity. The interaction of body and mind is not like that of two billiard balls striking one another on a pool table; they interact but do not thereby become a unity. It is far more plausible to view man, however, as a unity of body and mind because of the complex and intimate reciprocal interactions between the bodily and mental aspects of his nature. As Rhine saw it, in any event, matter and mind have properties common to both. But what are these common properties, this common ground?

Rhine did not find it easy, or even possible, to give more than a sketchy answer to this question. He affirmed, however (1947b), that "The nature of this common ground between mind and matter is still completely obscure. We can only infer its existence and regard it as a great research objective for the future" (p. 179). Rhine in fact offered two different hypotheses as to what this common ground might be.

It may represent an underlying order of neutral substituent energetics — a sort of nonpsychical and nonphysical substrate that is convertible into either mental or material manifestations. Or again it may reduce to a mere transition point, an abstraction [p. 179].

Let us examine these two disjuncts. The first one — the substrate hypothesis — is very reminiscent of the view that William James asserted in his well-known essay, "Does 'Consciousness' Exist?" (1922). In that essay, James used the term "pure experience" very much as Rhine used the term, "substrate." In this connection, James wrote:

As "subjective" we may say that the experience represents; as "objective" it is represented. What represents and what is represented is here numerically the same; but we must remember that no dualism of being represented and representing resides in the experience *per se*. In its pure state, or when isolated, there is no self-splitting of it into consciousness and what the consciousness is "of." Its subjectivity and objectivity are functional attributes solely ... [p. 23].

There is no way of knowing whether Rhine was actually acquainted with this essay. Its thesis, however, is so similar to Rhine's substrate view that it is possible that his view is an adaptation of James's. Rhine's "neutral substituent energetics" or "nonpsychical and nonphysical substrate" appear, in any case, to be the functional equivalent of James's "pure experience."

There is still the question of whether Rhine's substrate view should be interpreted monistically or pluralistically. Is there only one substrate behind the many human minds and bodies or is there a separate substrate for each human body and mind? This question cannot be answered. Rhine refers to "a sort of nonpsychical and nonphysical substrate" (singular) but he also refers to the common ground as "an underlying order of neutral substituent energetics" (plural). It is not possible to tell from such descriptions what his meaning really was. Of course, Rhine's failure to clarify this issue could be part of his intention in that he explicitly stated that the nature of this common ground is "completely obscure."

But this substrate hypothesis, as an answer to the question of what is common to both body and mind, is only one of two possibilities that Rhine offered. The "common ground," he also asserted, "may reduce to a mere transition point, an abstraction" (Rhine, 1947b, p. 179). What can this mean? Rhine did not offer an explanation for this brief statement. It would suggest, however, that there is no existing substrate as a common ground, but only a "transition point" where body and mind interact. There would be nothing on this hypothesis that "supports" the interaction; there would be just the interaction itself, and hence the "transition point" is only, as Rhine said, an abstraction and nothing more. Interaction of body–mind, on this second hypothesis, would be an ultimate fact of nature. It happens as an irreducible event.

Rhine did not choose one hypothesis over the other. He said that all that can be concluded with certainty is that the facts of parapsychology are such as to be incompatible with an "absolute dualism" (Rhine, 1947, p. 179).

It is relevant at this point to inquire about the spiritist survival hypothesis. Did Rhine believe that it is possible for mind to exist in separation from its body and thereby survive bodily death? At first sight, it would seem that Rhine's relative dualism would make the survival of a mind after bodily death an impossibility. But let us conceive of a living person in his terms, that is, as consisting of body, mind, and the substrate. After bodily death, why can the substrate not continue to exist but giving rise only to mental phenomena? There seems no logical reason for denying this possibility, though it would not be strictly a form of spiritist survival. Or, on Rhine's other hypothesis that a transition point, an abstraction, is the common ground for interaction of body-mind, why can there not be an elimination at death of all body-mind causal interactions, permitting body and mind each to go its way, one to the grave and the other to some form of spiritist survival?

It is not, however, necessary for us to inquire into the survival hypothesis. Rhine had explored it fully in the early part of his career as a parapsychologist. He soon recognized a problem in the investigation of spirit (mind) survival that has not yet been resolved, namely, that the sometimes impressive paranormal information communicated by mediums can as easily be explained in terms of an extrasensory perception hypothesis as in terms of a survival theory. As Rhine put it: "There is reasonably good indication that knowledge has been obtained through mediumistic utterances that would have to be considered parapsychical in its origin. There is no way known as yet to test the hypothesis that the source of the knowledge shown is discarnate" (Rhine & Pratt, 1957, p. 121).

Rhine's relative dualism is thus compatible with a survival hypothesis, or so it would seem, though he had found no conclusive evidence for belief in survival after bodily death. The lack of conclusive evidence one way or the other up to this time has not stopped some parapsychologists, for example, Professor Ian Stevenson, from a continuing search for such evidence.

Another philosophical problem with which Rhine wrestled was that of the causative principle. This issue runs through the history of philosophy and engaged the attention of such thinkers as Aristotle, Kant, Hume, Whitehead, Ducasse, and many others. Rhine, too, got involved with this problem, but specifically as it concerned psi phenomena rather than the physical world as such. As he wrote: "we now recognize the existence of two distinct types of causation (or determination): one, the more familiar energetic action which characterizes the physical universe...; and another which is found ... to transcend the physical principles we know" (Rhine, 1945, p. 226).

An alternative view that has seemed plausible to a number of parapsychologists is that of a theory of radiant energy; this was attractive to many because, if true, it would keep psi in the realm of the physical. This theory was opposed by Rhine, however, because he found it in discord with the facts of parapsychology. On a wave theory, the percipient in an ESP experience would receive wave effects in his brain from innumerable sources. But such a theory, as Rhine saw, fails to account for the selectivity that is found in ESP and PK occurrences. For this and other reasons, "there is nothing to favor a wave theory except the fact that it is ready at hand..." (Rhine, 1937, p. 210).

Rhine simply found it impossible to view physical energy as the causative principle in psi events. The source of this energy, he believed, must be the living individual, but not in his physical aspects. It is rooted in man's mind; it is "psychic" or "mental" energy. The percipient, not passive in ESP, displays a "definite volitional control over ESP ..." (Rhine 1964, p. 219). This psychic energy is intelligently selective in telepathy, clairvoyance and precognition. Rhine was not adverse to calling it "teleological," following a usage of Professor McDougall (Rhine, 1937, pp. 211–12).

The selectivity of psi energy can be recognized in many ways but also in the remarkable fact that, though this special energy does not operate on man's sense organs in ESP, it does operate on physical objects in PK phenomena. This mental energy is therefore clearly convertible on occasion to physical action. Rhine asserted in this regard that

> The mind, then, has a force that can act on matter. Whatever PK is, and however it functions, it does something to matter that is statistically measurable. It produces results in the physical environment that are unexplainable by any factor or energy known to physics. We must, nevertheless, suppose there is an energy present wherever work is done; and the PK records demonstrate that the falling dice were worked on by something more than the familiar forces which threw them. There must, therefore, be an energy convertible to physical action, a mental energy [Rhine, 1947b, pp. 107–8].

Rhine did not, as was noted, deny the existence of ordinary or mechanical causation, as it exists in the material continuum. It was in the realm of psi phenomena, however, where he found a break-down of physical modes of causal explanation and where a new kind of causative principle was required. Yet, in recognizing this fact, one should be reminded of Rhine's relative dualism, for he held that the physical and the mental have a common ground.

It is obvious that Rhine's view of psi causation has significant, indeed revolutionary, effects upon physics and philosophy. In intro-ducing a new causal agency into the data of physics, since physics is concerned with matter and motion, that field is left in an incomplete state unless it can somehow incorporate the psychokinetic occur-rences found in parapsychological investigations. When it is recalled especially that this mental energy is intelligent, teleological, one can well understand its revolutionary effects on orthodox physics, whether or not physicists attend to such discoveries as Rhine made. This psi causal agent also has a bearing upon philosophy in that it tends to verify empirically the belief in the teleology that some philosophers, such as A. N. Whitehead, brought into their causal theories.

Another major philosophical issue with which Rhine became involved was that of free will versus determinism. The importance of this problem is rooted in its relation to morality and to ethics. If, for example, mind is nothing more than the physical functioning of the brain, free choice would seem to be impossible. On the other hand, if one goes to the other extreme and assumes that a free choice is an un-caused choice, one ends up with a senseless view in that an uncaused choice would be caused by nothing—not by an awareness of the situation, or an appraisal of the consequences of alternative modes of action, or value considerations, or anything else. Neither of these possibilities will work as a basis for responsible choice when one is faced with a moral issue. Rhine avoided both of these positions in his attempt to solve the free will versus determinism issue.

This problem had its roots in parapsychology for Rhine. If, in precognition, one has an accurate awareness of a future event, then that future event must necessarily occur. But, if so, where does free-dom of choice and action lie? It would seem not to exist. And so, in the face of this fact, Rhine wrote:

> Hence it is crucial for us ... to know whether or not mind is just a physical brain function. For without freedom of choice our social philosophies would collapse. Without free volition there can be no morality, no real democracy, not even any science itself as a free

inquiry. If mental life is wholly a product of cerebral physics there would appear to be no escape from physical law anywhere in the course of human conduct. Freedom is then only a fancy, and ethics, under physical law, entirely a fiction [Rhine, 1947b, p. 9].

Rhine therefore concluded that one cannot enjoy the volitional freedom required by morality and ethics and, at the same time, have perfect predictability. The two notions, he believed, are absolutely irreconcilable (Rhine, 1947b, p. 82).

Rhine offered two suggestions as a resolution to the problem of free choice versus determinism; one of which was, however, inconclusive. The first was that the apparent foreknowledge in precognition was not always fully reliable and that it has "only a limited accuracy" (Rhine, 1947b, p. 82). In such cases, there would be at least a limited freedom.

There are cases of precognition that suggest this view. Milan Ryzl (1970), for example, cites the case of a railway employee who had a dream that two trains had collided with the loss of life at the terminal where he worked. The dream had alarmed the employee because of its vividness. Two days after the dream's occurrence, an overdue train got on the same track as an express that was arriving. Recalling his dream, he used a red flag to stop both trains when they were only a few yards apart. Without his action, the trains would have collided (p. 173). Rhine suggested, thinking of other but similar instances, that there was not "reliably perfect precognition" and there was "some scope left for volitional choice" (Rhine, 1947b, p. 82). Ryzl, on the other hand, said that the precognition he described was accurate as far as it went, and that those parts of the dream that were not verified by the objective events were *not* precognized. In this way, Ryzl "saved" the accuracy of precognition. Either Rhine's or Ryzl's interpretation seems possible. On Rhine's view, then, "We could ... not only see ahead with some effectiveness, but also choose our course with a degree of real freedom" (Rhine, 1947b, p. 82). There seems to be, besides the inconclusiveness here, a question of whether there is not a confusion between predictability and determination of physical events. The fact that one cannot know future events fully, as Rhine suggests here, does not seem to bear on the question as to whether those events are determined or not.

But this was only one way in which Rhine proposed to save free will from determinism. He also offered a better way and, in doing so, he fell back on his primary distinction between the physical and the mental continua. On this theory, he held that

> Only if the will has a nature different from the world on which it
> acts can it operate on free principles — free, that is, from the laws
> of the other system. Certainly, if we may say anything about pre-
> cognition, it is that it does not conform to physical laws. If, then,
> the mind can predict events, it is just that much more free from,
> because it is different from, the physical system upon which it
> acts [Rhine, 1947b, p. 84].

Given Rhine's views about mind and its own causative principle, this second explanation of freedom is better than the inconclusive first one. This view places freedom in the mental aspect of
man's nature. It is true that man's mind can be causally influenced
by physical nature, just as physical nature can be influenced by mind
through PK. But since the physical and the mental constitute two
disparate systems, there can exist a freedom of mind from the impact
of the physical world even though that freedom is limited. Rhine
described this limitation as a freedom ratio. It would appear that,
for Rhine, freedom meant this partial freedom of the mind from the
physical world.

One might, of course, raise the question: Even though the mind
is free from the physical world, at least to a degree, might it not be
that the mind has its own laws, properties, and potentialities which
in their turn determine mental events? Rhine, in fact, asserted that
there were such laws of the mind. The point could be made, however,
that such mental determinations are still independent, at least to a
degree, of possible interactions of the physical world on the mind; that
is, that these mental determinations are internal to the mind. This is
a plausible position and it avoids the fallacy of an uncaused will. This
view is not wholly unlike that of C. J. Ducasse (1953), who held that

> The course of action a man chooses in given circumstances is deter-
> mined not only by the nature of those circumstances, but also by
> the particular set of dispositions, tasts, past experiences, habits,
> purposes, impulses, and so on, which together constitute what we
> may call his particular 'volitional nature' at the time ... [p. 375-6].

With freedom of will established, Rhine is able to find a place
for morality and ethics in his philosophical reflections. Again, what
he affirmed in this connection is based on his central thesis concerning the nonmateriality of mind.

Rhine (1947b) regarded "the need for an effective morality" as one of our most urgent problems. But a solution to moral and ethical issues can arise only through "the science of human personality" (p. 219). Indeed, "Already the psi researches have gone far enough to show the possibility of a sound and reassuring scientific approach to ethical problems which in the past have been left to dogma, speculation, and tradition" (Rhine, 1947a, p. 1).

Though Rhine's moral views do not include a definitive moral code, they do reveal how parapsychology, with its insights into man's nature, can provide a basic guide to moral conduct. The essence of his ethical theory is presented in the following quotation (1947b):

> The more we are led on the one hand to think of our fellowmen as deterministic, physical systems — robots, machines, brains, — the more heartlessly and selfishly we can allow ourselves to deal with them. On the other hand, the more we appreciate their mental life as something unique in nature, something more original and creative than the mere space-time-mass relations of matter, the more we are interested in them as individuals, and the more we tend to respect them and consider their viewpoints and feelings [pp. 219–20].

To grasp this psychocentric conception of man through scientific knowledge of his nature is to provide a ground for happy and decent living, according to Rhine. And it is ESP and PK research that provides some experimental basis for benevolent feelings towards one's fellow men through the recognition of mind's nonmateriality and partial freedom. True, more research is needed to discover just how free man is and what his real ethical potential is. But the greater his freedom is, the greater is his ethical potential.

Another implication of Rhine's psychocentric view of man, especially important today with all of the ethnic divisions in our land, is the freeing of man from an emphasis on bodily traits, from "superficial group demarcations" (1947b, p. 222). For it is not the body that is the key to morality and free scientific inquiry, but the mind. Rhine's views on war and peace are an extension of these ethical ideas. And, similarly for our philosophy of government, which "depends entirely upon our view of the nature of the governed.... What is man? What is the human nature that must be dealt with by the functions of governing?" (1944, p. 247). And, he added, education, institutions and government are set up for man's mind.

Among the more important philosophic implications of psi are those that concern epistemology, the theory of knowledge. Rhine was, of course, well aware of these. He faced, first of all, those scientists and others who refused to believe that there were any actual psi data on which to build a science of parapsychology. Spontaneous cases of psi, which were the starting point for psychical research, were frequently declared to be fraudulent, delusive, or otherwise thrust aside. This was not so with the beginning data of the orthodox sciences. The geologist, for example, did not have to defend his belief in the existence of mountains, glaciers, meandering streams, layers of rock, and volcanoes. The parapsychologist as scientist was thus placed in the unusual position of having to justify the existence of the sort of data with which any science must begin — the *primitive facts* of science, as Ducasse called them (1941, pp. 118–9) in contrast with its derivative facts, which arise through experimentation, inference, and theory.

A second epistemological problem implied by psi phenomena, which should directly involve the philosopher who has traditionally attempted to theorize about the nature and limits of knowledge, is that presented by the existence of extrasensory knowledge of events in others' minds and of events in the external world. Such ESP knowledge fits into none of the orthodox epistemological categories, and its presence calls for changes in the theory of knowledge. Though there has been of late a marked increase in interest in this aspect of psi phenomena on the part of academic philosophers, inadequate attention to these facts still exists.

A third epistemological problem implied by the nature of psi phenomena need only be mentioned briefly here in that the non-physical character of psi has already been discussed. This problem is based on the incoherency of psi phenomena with the principles of orthodox science, that is, the fact that distance-time-mass-energy factors operate under different principles in psi than they do in physics. If an object can be moved by other than physical energy, as Rhine held that it can be, the physicist's account of energetic movement is thereby incomplete and incapable of subsuming natural phenomena that are claimed by him to be within his province. The same sort of incoherency between parapsychology and physics exists with respect to space and time in ESP occurrences and those in the "orthodox" physical world.

The implications of all of this is that there is a bifurcation in our scientific knowledge. There is physical science, on the one hand, with its own laws, forms of energy and materialist metaphysics, and parapsychology, on the other hand, with its emphases on para-psychic phenomena—phenomena not bound by the laws of the physical world, and which demand a nonmaterial explanation. This is the division that Rhine implied by his conception of psi. Are there of necessity two disparate kinds of science, physical and parapsychic, whose data and laws are incompatible?

In asking this question it is well to recall Rhine's relative dualism and his view that there must be a common ground of the physical and the mental because of their reciprocal interactions with each other. It is therefore possible that this bifurcation in science is not ultimately a necessity. This, in fact, is asserted by Rhine (1960) in *Dimensions of Mind*, where, in contrasting the physical and the mental, he wrote: "this distinction of nonphysicality is reasonably certain to prove to be transient, even though a temporarily very important, point" (p. 75). A few lines later, he added that this common ground of the physical and the mental "should ... become a principal object of scientific study for those in the field of parapsychology" (p. 76). And he further stated that psi would then be "an integral part of the universal system" (p. 76) which would incorporate all physical and psi events. Obviously, these are revolutionary implications of Rhine's work and they have led to much reflection by para-psychologists, an increasing number of academic philosophers, and others on how such a unity of science can be achieved.

Would such a unity reduce the physical and the mental to a single deterministic system, with a loss of freedom of will and moral responsibility? Rhine's answer, I think, would be no. This wider unity, based on the common ground of each of the two aspects, would not erase what needs to be saved for freedom. It would simply provide a coherency and lawfulness over the whole area of natural knowledge, including psi.

There have been criticisms of Rhine's philosophic views, but what philosopher has not had his critics? So let it be said simply that J. B. Rhine was a great and good man. At his death in 1980, the world lost a man with a touch of genius, a man of insight, great diligence, perseverance, courage, and a strong desire to know what life was all about. And his love for his fellow human beings made knowing him and having him as a friend a notable privilege.

REFERENCES

DUCASSE, C. J. *Philosophy as science*. New York: Oskar Piest, 1941.
DUCASSE, C. J. *A philosophical scrutiny of religion*. New York: Ronald Press, 1953.
DUCASSE, C. J. *The belief in a life after death*. Springfield, Ill.: Charles C. Thomas, 1961.
JAMES, WILLIAM. *Essays in radical empiricism*. New York: Longmans, Green, 1922.
RHINE, J. B. *New frontiers of the mind*. New York: Farrar & Rinehart, 1937.
RHINE, J. B. Editorial: Parapsychology and the government of men. *Journal of Parapsychology*, 1944, 8, 247.
RHINE, J. B. Editorial: Parapsychology and dualism. *Journal of Parapsychology*, 1945, 9, 226–7.
RHINE, J. B. Editorial: Parapsychology and ethics. *Journal of Parapsychology*, 1947a, 11, 1.
RHINE, J. B. *The reach of the mind*. New York: William Sloane, 1947b.
RHINE, J. B. Article: On the nature of man. In Hook, S. (ed.), *Dimensions of mind*. New York: New York University Press, 1960.
RHINE, J. B. ESP—what can we make of it? *Journal of Parapsychology*, 1966, 30, 84.
RHINE, J. B. *Extra-sensory perception*. Boston: Bruce Humphries, 1964. (Originally published in 1934 by Boston Society for Psychic Research.)
RHINE, J. B. & PRATT, J. B. *Parapsychology: Frontier science of the mind*. Springfield, Ill.: Charles C. Thomas, 1957.
RYZL, M. *Parapsychology: A scientific approach*. New York: Hawthorne Books, 1970.
SAGAN, C. Quoted in *Time*, October 20, 1980, 80.

The Work of J. B. Rhine:
Implications for Religion

JAMES A. HALL

The work of J. B. Rhine has clear implications for the study of theology and the practice of religion, although there has been little serious acknowledgment of this relevance. The scientific field of parapsychology owes the current definition of its borders to Dr. Rhine, and these borders clearly touch both the carefully cultivated fields of the sciences and the misty shorelines of the religions, shorelines with little stable definition but supporting vast shifting images of numinous awe and power. If science is the art of asking answerable questions, J. B. Rhine has posed the most *im*posing questions that have as yet been asked to either of these vast domains of human enterprise and endeavor. As Carl Jung wrote to J. B. Rhine on November 5, 1942 (Adler, 1973, Vol. 1, p. 322):

> I quite agree with you that once we are in possession of all facts science will look very peculiar indeed. It will mean nothing less than an entirely new understanding of man and the world.

J. B. Rhine (1945b) indicated quite early in his writings an awareness of the importance of parapsychological findings for the field of religion, particularly in reference to dualism (Rhine, 1945a), ethics (Rhine, 1947), and the possibility of human survival after bodily death (Rhine, 1960). He later made two major coordinated presentations of these concerns (Rhine 1975b, 1977–1978), so that there is no doubt that in his own mind the field of parapsychology has a relation to the field of religion that is analogous to "that of physiology to medicine, and physics to engineering" (Rhine, 1945b).

I first became aware of Dr. Rhine's deep concern with this relation of parapsychology and religion when he made a major address at the annual meeting of the Society for the Scientific Study of Religion (Southwest) at Phillips University in Enid, Oklahoma, in 1976. We talked a great deal at that conference and made basic plans for him to participate in an academic course on the psychology of religion at Perkins School of Theology, Southern Methodist University. In 1977, he generously spent an entire week at SMU, presenting the weekly convocation address in Perkins Chapel, consulting with members of the theological faculty, and addressing the Texas Society for Psychical Research on "Parapsychology and Religion," a meeting that fell with seeming synchronicity on Easter Sunday of 1977 (Rhine, 1976–1977).

Because of the deep and moving impression created by Dr. Rhine's visit, the sponsoring organization, the Foundation for the Study of Theology and the Human Sciences, began plans for a more focused symposium for the following year, one in which Dr. Rhine's concern about parapsychology and religion could be presented by him in a discussion forum with a select group of theologians, religious leaders, and representatives of the scientific community, particularly from the fields of psychiatry and psychology (Rhine, 1977–1978). This symposium on parapsychology and religion was held February 17–19, 1978, at Perkins School of Theology, SMU, convened by Albert C. Outler, Research Professor of Theology, and involved twenty discussants (Hall, 1977–1978a).

As we drove Dr. Rhine to the airport after this successful symposium he spoke of his sense of pleasure at having said what he wished to say about parapsychology and religion in an appropriate forum. I was also painfully aware that the symposium had been a strain on his remarkable physical energy and endurance. That he insisted on continuing the planned symposium in spite of recent health problems was a measure of the importance of the subject to his own deep purposes. He was unconcerned about any criticism that his presentation on religion might evoke in the scientific world. Several years before on the way to another airport he had said that his scientific critics never bothered him at all because he was always more critical of himself than any of them could possibly be. J. B. Rhine also encouraged the participation of Dr. K. Ramakrishna Rao in a subsequent symposium that took place only a few days after Dr. Rhine's sudden and unexpected death. We seriously considered postponing the symposium but concluded that "J. B." himself would have advised us to go right ahead with it.

In his 1977 Easter Sunday address to the Texas Society for

Psychical Research, which was transcribed for the *Journal of the Texas SPR* (Rhine, 1976–1977), J. B. Rhine traced the changing emphasis on Easter in his own experience:

> When I was a child I remember the concept of Easter as being a day of the promise of the literal resurrection. By the time I got into high school, it was a symbolic resurrection. By the time I got to college, where I was a pre-ministerial student, the concept was something else; not resurrection but a promise of a spiritual existence of some kind that wasn't very clear. Further on in my college career, I had to throw the whole thing out. I didn't know what to accept, I couldn't see the basis for any of it in my studies in the sciences to which I was drawn very strongly, especially psychology and biology. Still further on, by this time a graduate student, I heard about mediums and psychical research and the idea that life after death was something, an existence with which you could come to terms — you could do something about it [pp. 9–10].

In the same address, Dr. Rhine reviewed the early work with mediumship at the Duke Parapsychology Laboratory, primarily experiments with Eileen Garrett, the famous medium whose work with the Parapsychology Laboratory was financed by one of her own chief supporters. But the anticipated evidence for communication with discarnate personalities who had survived death was defeated by Mrs. Garrett's also scoring well on ESP tests that presumably required only her own psi powers, not the help of any incorporeal personal agency (IPA). Dr. Rhine (1976–1977) said: "We decided to put the question of Survival on the shelf as most every science has to do with its problems in earlier stages of its research, waiting for a time when methods are further developed" (p. 13). He wrote the chief supporter who had financed Mrs. Garrett, asking for funds to develop the basic methods needed if mediumship were to be thoroughly tested. As he succinctly put it: "She gave us the time but no more money" (p. 13).

Dr. Rhine was clearly not discouraged, however, about the possibility of re-opening the shelved question of survival. In 1975 he had indicated that he shared with William Perry Bentley an interest in investigating possible mediumistic evidence for survival (Rhine, 1974–1975, pp. 9–10). Rhine (1976–1977) suggested investing another fifty years of research on the survival question, adding: "I don't see how it could lose in bringing an answer to this question [of survival], whatever that answer is to be" (p. 15). He proposed two lines of parapsychological research that he felt might be fruitful in dealing with the question of survival (Rhine, 1976–1977, p. 14). These were (1) developing a tracer method that would "enable the subject to say not only what the message is, but where it came from ... a test of assurance, a confidence test," and (2) an animal experiment that would make the question of survival a biological question "as it properly should have been long ago." The general outlines of the proposed animal experiment would "let us ask if there is something about an animal that as its vital processes decline and death approaches keeps right on going as if it weren't dependent on the vital processes." Dr. Rhine pointed out that it would not be necessary to bring the animal to the point of actual death to theoretically test the proposed hypothesis. Even a demonstration that the simplest form of psi ability could function independently of the state of physical health would open the whole question of survival as a possibility.

Speculating on the possible findings of "what is really bedrock," Dr. Rhine (1976–1977, p. 19) said that he was leaning toward the view that the mind and body are a unity, "something like Spinoza's theory of the mind-body relationship," implying that "mind and body together make something that neither one of them possess" when separated. He labeled this possibility as like "the old idea of 'emergence.' " The terse, clear summary of his position (Rhine, 1976–1977) was the conclusion that "the scientists had the methods but not the problems and the theologians had the problems but not the methods" (p. 10).

J. B. Rhine published two papers explicitly dealing with the question of parapsychology and religion. The first (Rhine, 1975b) was virtually identical to the address given at Phillips University and primarily presents parallels between religious forms (as prayer) and various types of psi. These thoughts were expanded and elaborated in the second paper, that given at Southern Methodist University (Rhine, 1977–1978).

In the more expanded paper, Dr. Rhine discussed how parapsychology had already brought forward impressive evidence against the merely physicalist theory of man, thereby indirectly aiding the religious version of mankind. He stressed again, as he had done in 1975, the similarity between religious forms and types of psi (Rhine, 1975b): PK (related possibly to omnipotence), ESP (related to omniscience), clairvoyance (possibly related to the "all-seeing eyes" of a divine being), precognition (similar to prophecy, or knowledge of things to come), and all the various forms of psi relating to religious "miracles." "Thus," said Rhine (1977–1978), "on the whole, the types of psi that have been quite independently outlined by laboratory research closely resemble the kinds of exchange that religious men have assumed in the theologies that arose out of human experience long before the laboratories of parapsychology began their work" (p. 6).

Conditions of psi experience (most notably relaxation, sleep, trance, and other dissociated conditions) were seen as similar to religious traditions about the state of consciousness appropriate for contacting a divine order, as through a sacred oracle. Speaking of a "common foundation" of psi and religious experience, Rhine (1977–1978) said:

> Yet is now appears today that the chart of findings on psi communication fits rather closely into the pattern of interaction assumed in the major religions of mankind. Indeed, no matter what one thinks about the theological claims of these religions, he can now at least see that their founders must have built those great cultural systems on a rather good acquaintance with the same powers that have now been independently established as parapsychical [pp. 7–8].

Dr. Rhine then considered three questions from the point of view of the parapsychology of religion, seeing them as areas of probably fruitful future research:

> *First*, is the question of whether a person can exercise some volitional control over his situation. Is he in any meaningful sense (and in even the slightest verifiable degree) a free moral agent—free, that is, of the substituent deterministic forces operating in and through his organism?
>
> *Second*, is the problem of man's post-mortem destiny, whether or not death is the end of the personality as an individual agent.
>
> *Third*, is the question of the kind of universe it is in which we live. Is it in any verifiable way a *personal universe*, with a type of intelligently purposive agency within it to which man can with rational confidence turn for helpful communication in the midst of the trying emergencies of life [p. 9]?

He clearly indicated that these important questions are much more than problems for parapsychology alone, but added: "It does now seem safe to say with some confidence that this branch [of science] can continue to make advances into problem areas of religion where the footprints of no other science have ever been left" (p. 9).

J. B. Rhine thus clearly saw the relevance of parapsychology to the questions and beliefs that had been carried since the emergence of human consciousness by the forms of religious belief and worship. Without lessening his dedication to the principles of science he yet saw parapsychology as offering a way to possibly reconcile the unnatural split between mankind's greatest achievement, which is science, and mankind's greatest hopes and aspirations, which are still embodied in religious forms. J. B. Rhine thus was deeply concerned with the neglected field of natural theology, the concern that our study of the universe and our relation to it is also a way toward a sense of divine order that the great religions have believed on the authority of inspiration and revelation.

The evidence at this point is clearly inconclusive (Rhine, 1977–1978, pp. 21–22); there is enough evidence, however, to encourage parapsychology to pursue a deeper understanding of religious experiences and possibilities without sacrificing any of its dedication to the purest forms of science. The fact that neither the present community of science nor the present religious communities of faith sufficiently appreciate the deep importance of parapsychology is most likely a passing historical misunderstanding. As science, natural theology, and persons with religious commitment explore the largest meanings of human experience they must all increasingly appreciate the field of parapsychology. They also then will appreciate the gentle, honest vision of J. B. Rhine, which will increasingly be seen as a pioneering attempt to find the true place of mankind in the encompassing mystery of the universe.

In his Gifford Lectures on Natural Theology at the University of Aberdeen in 1951–1952, Michael Polanyi began a reassessment of scientific meaning and practice which has spoken both to science and to an increasing number of theologians. Polanyi (1958) spoke of opening horizons of religious inquiry through the deepening of scientific knowledge: "The greater precision and more conscious flexibility of modern thought, shown by the new physics and the logico-philosophic movements of our age, may presently engender conceptual reforms which will renew and clarify, on the grounds of modern extra-religious experience, man's relation to God." Polanyi added: "An era of great religious discoveries may lie before us" (p. 285).

In other Gifford Lectures at Edinburgh in 1979, still another scientist, Sir John Eccles (1980), Nobel laureate and distinguished researcher in neuroscience, turned his gaze in a similar direction:

Man has lost his way ideologically in this age.... I think that science has gone too far in breaking down man's belief in his spiritual greatness ... and has given him the belief that he is merely an insignificant animal that has arisen by chance and necessity in an insignificant planet lost in the great cosmic immensity.... We must realize the great unknowns in the material makeup and operation of our brains, in the relationship of brain to mind and in our creative imagination [p. 251].

Sir Karl Popper and Eccles (1977) had previously worked out a dualist-interactionist model of mind-brain relationship, a model that opens the possibility of the "relative sort of dualism" that in 1945 J. B. Rhine spoke of as an implication of the findings of parapsychology.

Natural theology is the most focused area in which the work of J. B. Rhine may (I think *will*) influence religious thought through the gradual and responsible exploration of the possible meanings of the divine/human interaction as observable in the world as we explore it scientifically. If this is indeed a religious universe, there is no intrinsic reason that science should not demonstrate such qualities (Hall, 1977–1978b, p. 40); if it is *not* such a universe, that too should ultimately come to awareness. In this scientific endeavor to find the meaning (if not the origins and limits) of mankind's place in the universe, a crucial factor is the faith that the community of science places on the integrity and reliability of individual scientists. The entire edifice of science ultimately rests on this basis of trust; and the trust of the community of science in parapsychology is built primarily on the foundation laid by the work of J. B. Rhine. In any future synthesis of science and religion, it is J. B. Rhine's unswerving loyalty to truth (Rhine, 1974, 1975a) and his "unquestioned integrity that has made parapsychology a respectable pursuit in the scientific world" (Hall, 1974–1975, p. 36).

Much remains to be done in parapsychology, and much additional work in other areas to begin a responsible investigation of the parapsychology of religion. Professor Frederick Streng (1977–1978, p. 32), a participant in the symposium at SMU, listed at least three things: a sensitivity to the assumptions now used to understand various forms of existence; the development of a vocabulary which allows mind, intuition, and will to play a role in the understanding of reality; and a continuing effort to accurately describe the phenomena of both parapsychology and religion, both in the laboratory and in ordinary life, and both in the past and the present. Albert

Outler (1977–1978, p. 48) added the need for a "really fruitful awareness of the paradox ... of the dialectic between the radical fact of mystery as the context in which we live and die and our insatiable hunger for intelligibility, verification, and scientific rigor." The mutual understanding of science and religion for the *human* origins and destinies of each field may point toward something that C. G. Jung anticipated: empirical indication of an ultimate unity of all existence, a goal Jung articulated through use of a term from medieval natural philosophy—the *unus mundus* (Von Franz, 1975, p. 247).

A significant honor was bestowed upon J. B. Rhine by the Society for Psychical Research, which had elected him to its presidency in the year of his death. In 1891 F. W. H. Myers, a founder of the SPR, reviewed a book that was then new, William James's *Varieties of Religious Experience*. Myers (1891–1982) spoke of the important and impartial work that had been begun, words that are equally applicable to the work of J. B. Rhine on the parapsychology of religion:

> It will be found that we have mainly concerned ourselves with such questions as, while admitting of statistical or experimental treatment, do nevertheless promise to throw some light, one way or the other, upon those deeper controversies as to the existence or character of a spiritual principle in man which have hitherto been mainly conducted on metaphysical than on empirical lines. In this task we have started — as I at least conceive our position — entirely without presupposition or prejudice [p. 112].

The impartiality of Dr. Rhine in considering the significant questions which parapsychology reopens is shown no better than in his answer to a question concerning his own conclusion about his own personal existence beyond the point of bodily death (Rhine, 1976–1977). Speaking to the Texas Society for Psychical Research on Easter Sunday of 1977, he said:

> As a matter of fact, I seldom ever thought about it [survival] in a personal way, and still less so since I quit conducting experiments with mediums. However, even in the days when we were working with mediumship, I never got deeply into the groove of thinking how this Spirit Survival might be because I didn't want to be carried away emotionally by such speculative thinking while the evidence was so inconclusive [p. 16].

In closing the symposium on parapsychology and religion at Southern Methodist University in 1978, Dr. Albert Outler spoke words of thanks to J. B. Rhine that also are an appropriate ending to my own present remarks. Dr. Outler (1977–1978) first summarized the accomplishments and problems brought into clearer focus by the dialogue of J. B. Rhine with the theologians and scientists who participated in the symposium. Then turning to Dr. Rhine he said:

> Most of all, and *of course*, we are *heartily thankful* to Dr. Rhine: for what he has contributed over the years, for his presence in our midst this week-end, for the inspiration he has given us for a continued search for truth — for that truth that lies within the perspective of science and rationality, but also that truth that reaches beyond those limits on out to those deeper and higher truths about human existence which hitherto have been too narrowly enclosed. For this and more, Dr. Rhine, we are, and will always be, in your grateful debt [p. 51]!

REFERENCES

ADLER, G. (ed.). *Jung letters* (2 vols.). Princeton, N.J.: Princeton University Press, 1973.

ECCLES, J. C. *The human psyche.* New York: Springer International, 1980.

HALL, J. A. Editorial. *Journal of the Texas Society for Psychical Research,* 1974–1975, 36.

HALL, J. A. Introduction: Symposium — parapsychology and religion. *Journal of the Texas Society for Psychical Research and the Oklahoma Society for Psychical Research,* 1977–1978a, ii.

HALL, J. A. Parapsychology, religion, and depth psychology. *Journal of the Texas Society for Psychical Research and the Oklahoma Society for Psychical Research,* 1977–1978b, 36–46.

MYERS, F. W. H. Review of William James's *The principles of psychology. Proceedings of the Society for Psychical Research,* 1891–1892, 7, 111–133.

OUTLER, A. C. Summary comments [of Symposium: Parapsychology and Religion]. *Journal of the Texas Society for Psychical Research and the Oklahoma Society for Psychical Research,* 1977–1978, 47–51.

POLANYI, M. *Personal knowledge: Towards a post-critical philosophy.* Chicago: University of Chicago Press, 1958.

POPPER, K. R., & ECCLES, J. C. *The self and its brain.* New York: Springer International, 1977.

RAO, K. R. The scientific status of parapsychology. Opening address at the symposium on parapsychology and religion sponsored by the Foundation for the Study of Theology and the Human Sciences, Dallas, Feb. 22, 1980. Unpublished.

RHINE, J. B. Editorial: Parapsychology and dualism. *Journal of Parapsychology,* 1945a, 9, 225–228.

RHINE, J. B. Editorial: Parapsychology and religion. *Journal of Parapsychology*, 1945b, **9**, 1–4.

RHINE, J. B. Editorial: Parapsychology and ethics. *Journal of Parapsychology*, 1947, **11**, 1–3.

RHINE, J. B. Incorporeal personal agency: The prospect of a scientific solution. *Journal of Parapsychology*, 1960, **24**, 279–309.

RHINE, J. B. Comments: A new case of experimenter unreliability. *Journal of Parapsychology*, 1974, **38**, 215–225.

RHINE, J. B. Perry Bentley as I know him. *Journal of the Texas Society for Psychical Research*, 1974–1975, 9–10.

RHINE, J. B. Comments: Second report on a case of experimenter fraud. *Journal of Parapsychology*. 1975a, **39**, 306–325.

RHINE, J. B. The parapsychology of religion: A new branch of inquiry. In *The centrality of science and absolute values*. Proceedings of the Fourth International Conference on the Unity of Sciences. New York: International Cultural Foundation, 1975b.

RHINE, J. B. Parapsychology and religion. *Journal of the Texas Society for Psychical Research*, 1976–1977, 9–22.

RHINE, J. B. The parapsychology of religion: A new branch of inquiry. (In symposium on parapsychology and religion.) *Journal of the Texas Society for Psychical Research and the Oklahoma Society for Psychical Research*, 1977–1978, 1–23.

STRENG, F. J. Prerequisites for the parapsychology of religion: Expanded vocabulary and new models of existence. *Journal of the Texas Society for Psychical Research and the Oklahoma Society for Psychical Research*, 1977–1978, 24–35.

VON FRANZ, M. *C. G. Jung: His myth in our time.* New York: C. G. Jung Foundation and G. P. Putnam's Sons, 1975.

J. B. Rhine's Impact

ARTHUR KOESTLER

A few years ago, John Beloff edited an anthology of essays by seven well-known researchers, to which I contributed a postscript. The title of the book, *New Directions in Parapsychology*, sounded matter of fact, yet it seemed to imply that the "old directions" had become inadequate and were perhaps leading into a dead end. One of the main reasons for this unsatisfactory state of affairs was underlined by Charles Honorton (Beloff, 1974):

"Until recently ... little systematic research has been directed toward the elucidation of subjective states associated with paranormal functioning. In view of the behavioristic *Zeitgeist*, it is perhaps not surprising that early proponents of the card-guessing paradigm ... largely disregarded their subjects' internal states...."

One might indeed say that parapsychology was more concerned with *para* than *psychology*. Given the circumstances, this was almost unavoidable. As John Beloff commented: "The Rhine school of parapsychology thought to beat behaviorism at its own game by showing that anti-behaviorist conclusions could be arrived at on the basis of impeccably objectivist data." To have obtained these data with dogged perseverance, undeterred by the hostility of academics and the derision of the ignorant, is the Rhine school's historic achievement. Yet it was only made possible by the self-imposed limitations which Honorton pointed out.

One of the cornerstones of scientific methodology is the formula *ceteris paribus* — "other things being equal." But other things are never equal where human subjects are concerned. Not even their reactions to the gross chemical impact of drugs are equal. Clinical studies have shown that about one-third of the American hospital population are placebo-reactors. Given the appropriate suggestion, they will react to barbiturates as if they were amphetamines, to amphetamines as if they were barbiturates and, with the proper suggestion, even to placebos as if they were one or the other. The states of consciousness of these placebo-reactors override the true effect of the chemical. It seems obvious that the effect of psi — whatever it consists of — is even more dependent on the "hidden variables" of the subject's general character, such as his disposition and particular state of mind at the time of the experimental test or spontaneous occurrence.

Thus one may wonder whether the parapsychologist's quest for the ideal experiment — repeatable at will, yielding predictable results — will not turn out to be a wild goose chase. In spite of his customary caution, John Beloff (1974) expressed the hope that parapsychology is "edging its way towards a solution of the problem of repeatability" (pp. 9–10). He may be right, but I do not feel so sure about it. A parabola edges its way towards its asymptotes without ever achieving union. The nearest we have come to a repeatable experiment is in the field of automated animal experimentation, described by John Randall. Perhaps with mice, gerbils and chicks the "hidden variables" interfere less with the functioning of the psi faculty. But people's psyches are more mysterious. Ask any writer, or painter, or scientist to define the precise conditions under which the creative spark will repeatably and predictably ignite the vapors in his mind! Yet creativity is a less elusive and mysterious faculty than psi.

The above is by no means intended to discourage the parapsychologist's patient efforts to elucidate the personality structures and states of consciousness which enhance the psi faculty, and the experimental conditions best suited to trigger it. On the contrary, I consider these efforts as perhaps the most promising among the "new directions" in parapsychology. I still remember with what enthusiasm I read about Gertrude Schmeidler's pioneer work some twenty years ago; "sheep" and "goats" appeared as a first step towards a taxonomy of potential psi subjects. In more than a quarter of a million card trials with more than 1100 subjects the sheep scored significantly and persistently higher than the goats. It looked so beautifully simple, almost self-evident: have we not always been taught that faith can move mountains — i.e., perform feats of PK? Unfortunately things turned out not to be as simple as that. Beloff and others found that in some studies the goats, perhaps out of sheer perversity, did better than the sheep; and a careful study of Rao's essay (Beloff, 1974) reveals that the singling out of any other personality factor led to similarly contradictory or inconclusive results. The combination of several factors, as attempted by Rao and Kanthamani, seemed a more holistic and promising approach. Yet ironically, Rao's composite portrait of the potentially high scoring ESP subject is in almost every respect the exact opposite of Pratt's description of the highest scoring person known at the time, Pavel Stepanek. The situation reminds me of a remark by the science fiction writer Poul Anderson: "I have yet to see any problem, however complicated, which, when you looked at it in the right way, did not become still more complicated."

But the parapsychologist need not worry unduly; other sciences have found themselves in similar predicaments. The subatomic world composed of electrons and protons looked complicated enough, but when the physicists looked at it in the right way, it became still more complicated, with dozens of "elementary particles" instead of two. The physicist's trouble is that the subatomic phenomena which he manipulates can no longer be fitted into the spatio-temporal framework of naive realism and conventional physics. The parapsychologist's trouble is equally fundamental. He too can manipulate, up to a point, the manifestations of psi in his laboratory, but he is unable to fit them into the framework of conventional psychology, and knows next to nothing of their physiological correlates, evolutionary origin, and biological value, that is to say, the purpose of psi in the general scheme of things. We do not even know whether, in evolutionary terms, psi is an *emergent* faculty—somehow related to man's spirituality—which gradually unfolds, like sentience and consciousness, with each upward step on the evolutionary ladder, or whether on the contrary extrasensory perception is an archaic and primitive form of communication which has been superseded by more efficient forms of sensory perception (but if this is the case, what about PK?). Needless to say, these questions are of fundamental importance, not only to the parapsychologist, but also to the philosopher and metaphysician. Thus the pursuit of parapsychology is an immensely worthwhile undertaking; and there are indications that, even if the researchers of the post-Rhine generation do not come up with final answers, they are learning to ask the pertinent questions.

Today, both the physicist and the parapsychologist are learning to live in a universe with a substructure of noncausal interactions—a fuzzy world of wavering contours, replete with little bubbles of indeterminacy, which provide intimations of an unexpected kind of freedom, for which in the world of classical physics there was no room. Once this lesson has sunk in, "nothing in science or philosophy could ever again be quite the same," to quote John Beloff (1974, p. 8) again. And I have no doubt that J. B. Rhine will be recognized by future historians as one of the pioneers of the new age.

REFERENCE

BELOFF, J. (ed.) *New directions in parapsychology.* London: Paul Elek, 1974 (reprinted by Scarecrow Press, Metuchen, N.J., 1975).

J. B. Rhine and American Psychology: The Three R's of His Limited Impact So Far

Irvin L. Child

The work of J. B. Rhine has attracted great attention in psychology, but only as a source of controversy, not as an integral part of general psychology. From the point of view of psychologists who are complete skeptics about the occurrence of psi phenomena, the impact of Rhine's work has of course been much greater than deserved; from the point of view of psychologists who are convinced that psi phenomena are genuine, the impact has been much less than the importance of Rhine's work should dictate. In the present context of honoring the memory of Rhine, the reasons that should justify a great positive impact are conspicuous in the very titles of many of the essays in this book. What I would like to concentrate on is why the impact has not been greater. I would summarize my theme in a threefold classification—repeatability, reasonableness, and right understanding—the three R's of the reserved response that psychology as a whole has made to Rhine's work, and to the further research this response has caused.

Repeatability

The most basic problem, the core issue, is the lack of dependable repeatability. This basic problem has been so often stated—necessarily, in view of its fundamental nature—that there may be little to add. To make it vivid, however, I will start by illustrating its contemporaneity, citing a recent experience of my own.

In the spring of 1979 Ariel Levi, a graduate student in social psychology at Yale who has an incidental interest in parapsychology, did a social-psychology experiment on factors influencing a person's expectation of success in performances that seem to be completely dependent upon chance. He used a Schmidt machine of the type that displays a number which starts at 1 and then is incremented, about 12 times a second, in steps of one; as each unit is added there is a one-sixteenth chance that the count will stop at that point. The chance distribution of numbers stopped at in a series of trials has a mean of 16; the most likely stopping point is the number 1, and each successive number above 1 has a relative frequency 15/16 times that of the preceding number. In Levi's experiment, a subject was to desire or hope for a stopping number higher than 16 on each trial. The subject was told that the probability of this outcome, if the machine was working entirely at random, is 36 percent. Just before each trial, the subject was asked to predict whether the outcome would be a hit (that is, above 16) or a miss, and to express the degree of confidence he felt in his hunch.

The main purpose of the experiment was to study the effect of three distinct factors on these expectations: (1) whether the subject was allowed to see the display of numbers and thus learn immediately whether each trial was a success or not; (2) whether the subject himself controlled the switch that set the machine going (although in no case was there any reason to believe realistically that the operation of the switch had any influence on the outcome); and (3) the kind of imagery the subject was instructed to engage in just before making his guess about the outcome. For each of these factors, previous social-psychology experiments and theoretical statements led to a definite expectation about the outcome of the experiments. Being able to see the outcome, and having a possibly illusory sense of control over it through handling the switch, should both favor an expectation of a successful outcome. Engaging in imagery of the actual goal, or perhaps imagery of instrumental processes directed at the goal, should also improve the strength of expectation in comparison with imagery completely irrelevant to the goal.

While Levi's main purpose in the experiment was to test in this specific situation the outcome of predictions based on prior work in social psychology, his interest in parapsychology led him also to record and analyze the actual outcomes of the machine under the varying conditions from trial to trial. When he analyzed this aspect of the data, he obtained some striking results. With subjects who had been asked to engage in imagery of the goal, that is, visualizing high numbers, the machine produced on the average higher numbers in in the feedback condition and lower numbers in the nonfeedback condition. When subjects were asked instead to engage in imagery of the internal operations of the machine, this outcome was reversed, feedback being associated with low numbers and nonfeedback with high. Levi had no definite predictions in advance about the outcome of this parapsychological side of the experiment. But after obtaining his striking results, he learned that Morris, Nanko, and Phillips, in an experiment with feedback conditions only, had obtained results identified with those Levi obtained in the feedback condition. While the details of the experiments were different, there was enough similarity in general purport that Levi's experiment could well be regarded as a successful replication of the other experiment.

Always hoping to find a dependable way of evoking psi phenomena in order that they may be studied, I was encouraged by this close parallel of outcome. Being in an unusually favorable situation for repeating an experiment almost exactly except for a change in experimenter, I decided to invest time in repeating Ariel Levi's experiment. I was able to use the very same room, the identical equipment, and for the most part identical materials and procedures, and subjects obtained from a similar source. The principal difference, apart from its being a year and a half later in time, was the identity of the experimenter, with all the differences in age, appearance, mode of interaction with undergraduate subjects, and the like which that implies. The outcome of this replication, with respect to the parapsychological side, appears at first glance to be a total absence of effect; so far as there is any suggestion of an effect, it seems to be opposite to what was obtained by Morris, Nanko and Phillips, and by Levi.

The history of psychologists' attitudes toward experimental parapsychology has largely been influenced by such instances of failure to replicate. So strong has been the impact of nonrepeatability that for many psychologists it quite wipes out the effect of what replicability has been found. Psychologists active during the 1930s and not closely following developments in parapsychology will probably have the impression, as I did at one time, that repetition of positive outcome in card guessing experiments was almost entirely confined to work done by Rhine and his associates at Duke University. Honorton has provided a very instructive summary of published experiments in card guessing during that period, in which he shows that there was a great deal of positive replication with other experimenters, and at other institutions. The skeptical attitude common among psychologists was, I think, often justified by the argument that during the same period many efforts by other individuals were not successful, and perhaps especially by the assumption that there were a great many experiments with negative outcome that never even reached publication. Careful consideration shows that the number of unsuccessful unpublished experiments could not have been great enough to negate the statistical significance of the positive experiments. But I think there is a psychological effect that occurs when people evaluate experiments with positive outcomes. If highly significant defect-free experiments with positive outcomes stand alone, they are more impressive than if they stand beside many similar experiments that yield no evidence of psi. It is easy in this situation to suppose that the positive experiments have some unknown defect. I cannot see why the objective fact I describe — the presence of two sets of experiments with different outcomes, one set arguing for the presence of psi processes and the other not — provides in itself any reason to ascribe the difference to one unidentified source rather than another. But the effect on people's evaluation of experiments seems to be very real, even if psychological rather than logical.

Lack of dependable repeatability, then, seems to put an end to many psychologists' interest in the work of Rhine and of other experimental parapsychologists. But on other problems, quite outside the realm of parapsychology, lack of dependable repeatability does not necessarily terminate the interest of psychologists. Consider, for example, the problem of what influences expectations of success, the problem that Ariel Levi was addressing in the social-psychology side of the experiment I have described. As I have said, previous experiments and theory in social psychology led to definite predictions about the influence of his experimental factors on expectations of success. But those predictions were in general not confirmed. Here is an experiment that was successful as a replication of a previous parapsychological experiment but as a replication — a conceptual replication — of previous social-psychology experiments it was not. Will social psychologists therefore be very skeptical about the reality of influences on expectation, or of the particular kinds of influence under study? I think we can safely assume they will not.

Reasonableness

Why the difference? It may be that in social psychology there is a larger body of prior experimentation with more uniformly positive results; but on specific problems a long history is not usually in fact required as a basis for interest. The key factor, I believe, is that the social-psychology predictions about expectation seem perfectly reasonable or possible in the light of general psychological assumptions and indeed in the light of popular beliefs, implicit or explicit, to which probably no one takes violent exception. On the contrary, of course, the very idea that psi phenomena might really occur seems in some way incompatible with general scientific understanding of the universe. And though the reality of psi phenomena is quite in accord with some popular beliefs, those beliefs are even among the general populace subject to great controversy. So an expression of doubt about the reality of psi should hardly come as a surprise to anyone.

It is striking indeed that among experimental psychologists, methodological purists may be less skeptical of ideas for which nobody has even devised satisfactory experimental tests than they are of parapsychological ideas for which experiments have been devised and applied with positive outcomes. Consider for example many of the hypotheses originating in Freudian psychoanalysis—notions about symbolism, about infantile sexual trauma, about repression and the unconscious. For many decades psychologists have tried to bring these concepts into the range of objective scientific research by devising procedures that might permit their value to be tested. Many of these efforts have been unsuccessful even in the eyes of the psychologists engaging in them, yielding no decisive evidence whatever about original psychoanalytic hypotheses. Where the psychological researchers have felt that they were getting somewhere toward giving a psychoanalytic hypothesis an empirical meaning, psychoanalysts have often argued that this appearance is based on misunderstanding of the psychoanalytic ideas, and perhaps that the psychoanalytic ideas are basically incapable of being tested in any objective way.

This is a close parallel to what some students of the paranormal say about the ideas they are exploring in expressing doubts about the special value of experimental parapsychology. Psychologists, however, who doubt the value of experimental parapsychology are even more likely to reject nonexperimental evidence for the paranormal. By contrast, in the case of psychoanalytic hypotheses, tolerance is more likely for the evidence from spontaneous cases, once a psychologist happens to be directly exposed to such evidence.

Consider an experience I had long ago which greatly influenced my general attitude toward psychoanalytic theory, and more particularly toward Freud's theory of errors as a product of unconscious resolution of conflicting motives. It happened during my senior year at U.C.L.A., at a time and place where the attitude of psychologists toward Freud was much like their attitude toward Rhine. I was given the privilege, in an independent study course, of receiving academic credit for reading Freud's works on my own. I was much impressed, although the instructor really didn't think I should have been. One evening that spring when I was at a friend's house, I took out a pack of cigarettes and offered one to a friend who was next to me, then took one myself, lit my cigarette and put the match out, leaving my friend with an unlit cigarette in his hand. I'm not such a paragon of etiquette and consideration for other people that it would be extraordinary for me to do a thing like that. But as a matter of fact I was sure I had never been discourteous before in that particular way. And it puzzled me. I thought about it again the next day, and then placed it in the context of the fact that the cigarette incident occurred on the very day when I had made a decision which involved going to Harvard as a graduate student. Then I remembered, too, an incident a couple of weeks earlier: I had been at the house of another friend, and at dinner his father was talking about the difficulty I would confront if I had to decide whether to go to graduate school at Harvard or Princeton or Yale or various other places to which I had applied. And had I ever heard, he went on, the story about what the difference is between a Harvard man, a Yale man, and a Princeton man? The Princeton man lights his friend's cigarette and then lights his own, the Yale man lights his own cigarette and then lights his friend's, the Harvard man lights his own cigarette and puts the match out. Well for me this experience of my own was enough to persuade me that the error I had made, unique thus far in my experience, was really related to thoughts I was not conscious of at all, a symbolic gratification of a wish I'd foregone.

This incident greatly increased my readiness to consider seriously a variety of psychoanalytic hypotheses which I might at first have rather scornfully rejected. Even if I had had a single seemingly psychic experience of approximately equal value as evidence, I doubt that my attitudes would have been equally influenced. And I think my responses here may well be typical of those of many psychologists. The absence of a dependable experimental test is less influential, the presence of spontaneous evidence is more influential, in attitudes toward the unconscious than in attitudes toward the psychic. The difference lies, I believe, in a feeling of reasonableness. The processes psychoanalytic theory points to do not in general seem impossible or genuinely incompatible with other psychological hypotheses. They merely seem either improbable in themselves, or too vague to permit direct experimental test. There seems always the possibility that eventually psychoanalytic ideas might be adequately reconciled with other aspects of psychology, that they might become a part of a general psychological theory that could be tested by experimental as well as clinical procedures.

Now the views put forth by J. B. Rhine were not completely lacking in possible detailed integration with other psychological ideas. Some of the factors he studied as influences in ESP were essentially the same as factors studied by other psychologists as influences on other psychological functions. For example, Rhine initiated experimentation on the effects of drugs on ESP performance. He had much to say, even in his first monograph, on motivational influences on ESP performance. A great deal of parapsychological research has involved close parallels with work in general experimental psychology.

Yet always there remains a basic gap, a sense that the phenomena being dealt with here seem unreasonable, seem in some fundamental way incompatible with the rest of psychology, physiology, and physics—a sense that, as the philosopher C. D. Broad put it, they seem to violate the basic limiting principles involved in science.

Some proponents of parapsychology have suggested that this gap is not as distinctive as psychologists make it out to be, that it parallels the gap between brain and consciousness. A neurological event and a conscious experience may be fundamentally different, and we have no definite knowledge of exactly how they are linked. If psychologists have no difficulty in dealing simultaneously with neurological events and conscious experience, if they find it reasonable to link the two in scientific statements, should they not find it equally reasonable to bring psi together with ordinary physical and psychological processes?

This challenge to the sense of so many psychologists that psi is unreasonable is not effective. This sense of the unreasonableness of psi reduces in the end to difficulties in repeatability. Surely the reason that many scientists can search happily for neurological events that influence conscious events, unworried by their seeming to be utterly different kinds of events, is that there is dependably repeatable knowledge of just this sort of connection. Certain chemicals, once absorbed by the brain, put an end to consciousness; a jar to the head sets off the firing of fibers in the optic nerve and leads to an experience of flashes of light. There is a host of correlations of specific conscious events with specific physical events both inside the nervous system and outside it, despite the basic discrepancy between the material and mental events. But there is no parallel to the apparent discrepancy between psi phenomena and physical or neurological events that can be fitted into our present scientific frame of reference, and there is as yet no comparable body of detailed knowledge that facilitates our overlooking the underlying discrepancy in this latter case.

Right Understanding

The third R accounting for the restrained impact of Rhine's work on American psychology is what I will call right understanding. Every profession or intellectual grouping is likely to have a distinctive sense of correctness in their approach to the solution of problems. They are likely to have an almost righteous zeal with which they seek to impose on others the solutions to which this "right understanding" leads them. Their right understanding is likely to be correct for some limited realm of events with which they are especially familiar; its righteous application to far different events may seem to outsiders to be far from correct. An instance of this may readily be found among parapsychologists: they have seen strong evidence for the occurrence of psi phenomena, and they may be tempted to extend their right understanding to a host of situations where outsiders would expect to see no evidence for psi phenomena. On the whole, I think parapsychologists have been commendably restrained in yielding to this temptation, and the caution characteristic of J. B. Rhine has been a valuable source of this restraint. But the right understanding of psychologists, it must be noted, finds broader social support for its extension.

What is this "right understanding" so common among psychologists? Psychologists, in comparison with other groups, are likely to be especially aware of possible sources of error and of alternative explanations for experimental findings which might deny the concept as psi.

This right understanding of psychologists is similar to the right understanding of magicians. Randi and some other magicians are fond of saying that magicians because of their mastery of techniques of deception are more aware than others of possible deceptions being practiced by a skilled magician purporting to be a psychic. Ability to detect tricks can obviously be very helpful to parapsychologists in those situations where they are working with people who are engaged in such deception, and in any event can help them assess correctly and arrange appropriately the security aspects of their normal procedures. But if there are indeed real psi phenomena, then the magician convinced that his hypothesis of deliberate deception applies to all apparent psi phenomena will be led astray. He believes that wherever magical skills provide a *possible* explanation they provide the *correct* explanation. The right understanding of magicians needs to be extended with restraint, or at least without self-righteous overconfidence.

The right understanding of psychologists consists of knowledge of a variety of ways in which normal psychological processes may lead to erroneous conclusions. This knowledge emerges from the psychology of perception, of reasoning, of judgment. Experiments done through the years have abundantly shown that many people confidently believe they have witnessed what they have not witnessed, draw unwarranted conclusions from what they have witnessed, and may distort their memory of what they have witnessed in ways that lead to false beliefs. Various kinds of psychological study converge in increasing this awareness of possible errors. There is the work of psychoanalytic origin, concerned with motivated misperception and distortion of memory. There is the nontheoretical work on psychology of testimony, growing out of the practical interests of students of psychology and the law. There is much recent work in social psychology on the frailties of human reasoning.

When the psychological study of such processes is applied to everyday beliefs in psychic phenomena, it is apparent that most such beliefs might be entirely due to such errors. All of this psychological work, had it been done a century ago, might have strengthened the suspicion with which the early students of psychical research in England regarded the anecdotal material that came to them. But it would lead to a stronger skepticism than those researchers had, and perhaps quite justify a complete renunciation of their sort of work as capable of leading to any substantial knowledge of psi phenomena. The outcome of this special skepticism might be indeed a renewed feeling that only careful experimentation, such as Rhine was so insistent in introducing into parapsychology, could be an adequate source of parapsychological knowledge. But if we must rely on experimentation, then we come back to the first point, that experimentation in this field has not yet been able to meet the expectation of dependable replication.

In view of all the special reasons for psychologists' being skeptical of results both of experimentation and of field work in parapsychology, it is perhaps surprising that so many psychologists are as tolerant as they are of the possible reality of psi phenomena. Some psychologists strongly reject the possibility of psi phenomena, and are hostile toward those who argue for it. But this hostility that characterizes the few may easily be mistaken for the lack of interest that characterizes the many. In the absence of dependable replication, the partial or occasional replication of more and more experiments in parapsychology attracts increasing interest from psychologists and others. Even the limited repeatability found thus far is a substantial challenge to the feeling that psi is beyond reason; surely, psychologists would almost unanimously agree that if reason and reality clash, reason must yield. Here the third of the three R's in the psychological attack, the self-righteous extension of right understanding, may end by turning back upon itself. Psychologists are not exempt from the findings of their own science, and their beliefs, like those of the zealous advocates of psi, may be less closely related than they think to evidence. I am encouraged to believe that as research develops further, interests in the experimental parapsychology, which so largely derive from the work of J. B. Rhine, will come to be wider and wider among psychologists.

J. B. Rhine
and European Parapsychology

Martin Johnson

In this essay I wish to explore J. B. Rhine's impact on parapsychology in Europe. Unfortunately time has not allowed me to carry out either an extensive or a penetrating study on this topic. However, I hope that this study will constitute the first step of an extended study on the topic.

I am going to pose some questions: What did J. B. Rhine know about European parapsychology? Was he well read? Did he follow developments on the European scene? What kind of work going on in Europe did he appreciate? In which ways did the Europeans respond? To most of these questions, I can only suggest answers in a rather subjective and impressionistic way. The question of how to measure the impact of an individual on a stream of events needs a far more careful analysis.

To reduce the impact of my own bias, I have tried to gather relevant information and opinions from some of the key figures and senior parapsychologists on the European scene. In that connection, I wish to thank John Beloff, Hans Bender, Erlendur Haraldsson, Arthur Koestler, Helmut Schmidt, Emilio Servadia, R. H. Thouless, D. J. West and George Zorab. They have been kind enough to respond to my query and have allowed me to use their statements.

In most cases, their statements are based both on personal experience of Dr. Rhine (that is, what kind of impression Dr. Rhine made on them) as well as their opinion of the impact Dr. Rhine exerted on parapsychology in a general sense.

Not all persons I turned to answered my query. Furthermore, a few persons, clearly known as antagonistic towards Dr. Rhine, have not been asked for their views. These facts may introduce a certain bias in my study, something that should be kept in mind in subsequent investigations of this issue.

The first question I want to pose is, what did J. B. Rhine know about European parapsychology? Reading Chapter 2 in *Extra-Sensory Perception* (Rhine, 1934), one certainly becomes convinced that Dr. Rhine had a profound knowledge not only of research carried out in the U. S. but also of the work being done in Great Britain, the cradle of parapsychology, and on the European Continent. He even gives a review of some investigations carried out in Russia. It is no surprise that he mentions the founders of the British Society for Psychical Research (SPR). The list of researchers within the SPR is extensive, which could also be expected. Moreover, Dr. Rhine was even then conversant with the work carried out in Germany as well as in France. His familiarity is not to be taken for granted, because of the language barriers that must have made it difficult for him to read the original reports. His condensed review of the work of Charles Richet, E. Osty, P. Janet, and R. Warcollier seems to me to be compiled in a scholarly way. Regarding the early work in Germany, he mentions contributions made by A. von Schrenck-Notzing, R. Tischner, von Wasielewsky, and C. Bruck. He also mentions W. Ostwald's interest in the field and touches upon his ideas of how to explain some of the phenomena. Regarding the work in Russia, the names of Bechterew, Chowrin, and Kotik are mentioned.

As a Dutch professor, I find it of special interest to notice that Dr. Rhine was acquainted with the pioneering experimental work that had been carried out at the University of Groningen by H. J. F. W. Brugmans and G. Heymans. However, may I remark that the names Brugmans and Heymans are slightly misspelled: two *n*'s instead of the correct one each!

Dr. Rhine returned in another connection to the Groningen work. He thought it important but, based on the information he had available, may have tended to underestimate its quality. At least, according to the recent investigation by Schouten and Kelly (Schouten & Kelly, 1978) the contrary view is supported that the statistics are better than they were thought to be and that reasonable precautions had been taken to eliminate the influence of sensory cues.

As a Scandinavian, I also find it interesting to find that Dr. Rhine was familiar with at least two of the main events on the parapsychological scene in Scandinavia. He refers to the work of A. Lehmann and F. C. C. Hansen, and to their attempts to explain away most of the findings within the field by refering to sensory cues. J. B. Rhine also mentions experiments with "travelling clairvoyance" under hypnosis carried out by the Swedish physician, A. Backman. However, he makes no reference to the interesting field study, carried out by Paul Bjerre, generally called the "Karin Case." According to Bjerre, he succeeded in producing poltergeist-like phenomena around "Karin" by means of post-hypnotic suggestions. In short it becomes quite clear from the reading of that "paradigmatic" book, *Extra-Sensory Perception* (See Mauskopf & McVaugh, 1980), that J. B. Rhine, even at that stage of his career, had a good grip on the history of parapsychology, irrespective of whether the various studies fell under the heading of "psychical research," "metapsychic," or "parapsychologie." Judging from *Extra-Sensory Perception* and subsequent books by Rhine, he made no secret of the fact that 'there lived heroes before Agamemnon' — at least a few. He was always keen to express his deep intellectual debts to William McDougall, his most important mentor. Regarding other Europeans, I think there are clearcut indications that he, at least, had a certain admiration for men like Henri Bergson, Hans Driesch, and Charles Richet. Whether one could really say that he felt indebted intellectually to these persons I am not sure. It is interesting to speculate whether Dr. Rhine would have been able to carry out the pioneering work behind his *Extra-Sensory Perception* if he had not been well aware of most of the investigations that preceded his own extensive research program. It goes without saying that J. B. Rhine remained a great authority on the history of his science for the rest of his life. I think that most readers of Wolman's *Handbook* would agree with me that Rhine's contribution, "The History of Experimental Studies," is admirably well written (Rhine, 1977).

If J. B. Rhine was so well informed of what had happened on the European scene before and around the time he wrote his paradigmatic book, it is no surprise that he remained so for the rest of his life. Over a period of more than forty years, he kept himself informed of what was going on in the field in all corners of the world. As I mentioned in the obituary I wrote (Johnson, 1980) J. B. Rhine had an extremely wide-ranging correspondence. He corresponded with almost everyone who took a more or less professional interest in parapsychology. May I also say that he was a real master as a letter writer.

Within the United States he travelled extensively, but his trips abroad were rare. However, one could say that he compensated for that by inviting a great number of people to visit him. In this way, he could keep himself well informed about the people in the field, what they honored and disdained, and how capable they were. He could also, by means of these invitations, formally or informally exert an educational influence. In addition, visitors could contribute articles about their work to the *Journal of Parapsychology*. Direct examples of Rhine's educational activities which have had an impact on an international scale were the Review Meetings at the FRNM during the late sixties and early seventies and the summer school that was introduced during the seventies. Besides drawing people to the Parapsychology Laboratory and to the FRNM, Dr. Rhine arranged small research grants. Through his extensive correspondence, by invitations, and by rendering small grants, he could offer leadership to a higher degree than anyone else in the field.

Dr. Rhine possessed a charismatic personality that undeniably must have been important in influencing people. He could also be very stubborn but if he so desired, extremely diplomatic. Sometimes he did not so desire. He could be exceedingly outspoken, to say the least. Reports of some encounters between Rhine and staff members and visitors certainly contributed to his reputation as a controversial figure.

J. B. Rhine's relation to European parapsychology was certainly not entirely uncomplicated. The same can be said to a certain degree about his relation to at least some of the work which has been carried out on the Continent. Rhine's strong emphasis on the professionalizing of parapsychology (and that it was *he* who did so!) was certainly a thorn in the flesh of many representatives of the admittedly more amateuristic private societies.

Another reason for dissonance was Dr. Rhine's attitude regarding the value and use of spontaneous cases. This is clearly stressed by Mr. Zorab in statements he has given me for this essay. Rhine's opinion on hypnosis and paranormal phenomena was also not appreciated by many Europeans. Moreover, his opinion, by and large, on the use and needs of "sensitives" was somewhat contradictory to the European tradition, and his relative lack of interest in field studies also aroused strong feelings. His strongly negative attitude towards interpretations of the paranormal in terms of psychoanalytic assumptions disturbed many psychologists following an in-depth psychological approach with psychoanalytic thinking as an important ingredient. I remember that in one of our conversations Rhine flatly described orthodox psychoanalysis as a "pseudoscience." One should here stress, however, that that position is not uncommon at all. To most "Popperians" that is certainly the case, as it is more or less impossible to put many of the assumptions to a critical test of refutation (See Farrell, and Comment: Cioffi, 1970). The view that Rhine totally neglected the spontaneous cases can substantially be refuted by the fact that he encouraged his wife to devote much of her work to the collection of cases. As a matter of fact, she turned into one of the world's leading experts in this area. His strong emphasis on laboratory control made some of his antagonists see him as a somewhat restricted scientist, being obsessed by the execution of tedious and repetitive card-calling and dice-throwing experiments. *Extra ecclesiam nulla salus* — outside the laboratory, no parapsychology — is a travesty by which I have heard a few try to ridicule Dr. Rhine. Dr. Rhine never denied the possible heuristic value of field studies and the study of spontaneous cases, but he felt hesitant about how to evaluate such observations in a strictly scientific way.

It seems reasonable to me then to assume that Dr. Rhine's "scientisms," or ideals of science, were interpreted by some Europeans as somewhat restricted and also as conflicting with the ideal of science within "Geisteswissenschaft," an ideal propagated by philosophers like W. Dilthey, W. Windelband, and E. Spranger.

Some other reasons for criticism of Rhine are touched upon in D. J. West's answer to my query, below. Some of the aspects I have touched upon could explain the surprising fact that Dr. Rhine had to wait until the last year of his life for the distinction of becoming the president of the SPR (in London), a distinction several foreigners have obtained for a fraction of what J. B. Rhine contributed to parapsychology.

Another impact of Rhine on an international scale is the fact that he was the founder of the Parapsychological Association. He declined to have any official function on its council and I think that will clearly refute the view that he created the PA just as a means of extending his power.

And now, let us turn to some of the testimonies given by some of the key persons and senior parapsychologists from Europe.

John Beloff: It was in the spring of 1941, if I remember correctly, that I first came across his book *Extra-Sensory Perception*. I would have been 21 at the time. I was then in the army, stationed at a small town on the South Coast where I found the book in the local lending library. It made a strong impact on me, the more so as my whole upbringing had led me to distrust something as unscientific as psychic phenomena. And yet here was scientific evidence that ESP was a fact, however inexplicable. Of course I had no idea at the time that I would ever become involved in the field (assuming I was to have any future at all, which in those dark days seemed none too sure). Anyhow, thereafter, the name of Rhine was for me synonymous with parapsychology in its scientific guise. It was not until much later in life that I came to have doubts about the Rhine approach or see its limitations. But, even today, I would argue that the course which Rhine followed was defensible, given the situation that obtained and that a strict Rhinean methodology was a necessary phase in the development of our field.

Going back to my files after receiving your phone call, I note that the first communication I ever had with Rhine himself was a letter he sent me dated January 5, 1963. He had just read an enthusiastic review of my book *The Existence of Mind* in the *J.S.P.R.*, written by the late Sir Cyril Burt (Burt was then a highly revered elder statesman of British psychology; the disclosures that after his death destroyed his good name were then a thing of the distant future!). He simply wanted to know more about me and to inquire whether I would be interested in visiting the Duke Laboratory at some later date. I duly replied at length on January 13 (I had then just moved from Belfast to Edinburgh). In that letter I mentioned my interest in Ryzl's recent work in Prague and in the question it raised as to whether hypnotism could be used to develop ESP ability. I wrote: "Perhaps I am being too sanguine but to me it looks as if there was now a sporting chance that hypnotism may prove to be the key to that great desideratum of parapsychology: the repeatable experiment." Alas, events were to prove that I was, indeed, being much too sanguine!

Rhine next wrote on August 27, 1963. He was mildly encouraging about my interest in Ryzl but rather less so about hypnosis in general, pointing out that Ryzl no longer used hypnosis with Stepanek and expressing the opinion that the main benefit of using hypnotism was to bring the subject and experimenter into closer cooperation.

I first met J. B. in July 1965 at Durham, where I was spending a month of my summer vacation. Since that time I regularly exchanged news and views with Rhine two or three times a year and I visited the Laboratory again in the summer of 1969.

On one question, at any rate, I could definitely claim to be a follower of Rhine. Like him I have, as you know, always regarded parapsychology as the test case for materialism. By this I mean that if we are to reject the materialistic view of man as just a complicated natural machine whose workings are governed exclusively by physical laws, neither religious faith nor philosophical arguments can provide adequate grounds for doing so. Only parapsychology — that is, only a clear demonstration that the mind has powers that cannot be explained in terms of the powers of the brain — can effectively refute the materialist thesis. That is what for Rhine made parapsychology all important and, in this respect at least, I am still much closer to Rhine than I am to the present day leaders of the field such as Schmidt, Stanford or Braud.

Hans Bender: The news that the "great old man" of parapsychology, J. B. Rhine, had gone over to the other side deeply moved everyone related to psi research, and especially those more or less close to his generation. No other scientific discipline is so strongly tied to the personality of its pioneers than is the research into the frontiers of the mind. After the extinction of the living flame one always asks anxiously if the work will continue to go on. We need not worry about that in regard to J. B. Rhine's tremendous work. J. B. has lit so many torches all over the world that they will burn on with their own strength, and he has found in his successor at the FRNM, K. Ramakrishna Rao, the man who will carry on the fire in his own sense. Rhine's concentration on controlled and standardized quantitative techniques of experimenting, along with his high scientific ethic, led to the statistical proof of the existence of ESP and psychokinesis. His approach was encouraging for scientists who felt attracted to the field of parapsychology from the very beginning of his work. I am an example of the positive suggestions which emanated from Rhine's work: in 1934 when I was conducting the first experiments in clairvoyance to be made in a German university, Gerda Walther, from the Psychological Institute of Bonn, sent me Rhine's first report about the Duke ESP experiments, entitled *Extra-Sensory Perception*. I was deeply impressed, and this fascinating book essentially helped me to make up my mind for a long-term project; I decided to devote my scientific activities to establishing parapsychology in the academic frame. J. B. continued to encourage me; after having searched after my whereabouts in the chaos of the war's end, he came to the inauguration of the Institut für Grenzgebiete der Psychologie und Psychohygiene in Freiburg, my native town. Established as a free institution in 1950, this organization was the precursor of a chair for psychology and border areas of psychology at Freiburg University in 1952. I am certain that it would not have been possible to establish parapsychology as part of psychological education without the background of Rhine's breaking through the front of established science.

In the sixties and seventies I saw J. B. several times in the States. My participation in one of the famous "coffee hours" in the Parapsychology Laboratory in 1961 and the discussions I later had in his circle were unforgettable. In spite of his methodological restriction, J. B. always respected the high interest I have for qualitative research. He left nonexperimental aspects of the work to his wife, Louisa E. Rhine, who, like her husband, has found worldwide recognition.

Erlendur Haraldsson: I am sure that I must have heard of Dr. Rhine already as a teenager, but at that time I did not pay much attention to his name. Like many other parapsychologists, I became interested in the paranormal because of some personal experiences.

In 1958 I went to Germany to study philosophy, German, and later on, psychology. I studied in Freiburg and thus came in contact with Professor Bender and attended some of his lectures on parapsychology. In 1961 I wrote to Dr. Rhine and inquired where I could buy a deck of ESP cards. He wrote a friendly letter and sent a few decks of ESP cards. At the same time he asked me for information about "Dreaming Joe," an Icelander who at the beginning of the century attracted some attention because of his alleged clairvoyant dreams. I was able to pass some pieces of information on to Dr. Rhine. We continued to exchange letters occasionally. In 1968 I wrote and told Dr. Rhine that I was finishing my studies in psychology. He wrote and offered for me to come and work for half a year. I suggested three months, which he accepted. It turned out later on that I was to stay at his institute for a full year. I came there in August 1969 and left one year later for Charlottesville.

What kind of impression did Dr. Rhine make on me? When I got to know Dr. Rhine he soon reminded me of Mulla Mustafa Barzami, the great leader of the Kurds in Iraq whom I had met earlier when I, as a journalist, studied the Kurd's situation. I felt Rhine was a man one could learn much from, a man of great qualities and strength. He was of the greatest importance for the development of my interest in experimental parapsychology. I can only remember one occasion when we did not agree. I was planning my plethysmographic experiments. I wanted to have a great number of subjects but Dr. Rhine suggested that I should restrict the number of subjects to be able to maintain a psi-conducive atmosphere all through the experiment. In retrospect, I think Rhine was right.

Broadly speaking I think that Dr. Rhine made his greatest contribution to parapsychology by professionalizing the field and by creating an in-group spirit. He also made many methodological contributions. He remained the great statesman of parapsychology for several decades. He was certainly also one of America's best known professors, not least among laymen. I cannot say that he played the role of a father figure in my life, since I had reached a rather mature age when I met him. However, I admired him and looked up to him as the father of modern, experimental parapsychology.

Arthur Koestler: Rhine's work meant to me first and foremost that I could continue to believe in telepathy without a guilty conscience.

Helmut Schmidt: I find it nearly impossible to reconstruct my perception of parapsychology and of J. B. R. during my time in Europe. I am fairly certain that my first encounter with quantitative parapsychology was provided by his article in *Reader's Digest* which appeared shortly after the war, and soon afterwards I got a copy of *Die Reichweite des menschlichen Geistes*.

A somewhat stronger push towards parapsychology, however, came from a lecture by Wolfgang Pauli and from the books by Soal-Bateman and Amadou. My first direct contact with J. B. R. took place only some years after I had left Europe.

Emilio Servadio: In the very first issue (1938) of the *Bulletin* of the Società Italiana di Metapsichica (now Società Italiana di Parapsicologia, or Italian Society of Parapsychology), one of the founders of the Society—Professor Giovanni Schepis—published a lengthy essay on "The Statistical Approach in Parapsychology," mainly based on the work of Dr. Rhine and his collaborators. In 1946, a short time after my return to Italy from India, I gave a public lecture, "Una Svolta in Metapsichica" (*A Turning Point in Parapsychology*) at the headquarters of the Società Italiana Dante Alighieri in Rome. In my lecture, I pointed out the great importance of Dr. Rhine's work.

In 1949, in a series of books on parapsychology published by the House of Ubalidini-Astrolabio in Rome under my supervision, an

Italian version of Dr. Rhine's book *The Reach of the Mind* appeared, with a foreword that Dr. Rhine himself found quite good and very flattering. The title of the Italian edition was *I poteri dello spirito*. Other books by Dr. Rhine have also been published in Italian. In many books or papers on parapsychology written by Italian authors (Inardi, Cassoli, myself, and many more), the work of Dr. Rhine and of the American school of parapsychology was duly mentioned and commented upon.

When Dr. Rhine died, an obituary of some length appeared in the Roman newspaper *Il Tempo*. It was written by Anna Maria Turi, who has specialized in popular articles on parapsychology.

R. H. Thouless: My first contact with Rhine was when I was asked by the S.P.R. to review his book *Extra-Sensory Perception* (1934). I was an experimental psychologist and, as such, skeptical of the reality of ESP. The reading of Rhine's book did not altogether remove this skepticism, but I said in my review that Rhine had made a case that needed answering. Some of the experiments seemed to me to be inconclusive, particularly when the subject was informed as to his success during a run. Rhine made a good-natured reply to my criticisms and we remained good friends till the time of his death.

I think Rhine's main impact on me, as on other European parapsychologists, was to sharpen interest in the experimental approach to parapsychology. Both Soal and I tried to repeat Rhine's card-guessing successes, initially with completely negative results. However my mind remained open as to the possibility of ESP, and in a few years I began to get sufficiently positive results to remove my remaining doubts. It was not until after the end of the 1939 war that I was able to visit Durham, N.C., and to make personal contact with Rhine. This was the first of many visits that increased my conviction that ESP research was really on to something of first-rate importance. I think I owe that conviction, still retained, in large measure to J. B. Rhine.

D. J. West: By virtue of his strong personality, his long and unswerving devotion to the promotion of parapsychology, and the key position he held for many years as head of its only recognized academic research center, J. B. Rhine was for many of my generation a sort of charismatic father figure. My contact with him was closest in the early fifties when his preëminence in the subject was unchallenged.

I admired him for his charm, his dedication, his gift for enlisting the enthusiasm of the young, his immense diligence and patience in dealing with endless visitors and correspondents and his skill in fundraising without loss of independence.

I did not agree with all his ideas. In his sensitivity to the need for a solid public image, I believe, he was reluctant to comment on some of the obvious weaknesses of the experimental evidence, such as the decline in scoring as experimental techniques improved, the justified criticisms of the earlier pioneering work at Duke, or the obvious lack of repeatability. He tended to link experimental results with a somewhat naive and perhaps religiously inspired philosophical dualism, which was off-putting to those who wanted to preserve objectivity and remain in the mainstream of scientific thought.

Rhine was always under attack from hostile critics of the unbelieving orthodoxy, as well as from "friends" of the subject who wanted him to pursue different lines of research or support different views. His response was to adopt a rather more inflexible line than was perhaps healthy. His adherence to statistical experiments — guessing and dice throwing — and his reluctance to become involved in other matters, such as the macrophysical effects associated with mediums, was one example. He accepted too readily the view that successful ESP experimenting is a gift of personality and that experimenters who do not succeed are regretably expendable. For most of his later life he gave up experimenting himself, perhaps believing he had lost his touch. He was, perhaps, a little too hard on those of his young disciples who were too innovative, too critical, or too questioning of the direction of current research. However, his obstinate adherence to the need for empiricism and experiment is something parapsychologists should all recognize with gratitude.

Despite all the criticisms levelled against him, Rhine was a successful leader who inspired lasting loyalty in the small band of workers who stayed with him through good times and bad. No small part of his success was attributable to the steadfast, tasteful, and effective support of his wife Louisa, who took such an active part in all his professional enterprises.

George Zorab: The first time I heard about Rhine was when I attended a lecture of Dr. P. A. Dietz who at the time, together with Dr. W. H. C. Tenhaeff, was one of the most prominent parapsychologists in the Netherlands. It was in 1938. Dietz, a biologist and psychiatrist, was quite enthusiastic about Rhine's experimental ESP research, and he expressed his conviction that the statistical approach would be far more appropriate in convincing the scientific world of the authenticity of ESP than the so-called qualitative experiments that had so far been conducted, and the study of the spontaneous cases.

After the end of World War II, I was named Secretary of the Dutch S.P.R. The various parapsychological journals issued in the countries of the Allies were again available, and we in Holland were informed of the progress in the field. Thus the then already extensive experimentation in what Rhine had termed PK became known over here, exciting an enormous enthusiasm among the general public who in great numbers flocked to the many lectures organized by the Council of the Dutch SPR.

It was a great honor for the Dutch SPR that Rhine, planning his world tour in 1951, decided to visit Holland and lecture to the students of the University of Utrecht.

I well remember the moment that I met Rhine for the first time. It was in the spring of 1951. Tenhaeff and myself went to the Hook of Holland to meet J. B. and Louisa Rhine. They had boarded the daytime Harwich boat in order to set foot on Dutch soil at about 6 p.m. As we were waiting, we saw the Rhines enter the waiting room: Rhine, a tall and handsome figure, wearing one of those broad-brimmed cowboy felt hats; Louisa, his wife, much smaller than her husband, at his side. When they came up to greet us, I was immediately impressed by his kindness and charming manner. After some talking we left the station. Tenhaeff accompanied the Rhines to Amsterdam by train, and I motored to The Hague. The Rhines were scheduled to stay with Professor Heyn, who had a large flat in Amsterdam, during their stay in Holland. I soon discovered that Rhine and Heyn had become staunch friends, and greatly appreciated one another. This friendship lasted quite a time, Rhine inviting Heyn to visit him in Durham, and so on.

For the Rhines the visit to Holland was a busy time. The first day was devoted to giving a lecture to the students of the University of Utrecht. Rhine's subject was precognition. He informed the audience of the results of the precognitive experiments between Durham and Yugoslavia. The results were reasonably significant. Those present were quite impressed. The next day was devoted to a sitting with Croiset. A large number of important members of the S.P.R. were present. The experiment consisted of Croiset's being taken outside the conference hall accompanied by two persons selected by the audience who had to act as Croiset's guardians, and also a person present in the hall (there were about 50 people in that hall) was nominated to be the subject to be recognized by Croiset. The experiment was not a success, and I could see that Rhine at the time had no great opinion of Croiset's ESP gifts. The visit ended with a gala dinner preceded by lectures by Rhine, Heyn, and several others. The conference in Amsterdam was crowded, and several times Rhine received an enthusiastic ovation.

The second time I met Rhine and his wife was at the 1955 Cambridge Conference on spontaneous cases sponsored by the Parapsychology Foundation. It was at Newham College, and here I had the pleasure of meeting the daughter of Mrs. Verrall, who possessed the same ESP gifts as her mother. I had long talks with her, as she was a link between the pioneers and the newer generation. She was one of the few with whom Myers had played, telling her tales till she fell asleep.

Louisa was busy collecting spontaneous cases at the time, not with the idea, as Rhine told us in one of his lectures, that studying them would be of much value for the progress in parapsychology, but because this kind of case could well be important for supplying suggestions for statistical experimentation.

Several parapsychologists present at the Conference — Servadio, Gerda Walther, Zorab, and others — could not support the view of J. B. and Louisa that spontaneous cases did not need to be severely tested and followed up before being published or added to the paranormal case material. According to the Rhines, it was sufficient just to note down the case as related by the person, who had either experienced the case himself, or had heard about it secondhand. The outcome of these discussions was that some time after the Conference, Gardner Murphy, who had also attended the meeting, persuaded Mrs. Garrett that the Parapsychology Foundation would install a committee for the study and collection of spontaneous paranormal cases. Gardner Murphy then asked me to be that committee's president, an offer I gladly accepted. Members of the committee were W. Ebon and Dr. E. Dingwall.

Rhine also invited Kooy to come to Durham and lecture to some gathering there on his space-time world idea. Kooy was Rhine's guest for about a week. This took place after his article was published in the *Journal of Parapsychology*.

Martin Johnson: The first time I came across the name of J. B. Rhine must have been in 1947. I was then 17 years old. I had just started my job as a laboratory assistant at one of the laboratories in Skelleftehamn, northern Sweden, belonging to the Boliden Mining Corporation. My absorbing interests at the time were nuclear physics, astronomy, and parapsychology.

The beautiful, clear, night skies during the long periods of darkness, just south of the Arctic Circle, may explain why astronomy attracted my interest. As to the paranormal, I believe that an up-bringing in Swedish Lapland certainly was conducive to such an interest. In addition, my grandmother on my father's side was considered to be a "psychic." But back to my encounter with the name J. B. Rhine. In the village library I found a book, *Universums Själ* (The Soul of the Universe), written by the Swedish-American astronomer, Dr. Gustaf Stromberg, of Mount Wilson Observatory. The preface was written by the distinguished Swedish astronomer, Dr. Knut Lundmark, who later became one of my great mentors as well as a fatherly friend. The book was first published in Sweden in 1938. Regarding Dr. Rhine, Stromberg wrote:

> Recently some new evidence has been uncovered which makes it almost necessary for us to regard mental phenomena as transcending physical space. The carefully conducted scientific investigation by Rhine and his associates at Duke University have shown the reality of the phenomena *telepathy* (transfer of thoughts and mental pictures) and *clairvoyance* (seeing at a distance without the use of the eyes)."

How inspiring to find that a noted astrophysicist, who could recall Albert Einstein as a personal friend, would consider so seriously the results obtained in this area!

About the same time I also read a book written by Sweden's only active parapsychologist at the time, Dr. John Björkhem (1939). The book was *Det Ockulta Problemet* (The Occult Problem). Here for the first time I became a little more acquainted with Dr. Rhine's statistical approach, which I immediately appreciated. I decided to carry out some card-calling experiments. In accordance with the spirit of the times, in Sweden at least, the subjects were put into a hypnotic state during the card-calling procedure. However, I did not know exactly how to evaluate the results.

In the early fifties, the Rhines were on their world tour and also paid a visit to Sweden. At that time, I attended a college in Lund. I heard news about the lecture that Dr. Rhine had delivered at Lund University, but regretfully the Rhines had already left.

In 1950, I read an interesting article that appeared in the Swedish edition of *Reader's Digest, Det Bästa*. It seems to have been the same one that evidently had an impact on Dr. Helmut Schmidt's interest in parapsychology (See Rhine, 1948). The card-symbols were depicted in that article — and now I could manufacture my own deck of Zener cards! My interest in the paranormal increased as a result of several personal experiences suggestive of psi. Around 1953, I started corresponding with Dr. Björkhem. In the same year, he got an invitation and went to the Duke Laboratory. After returning from the U.S., he was kind enough to send me a copy of Betty Humphrey's *Handbook of Tests in Parapsychology*, a couple of ESP decks and a few copies of the *Journal of Parapsychology*.

With the help of Dr. Björkhem I had an opportunity to pay a short visit to the Parapsychologisch Instituut, in Utrecht, The Netherlands, in 1956. During my stay, I had the occasion to carry out an improvised experiment with Dr. Tenhaeff's celebrated subject, Mr. G. Croiset (Harrison Pollack, 1962). It was an experiment designed to test the "impregnation hypothesis," a kind of token-object test. It was also designed to eliminate all possible sensory cues. Because of lack of funds, however, the apparatus needed to evaluate the results electronically could not be built for several years. The outcome of the experiment indicated at any rate, that something more than chance probably had influenced the outcome. For several years I was deeply involved in other matters, but my friend Mr. Hans Sjöbäck, now one of the professors at the Department, thought it was a fine piece of work. He told Mr. Aage Slomann and Mrs. Signe Toksvik in Copenhagen about the experiment, and without my actual knowledge of it, they wrote a letter to Dr. Rhine, informing him about the experiment. That constituted the beginning of my contact with Dr. Rhine which was to continue until his death.

The first letter from Dr. Rhine was addressed jointly to myself and Mr. Sjöbäck. It was dated June 22, 1962. That led to further correspondence, and in October 1962, I received an invitation to pay a visit to the Parapsychology Laboratory at Duke. My wife and I arrived on July 5, 1963. I recall that we both were quite impressed by Dr. Rhine's thoughtfulness in sending a letter to our temporary address in New Jersey, to welcome us to the New World. This was the first of several visits to Dr. Rhine and Durham. We corresponded more or less regularly, and in my archive, I have been able to trace 90 letters written by Dr. Rhine.

I am grateful and proud to state that over the years rather close ties developed. I am proud to have been invited as the first "visiting discussant" at one of the review meetings which took place in the late sixties and early seventies. I was also asked to go to Moscow on one occasion as a representative of the Institute of Parapsychology. I was also one of the first, at least of those outside the U.S., to learn from Dr. Rhine about the Levy affair. During this period I got much encouragement from Dr. Rhine. He even financed one of the investigations I carried out at Lund University, although he was not especially keen to see that study pursued (Johnson, 1972).

I am also informed that Dr. Rhine, when consulted by the board of the University of Utrecht, ranked me number one among the listed candidates for a regular chair in parapsychology. I am sure that his backing was one of the crucial factors that eventually led to my nomination.

When I looked through Dr. Rhine's letters I was very much reminded of how helpfully and kindly he always treated me. Together with Dr. Knut Lundmark he ranks as the greatest source of inspiration in my career as a scientist. Without J. B. Rhine I do not think that I would have remained in the parapsychological field at all.

Did we always agree? Certainly not, but I believe that there was a mutual respect for each other's opinion. I do not think that there are many hard facts in parapsychology, whereas Dr. Rhine's view was a much more optimistic one. We certainly also disagreed regarding publication policy in parapsychology. Even if the stated publication policy of the *European Journal of Parapsychology* is contrary to Dr. Rhine's conviction of what a publication policy should be, it did not create bad feelings. That is clearly illustrated by the following quotation from his Christmas letter to me, of December 10, 1975:

> You must indeed feel very good about 1975, as it draws to a close. You will end as the Professor of Parapsychology, President of the Parapsychological Association, and the editor and founder of the *European Journal of Parapsychology*. I sincerely congratulate you and want your success to continue, although not necessarily so tangibly.

I think this letter represents an act of utmost magnanimity, in a situation where there was disagreement between a senior and junior colleague — and in a situation when the junior one was clearly much indebted to the senior.

The most important general impact on parapsychology by J. B. Rhine both in the U.S. and elsewhere, seems to me to have been admirably condensed by Dr. Brian Mackenzie (Mackenzie, 1978):

> With Rhine as a focal point parapsychology developed its own values, standards, procedures, problems, language and audience. Problem selection was initially based upon the choice of the best definable issues, and thereafter largely upon the results of immediate previous research. The isolation of "extra-sensory perception" (a term which Rhine coined) as the area for concentration among the paranormal problems and phenomena which were topics of popular and amateur interest, was the first important result of such professional restriction of attention [p. 206].

As I have already stressed, Rhine brought about a change from the amateuristic approach which had so often characterized the private societies toward a more professional approach. Dr. Rhine influenced people not only by his published articles and editorials but also by his charisma face-to-face. As I mentioned, he had an extremely wide-ranging correspondence with almost all who took a more or less professional interest in the field. Impressively, many Americans as well as non-Americans were brought into our field through Dr. Rhine's publications and correspondence. Of considerable educational importance were the review meetings that were arranged at the F.R.N.M. during the late sixties and early seventies. The system of inviting a "research fellow" for a period of training or for carrying out of a piece of independent research work has certainly had an impact on current parapsychology in several ways. May I mention here that the Utrecht laboratory has adopted the system to a certain extent. One of its positions is earmarked for a visiting research associate. The introduction of the summer school at the F.R.N.M. has certainly also been of importance for recruiting new parapsychologists.

J. B. Rhine should also be commemorated as the founder of the Parapsychological Association, the only recognized international organization of professional parapsychologists in the world. The P.A. today undeniably plays an instrumental role in maintaining professional and ethical standards in parapsychology and in the reporting of research findings in our field.

It is my sincere conviction that J. B. Rhine has an important place in the history of ideas — independently of what may happen to parapsychology in the future.

Whenever I think of J. B. Rhine, I always vividly recall the first time, July 20, 1963, he invited my wife and myself to join him on one of his legendary cross-country tours in his truck. I think we passed the test reasonably well. In the middle of his wood we witnessed together a partial eclipse of the sun. At the very moment I experienced deeply the convergence of my interest in the exploration of outer space with my interest in the exploration of "inner space."

To round-off my thoughts, I would like to stress that I consider Dr. J. B. Rhine's work a heroic contribution to the history of ideas and science.

I have indicated that he remained somewhat controversial as a research worker, school builder, and philosopher. However, by the majority of the people who have some background in the field, his work as a scientist and research leader was much admired. He did not receive many awards such as honorary degrees from universities, but many competent and original scientists recognized his extraordinary work as important. C. G. Jung (1964) viewed Rhine as the person who had conclusively proved the existence of paranormal phenomena (p. 238). The Nestor of German parapsychology, R. Tischner (1950), viewed Rhine as "the Lavoisier of parapsychology." According to Tischner, Rhine had done essentially the same for parapsychology as Lavoisier did for chemistry. (Lavoisier introduced the scale balance and thereby quatitative measurement to chemistry.)

I am not fully convinced that J. B. Rhine was the man who made parapsychology a science. On that issue only the future can judge. However, he was the person who, more than anyone else so far, made parapsychology a recognized science, by the persistence of his extensive research program and by stressing that the same methods should be used in this area of research as those which had turned out to be successful in the established sciences.

From our correspondence during the last years of his life I clearly got the impression that he was fully aware of the problematic situation in which parapsychology as a science finds itself. Rhine had certainly hoped to see a real breakthrough in parapsychology — conceptually, financially, and sociologically. This hope was to a large extent thwarted. His realization of the actual situation in parapsychology, his tremendous deep involvement and identification with the field, seems to me very well to explain his last words: "we must go on, ... go on" (Rao, 1980, p. 2).

I believe that it is very appropriate to end my thoughts with another quotation of Dr. Thouless (1972): "No one can write on the subject without owing a considerable debt to that distinguished pioneer J. B. Rhine."

REFERENCES

BJORKHEM, J. *Det ockulta problemet*. Uppsala: Lindsblads, 1939.
FARRELL, B. A., & COMMENT: CIOFFI, F. Freud and the idea of a pseudo-science. In *Explanations in the behavioural sciences*. Cambridge, England: Cambridge University Press, 1970.
HARRISON POLLACK, J. *Croiset the clairvoyant*. Garden City, N.Y.: Doubleday, 1964.
JOHNSON, M. *Three papers on the token-object phenomena*. Research Letter of the Parapsychology division of the University of Utrecht, June 1972, 1–33.
JOHNSON, M. J. B. Rhine (1895–1980). *European Journal of Parapsychology*, 1980, 3, 119–26.
JUNG, C. G. *Mitt liv. Minnen, drömmar, tankar* (Swedish edition of Jung's *Erinnerungen, Träume, Gedanken*). Stockholm: Natur & Kultur, 1964.
MACKENZIE, B. Parapsychology and the history of science. *Journal of Parapsychology*, 1978, 3, 194–209.
MAUSKOPF, S., & McVAUGH, M. The elusive science. Baltimore: Johns Hopkins University Press, 1980.
RAO, K. R. J. B. Rhine: A tribute. *Psi News*, 1980, 3(2).
RHINE, J. B. *Extra-sensory perception*. Boston: Bruce Humphries, 1934.
RHINE, J. B. *Vetenskapen om det övernaturliga* (a condensed form of *The Reach of the Mind*). *Det Bästa* (Swedish edition of *Reader's Digest*) May 1948, 83–97.
RHINE, J. B. The history of experimental studies. In B. B. Wolman, *Handbook of parapsychology*. New York: Van Nostrand Reinhold, 1977.
STROMBERG, G. *The soul of the universe* (manuscript in the author's possession).
THOULESS, R. H. *From anecdote to experiment in psychical research*. London: Routledge & Kegan Paul, 1972.
TISCHNER, R. *Ergebinisse Okkulter Forschung*. Stuttgart: Deutsche Verlagsanstalt, 1950 (see also review in *Journal of Parapsychology*, 1950, 14[4], 287).

J. B. Rhine and Pseudoscience: Some Zetetic Reflections on Parapsychology

MARCELLO TRUZZI

Though celebrated by many as a revolutionary harbinger of a "future science," Professor J. B. Rhine's laboratory science of parapsychology has frequently been viewed as a pseudoscience. Such criticism has come from opposite quarters. On the one hand, occultists and mystics condemned Rhine's efforts to bring the "ineffable" into the laboratory. From their standpoint, the fundamental character of psychical phenomena does not lend itself to investigation through scientific methods. Interestingly, though Rhine ignored pressure from this group (Rhine, 1947), recent events within parapsychology suggest that some frustrated experimentalists (such as Mishlove, 1981, and Pratt, 1974) may be moving towards a more "humanistic" view. On the other hand, many scientists perceived Rhine's efforts as seeking to return elements of metaphysics (particularly the idea of Cartesian mind–body dualism rejected by most contemporary psychologists) into a dominant scientific world-view that wanted no part of such matters. So, ironically, these critics identified Rhine's work with much of the very occultism from which he sought to disentangle his laboratory approach. In this essay, I will not consider the critics who claim Rhine's work was too scientific; I will look only at those who charged it was not scientific enough.

Criticism of parapsychology as pseudoscientific has gone through several different phases, and the early period of scientific ambivalence has been well documented by Mauskopf and McVaugh (1977 and 1979). During the last 20 years (with the important exception of psychologist C. E. M. Hansel's attack), the sharpest criticism has come more from conjurors and science journalists than from the scientific community. But a recent attempt by a leading physicist,

John A. Wheeler, to obtain the disaffiliation of the Parapsychological Association from the American Association for the Advancement of Science (Wheeler, 1979a) renewed concerns about the basic scientific legitimacy of parapsychology. Though that disaffiliation effort met with quiet defeat, specific charges — erroneous and since corrected, if not entirely apologized for (Wheeler 1979b) — were hurled against Professor Rhine and many old issues were renewed.

The term "pseudoscience" is used by critics to describe claims of knowledge that they find unacceptable. Just as sociologists concerned with deviant behavior have come to emphasize the labelling process — the interaction between those who violate norms and those who institute sanctions against them — so have sociologists concerned with belief systems come to recognize that what we label *knowledge* or *nonknowledge* is often the end result of negotiation through social processes. Nowhere is this concept more significant than within the sociology of science, for current analyses of scientific norms by sociologists — work paralleled by the similar findings of modern historians of science — lead us to reject the once simple idea of a relatively clear-cut "scientific method" carried on by rational and unbiased practitioners on an objective external world mapped by scientific theories which progressively and smoothly change to cover more facts better. This simple Received View of scientists, coming from the logical positivist tradition (see, for example, Suppe, 1977, and Brown, 1979) which is said to describe the Story Book picture of science (see Brush, 1974) will never be the same. Among such critics as Thomas S. Kuhn, Paul Feyerabend, Imre Lakatos, and Barry Barnes, our view of science as *actually* practiced is undergoing challenging review and reappraisal. In light of this, the criteria for determining when we are dealing with a pseudo rather than a proper science have become greatly confounded.

Things are further complicated if we look at how scientists use the label pseudoscience. I have elsewhere argued (Truzzi, 1977) that if purported sciences are categorized according to whether or not they are institutionally accepted by the general scientific community, and this is crossed with whether or not they are methodologically correct in following scientific procedures of evidence and investigation, one creates a matrix with four cells. There will be two cells where there is agreement between institutional and methodological judgments; the positive case of "normal" science and the negative of quackery (true pseudoscience). There are also the cases where a science is accepted institutionally despite deficient methodology (good examples include much of psychiatry or sociology) and where a science is not accepted institutionally while it actually is methodologically quite proper. Since we normally would consider pseudosciences to be those that fail to follow scientific method, the third case is one of a pseudoscience perceived as legitimate while the fourth is of one condemned as illegitimate, a pseudoscience, when it actually is not. Proponents of parapsychology claim it to be a case of institutional nonacceptance despite methodological propriety whereas its critics claim it is simply quackery (negative on both grounds).

To most laymen, however, the issue seems far simpler. Pseudosciences are those practiced by frauds and charlatans, or at least by cranks or crackpots. Closer examination of the matter forces us to realize that this approach may be little better than explaining the existence of crime by saying that it is caused by criminals. Unfortunately, this simplistic attempt at understanding so-called pseudosciences by concentrating on the character of its practitioners has also been found in the pages of such professional journals as *The Scientific Monthly* (Lafleur, 1951), *American Scholar* (Bernstein, 1977/8), *New Scientist* (Harvey, 1978), and *Science* (Gruenberger, 1964). But most sophisticated discussions have recognized that the characteristics associated with cranks (obstinate adherence to a generally rejected idea), crackpots (irrational arguments or premises), incompetents (errors in investigation), or charlatans (fraudulent presentation of data) have all sometimes been found among respectable and even great scientists. In short, pseudoscience and science can not be distinguished on the basis of the character of their practitioners.

While most scientists have concentrated on the methodological character of the purported science, and laymen (e.g., conjurors and journalists) have tended to consider the psychological motives and character of the claimants, the former approach may have problems as great as the latter. A growing number of sociologists of science (particularly the British writers) have moved towards a cultural relativism (if only as a heuristic device), and some philosophers of science (most notably Feyerabend, 1975) have argued against the existence of any kind of true scientific method which can be used as a yardstick to judge when something is or is not a science. Similarly, most contemporary historians of science find that methodological examination reveals no foolproof way of ascertaining a priori whether unorthodox ideas in science will prove truly revolutionary or ultimately be rejected. The matter was put clearly by a critic of parapsychology, some years ago when he said:

> Picking winning scientific theories is not unlike picking winning horses. Some do it better than others, but how much of that is luck and how much is brains is known to nobody.... Still it seems to be a fact — an established orthodox fact, if you will — that there is *no* method of judging scientific theories that is both easy and sure, and no method at all that is completely certain [de Camp, 1954, pp. 117 and 129].

What then are we to make of the label pseudoscience? If we now have so much ambiguity in defining science, surely we have at least as much in recognizing false science. In fact, the label pseudoscience is commonly used in a way that is simply pejorative and pre-judgmental. When one considers the accepted scientific ideas today that were once called pseudoscientific by their critics, my point becomes quite clear (for excellent case studies, see Goran, 1971). It is for this reason that I have generally preferred the term *protoscience* to describe enterprises that aspire to scientific recognition and accept-ance, that seek to play by the rules of science insofar as these are manifest, but about whose claims the general scientific community may yet remain unconvinced.

Parapsychology is clearly such a protoscience. Though it attempts to establish itself through scientific methods, its claims remain unconvincing not only to most scientists, especially psy-chologists (Wagner and Monnet, 1979), but also to its more critical practitioners (Schmeidler, 1971). There is general recognition within parapsychology that there is no fully replicable experiment (psi on demand) (Rhine, 1955), that there is no generally accepted theoretical model providing mechanisms for psi (Rao, 1978) and that this lack will probably prevent full acceptance of parapsychology by the general scientific community.

Since the term pseudoscience continues to be used in discussions of parapsychology's status, it might prove fruitful to examine the term as it is being used to get a better idea of what is really meant. We may call something a false science for many different reasons, just as any number of points, from experimenter fraud to subtle statistical or design errors, can lead us to reject an experiment. In the broadest view, I would suggest that critics who allege that a proto-science is actually a pseudoscience can be separated by the focus of their attacks: empirical, conceptual, and methodological. Though some critics of parapsychology combine these targets, most tend to concentrate in one area.

Empirical critics take issue with the basic facts being alleged. They are commonly concerned with matters of possible fraud, both by subjects and experimenters, incomplete or incompetent observation, and purported contradiction between the events claimed and empirical generalizations (such as the laws of physics) accepted by most scientists.

Conceptual critics take issue with the basic units of analysis (the variables) posited by parapsychologists; this attack is mainly on a priori grounds and seeks to call into question definitional congruence between ideas like psi, precognition, and clairvoyance, and the normal prerequisites of scientific analysis.

Methodological critics take issue with the operational and procedural aspects of research including such matters as the use of theoretical rather than empirical statistical distributions, problems of falsifiability, and related matters.

Since claims of a science can be false empirically, conceptually, or methodologically, failure in any of these areas can lead to the label pseudoscience. And since there are a variety of points of attack within each category, a single pseudoscience may be viewed as false in several different ways. Let us now look briefly at these various forms of criticism leveled at parapsychology.

The Empirical Critics

The three major complaints of the empirical critics about the claims of parapsychology state that positive results are either impossible, or the result of fraud or incompetence. The argument for impossibility is based upon alleged contradiction of well established scientific laws. In this sense, the presence of psi is roughly equated with that of a miracle, and some version of the Humean argument against miracles (Hume, 1967) is invoked, attempting to show that parsimony leads one to conclude that either fraud or incompetence is a more plausible explanation. Since most parapsychologists see psi as natural rather than supernatural and do not see it as contradicting but rather extending our views of the laws of nature (Palmer, 1978), this criticism badly distorts the Humean argument which defined a miracle as more than a fact "which ... partakes of the extraordinary and the marvelous." Though it has recently been argued that psi violates the "basic limiting principles of science" (Flew, 1980), thus fitting Hume's basic idea of a miracle, this has certainly not yet been unequivocally demonstrated. In any case, as I have argued elsewhere (Truzzi, 1978), extraordinary events should not be judged impossible a priori if science is to remain inductive and descriptive rather than prescriptive.

Rooted in at least a strong presumption that psi is *likely* to be impossible (or at least extremely improbable), empirical critics of parapsychology (e.g., Hansel, 1980, and Price, 1955) assert that psi research is a fraud. This approach, since it requires no explicit evidence for fraud, has been criticized as nonfalsifiable (Pinch, 1979) and therefore scientifically untenable. This position has frequently been based on the idea that fraud is likely given the past frequency of fraud in parapsychology and psychical research. But, as I have argued elsewhere (Truzzi, 1980), most of the convincing exposures of fraud in parapsychology (and perhaps even in psychical research) have been made by critical proponents of the paranormal. Thus, the disclosure of past frauds is really excellent evidence for the vigilant social control mechanisms within parapsychology. This was particularly well demonstrated in the revelations of fraud by a member of the Institute of Parapsychology, when caught by his colleagues, and Rhine's strongly negative reaction when the events were uncovered (Rhine, 1974c).

The empirical criticism of incompetence (as distinguished from purely methodological incompetence) usually refers to the lack of adequate controls taken to insure against sensory leakages of one kind or another. This argument has been particularly strongly stated by conjuror critics (such as Diaconis, 1978, 1979, and 1980, Randi, 1980, Christopher, 1970, and Rinn, 1950). The argument here is that parapsychologists are simply not properly equipped to deal with deception and misdirection, and that the presence of a skilled deceptionist-experimenter is a necessary element for any responsible psi experiment, though not sufficient, in the minds of these critics, to guarantee honest results. From the point of view of the magician, reading an article about an experiment is much akin to reading the description of a magic effect in a conjuror's catalog. One knows the facts are literally true as described, and the description would seem to preclude any possible trick method of achieving the effect. Yet the catalog description is admittedly that of a trick; this puzzle is created mainly by omitting special details in the description. Typically, the layman — and even some advanced magicians — would read such catalog copy and be puzzled and unable to imagine any way the trick might be done. But magicians also know that actually seeing the trick being done makes it far more likely (even if not certain) that they will perceive the modus operandi. For this reason, the skeptical magician is likely to insist that he or a magician he respects be present during a psi experiment to eliminate alternatives to psi from operating.

I consider this a very serious criticism of psi research. Though Rhine was generally cooperative with the magical fraternity, neither he nor most parapsychologists appreciate the full scope of this problem. Those who do recognize it seem to depend upon eventual replications as a solution rather than seeking more involvement of conjurors in their research designs. As one long involved with conjuring, I have much sympathy with this criticism, but there are important limits to its value.

It is quite one thing for a conjuror to be *unimpressed* by a research report and to doubt its descriptions, based on the absence of a specialist in deception to guard against vital forms of misdirection likely to be omitted in the research report. It is quite another thing to *dismiss* such reports. *Any* research report will contain omissions, and the presence of a conjuror is not sufficient to guarantee controls. Critics like Diaconis are surely right in assigning a low probability for validity to any research report of psi that did not involve a specialist in deception, and Diaconis is correct in asserting that he may rationally choose to ignore such reports. His skeptical threshold is low, and every scientist can and must make judgments as to what research should have low priority and be ignored. The problem comes when other scientists (mostly nonmagicians) read Diaconis's critique and then presume it is reasonable for them not merely to ignore but to actively dismiss such research reports that do not involve a conjuror. It may be that psi researchers without assistance of conjurors are like blind men conducting experiments on color vision, but such experiments may still have some evidentiary value.

As with the argument for fraud, the magician's argument needs to be stated in a falsifiable way. A major problem here is that not all magicians are equally competent, and even the best magicians frequently get fooled by other magicians. Actually, the magician's argument may be more flimsy than the fraud argument. The simple argument that a magician was not present and that vital omissions *may* be in the research report does not even give us an alternative scenario we can falsify; it is really based on the assumption (the faith) that there is *some* way a magician might have been able to do the trick. It is not so much that the magician doubts psi, per se, as that he has almost unlimited confidence in the creative capacities of the conjuror. Let me stress that this is not an irrational posture, for the folklore and history of magic cites case after case of innovation against what seemed insurmountable controls by audiences (one needs only think of the escape challenges given to Houdini by those who thought he was completely controlled). As with fraud claimants, it is necessary to get the magician to agree to falsifiable criteria for dismissal. Most important, it is necessary to realize that those who wish to dismiss a psi research report based on a magician's decision to ignore a report are actually basing their dismissal on faith in the magician, rather than on any arguments for alternative explanations he might have put forward.

Though these problems can be met through the development of a regularly replicable experiment, the approach apparently favored by Rhine, there surely is a great deal more room for the involvement of magicians (not all of whom are disbelievers by any means) and other skeptics in psi research, particularly in the planning of research designs in ways that can obtain the prior agreement of skeptics as to what explicit results would signify.

The final variety of empirical critics are those who argue that the legitimacy of psi research depends upon the reality of its postulated variables. The argument of John Wheeler (1979a), and more recently Paul Kurtz (1978), is that for parapsychology to be a true science, psi must exist. I have discussed this critique elsewhere (Truzzi, 1980), so suffice it to say here that this criticism is based on a definition of parapsychology very much out of line with that of many psi researchers. More important, it completely disregards the arguments used by the Parapsychological Association to obtain affiliation with the American Association for the Advancement of Science. The legitimacy of a science depends centrally upon its methods of investigation and not upon the truth of its hypotheses; otherwise negative results would be scientifically meaningless, and that is absurd.

The Conceptual Critics

The conceptual arguments against parapsychology have mainly been brought by analytical philosophers. Here the concern is with the a priori character of parapsychological presumptions and endeavors. A review of these issues can be found in Ludwig (1978), and Brier and Giles (1975). An excellent recent example is the review by Antony Flew (1980). His attack begins with the problems of defining psi negatively, that is, understanding how results may remain in the absence of normal means of sensing or knowing. Though his careful analysis of terminology reveals many problems, it has not yet conclusively demonstrated conceptual contradictions even in the notion of precognition, where I find the arguments against backward causation to be particularly strong if not persuasive (see Brier, 1974). Though I know of none who would argue that parapsychology is a pseudoscience purely on the basis of conceptual criticisms, some of the analytical arguments are very important in dealing with particular issues in psi research.

Though J. B. Rhine made some attempt to deal with such conceptual problems, his discussion of telepathy being a notable example (Rhine 1974b), many such issues are of quite recent origin, and parapsychologists would do well to pay greater attention to them than has been the case.

The Methodological Critics

This category of criticism includes most of the better known objections made to psi research. These have been reviewed many times (e.g., Ransom, 1971, and Palmer, 1978) and will not be recataloged here. Most prominent certainly, are the issues of insufficient replicability (about which most parapsychologists and their critics probably agree), and the absence of an acceptable general theory providing mechanisms or predictions to guide research. Most important for purposes of my discussion here is the relation of such objections to the major current definitions of pseudoscience.

From the verification perspective found among logical empiricist philosophers of science, operationalism is necessary but not sufficient. Nonoperationalizable science would be a contradiction and is really metaphysical and meaningless, thus a pseudoscience. Though operationalization of constructs in some areas of psychical research remains problematic, the laboratory approach of parapsychology can not be judged a pseudoscience by this criteria. In fact, J. B. Rhine's insistence on operationalization of psi constructs, particularly his concern with the untestable character of telepathy (Rhine, 1974b), is a major factor distinguishing his work from that of many psychic researchers. Though critics might question the validity of statistical measures demonstrating psi rather than some alternative process at work (such as sensory leakage), this is a matter of interpretation rather than measurement.

The philosophy of science that emphasizes falsification rather than verification, centered around the writings of Sir Karl Popper (1959), designates as pseudoscientific those conjectures about the empirical world that are unfalsifiable. Though most parapsychologists would not be guilty of this error, this clearly represents a danger for psi research. Critics like Martin Gardner (1975) have pointed out that given all the alternative ways psi researchers can find evidence for psi (e.g., psi-missing and displacement effects), it may be too difficult, if not impossible, to find a way to show a convinced researcher that there is no psi effect in his data. There is another source of danger, too. Following Popper's falsification criteria, negative results are actually more important than positive results, for negative results force theoretical reconstruction while positive results merely corroborate rather than verify conjectures. J. B. Rhine's policy (Rhine, 1952, 1975, and 1976) that negative research results should be fully published in the *Journal of Parapsychology* only if they contributed something constructive or novel to our understanding was much criticized by some fellow parapsychologists (Beloff, Broughton & Millar, 1976, and Johnson, 1976), but the policy remained the same. Negative findings in an experiment similar to an earlier one where positive results were found invalidate generalization from the earlier study, so full and careful comparison of the two studies, seeking possible sources of difference, must be conducted if anything positive is to be salvaged from the first study. In any case, from a Popperian standpoint, the parapsychologist, like any other scientist, must be willing to state what tests would falsify his conjecture that psi exists. Failure to specify and then to publish such negative results may move parapsychology towards what Popper would define as a pseudoscience.

Finding the falsifiability criterion full of problems much like those with verifiability (absolute falsification of a theory is actually infrequent in science), some modern philosophers of science have proposed other approaches. Rather than seeing science as simply a series of conjectures and refutations — as does Popper — Imre Lakatos (1973 and 1978) sees it as a general research program. Scientific programs are progressive while pseudoscientific ones are degenerating. A progressive program predicts novel facts; its theory generates the discovery of new rather than known facts. Lakatos's perspective on parapsychology suggests a gloomy picture. Instead of working on a theory which might alert us to novel facts, psi research seems primarily interested in establishing the existence of alleged "old" facts. At first inspection, parapsychology looks more like a degenerating rather than a progressive research program. If Lakatos's view of scientific change is correct — and I find much to recommend it — the future of parapsychology may center around its new theoretical developments, the most promising of which may be found in the so-called "new physics." So far, the quantum physics extrapolators into psi research have been more interested in explaining dubious past psi claims, such as the metal-bending effects associated with Uri Geller and others (e.g., Hasted & Robertson, 1980) than in novel data-generating experiments. The work of E. H. Walker (1976) may be a good and promising exception. Unfortunately, such efforts have found little support in the physics community from those like John Wheeler who might have been expected to lend more comfort to these efforts to extend quantum theory.

What can be made of all this? As a philosophical zetetic, one who expresses doubt and demands continuous inquiry, I fear my discussion so far may present you with more questions than answers. But this may be the route toward solving parapsychology's problems. Arthur C. Clarke recently wrote a penetrating comment about UFOlogy that I think also applies to parapsychology. He wrote that when there are so many different and unsatisfactory answers available, there is probably something wrong with the questions (Clarke, 1980, p. 9). I think we need to reconsider some of our analyses to better understand what questions we really should be considering.

One question that emerges as foremost in my own mind concerns the proper place of parapsychology among the other sciences. Let me suggest a direction that I would encourage. I am convinced that psi research has been dysfunctionally cutting itself off from other areas of scientific investigation. I have already noted that psi investigators need to involve their critics, especially conjurors, in the design and execution of their research. They should also seek to integrate their concerns more with those of general psychology. Thirty-three years ago, J. B. Rhine wrote: "We may hopefully regard it as only a matter of time until parapsychology is fully integrated with general psychology. Any other development is quite unthinkable if we are to count on progress" (Rhine, 1949, p. 221; similarly, see Rhine, 1952). Yet by 1968, he concluded that full autonomy of parapsychology from psychology was the way to success and recognition. This may have been a great mistake. Until fully replicable demonstrations of psi are available, any autonomy is premature. Instead of conducting experiments designed to have constructive outcomes for psychology in general, psi research seems to be committed to a doctrinaire (and dubious) antiphysicalist dualism and a policy of looking only for "psi or nothing" that may leave it with "nothing." Instead, I would urge a more constructive approach that would advance our knowledge within general psychology even in experiments that might not produce the sought after psi. The way things are now, negative findings and alternative explanations may be viewed as failures when they may actually bring us important scientific advances. If alternatives to psi explanations for experimental results mean new understandings about things like statistical distributions, subtle forms of sensory leakages, unexpected experimenter effects, and so on, don't such findings advance our knowledge? After all, even if psi does not exist at all, surely the question why so many people think it does must represent an important problem for psychology.

But I recommend greater integration for parapsychology than merely with psychology. It is still premature to guess where the ultimate impact of psi research will be. It may well contribute more to methodology than to substantive areas, and the substantive areas that might benefit could include statistics, sociology, and physiology, as well as psychology. Going even further afield, parapsychologists may find that they have benefits to derive and give to other protosciences interested in anamalous areas. Such interaction with other deviant science areas can be dangerous and needs to be done very cautiously. But parapsychologists who are correct in seeking to dissociate psi research from occultism and mysticism sometimes dismiss other protosciences like cryptozoology and cosmobiology in the same cavalier fashion that irresponsible critics have dismissed parapsychology. Dogmatic dismissal is just as "pathological" (see Hyman, 1980) when done by maverick scientists against one another.

In the final analysis, all we can ask of one another is to demonstrate openness to evidence and commitment to inquiry. And we must apply that openness to ourselves and the possibility that we may be wrong, as well as to those we wish to share our views.

REFERENCES

BELOFF, J., BROUGHTON, R., & MILLAR, B. Letter to the editor. *Journal of Parapsychology*, 1976, **40**, 88–91.

BERNSTEIN, JEREMY. Scientific cranks. *American Scholar*, 1977/8, **47**(1), 8–14.

BIERMAN, DICK. Letter to the editor. *Journal of Parapsychology*, 1976, **40**, 91–92.

BRIER, BOB. *Precognition and the philosophy of science*. New York: Humanities Press, 1974.

BRIER, BOB, & GILES, JAMES. Philosophy, psychic research, and parapsychology: A survey. *Southern Journal of Philosophy*. 1975, **13**, 393–405.

BROWN, HAROLD I. *Perception, theory and commitment: The new philosophy of science*. Chicago: University of Chicago Press, 1979.

BRUSH, STEPHEN G. Should the history of science be rated X? *Science*, 1974, **183**, 1164–72.

CHRISTOPHER, MILBOURNE. *ESP, seers & psychics*. New York: Thomas Y. Crowell, 1970.

CLARKE, ARTHUR C. Introduction. In S. Welfare and J. Fairley, *Arthur C. Clarke's mysterious world*. New York: A & W Publishers, 1980.

DE CAMP, L. SPRAGUE. Orthodoxy in science. *Analog Science Fiction*, May 1954, 116–29.

DIACONIS, PERSI. Statistical problems in ESP research. *Science*, 1978, **201**, 131–36.

DIACONIS, PERSI. Rejoinder to Edward F. Kelly. *Zetetic Scholar*, 1979, **5**, 29–31.

DIACONIS, PERSI. Persi Diaconis replies to Edward F. Kelly and Charles T. Tart. *Zetetic Scholar*, 1980, **6**, 131–32.

FEYERABEND, PAUL. *Against method*. London: New Left Books, 1975.

FLEW, ANTONY. Parapsychology: science or pseudoscience? *Pacific Philosophical Quarterly*, 1980, **61**, 100–14.

GARDNER, MARTIN. Concerning an effort to demonstrate extrasensory perception by machine. *Scientific American*, 1975 (Oct.), 114–18.

GORAN, MORRIS. *The future of science*. New York: Spartan Books, 1971.

GRUENBERGER, FRED J. A measure for crackpots. *Science*, 1964, **145**, 1413–15.

HANSEL, C. E. M. *ESP and parapsychology: A critical re-evaluation*. Buffalo, N.Y.: Prometheus, 1980.

HARVEY, BILL. Cranks—and others. *New Scientist*, March 16, 1978, 739–741.

HASTED, J. B., & ROBERTSON, D. Paranormal action on metal and its surroundings. *Journal of the Society for Psychical Research*, 1980, **50**, 379–98.

HUME, DAVID (L. A. Selby-Bigge, ed.). *An inquiry concerning human understanding*, 2d ed. New York: Oxford University Press, 1967.

HYMAN, RAY. Pathological science: Towards a proper diagnosis and remedy. *Zetetic Scholar*, 1980, **6**, 31–39.

JOHNSON, MARTIN. On publication policy regarding non-significant results. *European Journal of Parapsychology*, 1976, **1**(2), 1–5.

KURTZ, PAUL. Is parapsychology a science? *The Skeptical Inquirer*, 1978, **3**, 14–32.

LAFLEUR, LAWRENCE J. Cranks and scientists. *The Scientific Monthly*, 1951, 73, 284–90.

LAKATOS, IMRE. Science and pseudoscience. *Open University radio talk, British Broadcasting Company*, 1973. (Mimeo.)

LAKATOS, IMRE (J. Worrall and G. Currie, eds.). The methodology of scientific research programmes. *Philosophical papers, volume 1*. New York: Cambridge University Press, 1978.

LUDWIG, JAN (ed.). *Philosophy and parapsychology*. Buffalo, N.Y.: Prometheus, 1978.

MARTIN, MICHAEL. The use of pseudo-science in science education. *Science Education*, 1971, 55, 53–56.

MAUSKOPF, SEYMOUR H., & MCVAUGH, MICHAEL R. Parapsychology and the American psychologists: A study of scientific ambivalence. In B. Shapin and L. Coly (eds.), *The philosophy of parapsychology*. New York: Parapsychology Foundation, 1977, 216–36.

MAUSKOPF, SEYMOUR H., & MCVAUGH, MICHAEL R. The controversy over statistics in parapsychology, 1934–1938. In S. H. Mauskopf (ed.), *The reception of unconventional science* (AAAS Selected Symposium 25). Boulder, Colo.: Westview Press, 1979, 105–23.

MISHLOVE, JEFFREY. The schism within parapsychology. *Zetetic Scholar*, 1981, 8, 78–85.

PALMER, JOHN. Extrasensory perception: Research findings. In S. Krippner (ed.), *Advances in parapsychological research*, vol. 2, *Extrasensory perception*. New York: Plenum, 1978, 59–243.

PINCH, TREVOR J. Normal explanations of the paranormal: The demarcation problem and fraud in parapsychology. *Social studies of science*, 1979, 9, 329–48.

POPPER, KARL. *The logic of scientific discovery*. London: Hutchinson, 1959.

PRATT, J. B. Some notes for the future Einstein for parapsychology. *Journal of the American Society for Psychical Research*, 1974, 68, 133–55.

PRICE, GEORGE R. Science and the supernatural. *Science*, 1955, 122, 359–67.

RANDI, JAMES. *Flim-flam: The truth about unicorns, parapsychology and other delusions*. New York: Lippincott & Crowell, 1980.

RANSOM, CHAMPE. Recent criticisms of parapsychology: A review. *Journal of the American Society for Psychical Research*, 1971, 65, 289–307.

RAO, K. RAMAKRISHNA. Theories of psi. In S. Krippner (ed.), *Advances in parapsychological research*, vol. 2. *Extrasensory perception*. New York: Plenum, 1978, 245–95.

RHINE, J. B. Impatience with scientific method in parapsychology. *Journal of Parapsychology*. 1947, 11, 283–95.

RHINE, J. B. The relation between parapsychology and general psychology. *Journal of Parapsychology*, 1949, 13, 215–24.

RHINE, J. B. Parapsychology and scientific recognition. *Journal of Parapsychology*, 1952, 16, 225–32.

RHINE, J. B. Some present impasses in parapsychology. *Journal of Parapsychology*, 1955, 19, 99–110.

RHINE, J. B. Psi and psychology: Conflict and resolution. *Journal of Parapsychology*, 1968, 32, 101–28.

RHINE, J. B. Security versus deception in parapsychology, *Journal of Parapsychology*, 1974a, **38**, 99–121.

RHINE, J. B. Telepathy and other untestable hypotheses. *Journal of Parapsychology*, 1974b, **38**, 137–53.

RHINE, J. B. A new case of experimenter unreliability. *Journal of Parapsycholory*, 1974c, **38**, 215–25.

RHINE, J. B. Publication policy regarding insignificant results. *Journal of Parapsychology*, 1975, **39**, 135–42.

RHINE, J. B. Publication policy on chance results: Round two. *Journal of Parapsychology*, 1976, **40**, 64–68.

RINN, JOSEPH F. *Sixty years of psychical research: Houdini and I among the spiritualists*. New York: Truth Seeker Co., 1950.

SCHMEIDLER, GERTRUDE. Parapsychologists' opinions about parapsychology. *Journal of Parapsychology*, 1971, **35**, 208–18.

SUPPE, FREDERICK (ed.). *The structure of scientific theories*, 2d ed. Urbana: University of Illinois Press, 1977.

TRUZZI, MARCELLO. Editorial: Parameters of the paranormal. *The Zetetic*, 1977, **1**(2), 4–8.

TRUZZI, MARCELLO. On the extraordinary: An attempt at clarification. *Zetetic Scholar*, 1978, **1**, 11–22.

TRUZZI, MARCELLO. A skeptical look at Paul Kurtz's analysis of the scientific status of parapsychology. *Journal of Parapsychology*, 1980, **44**, 35–55.

WAGNER, MAHLON W., & MONNET, MARY. Attitudes of college professors toward extra-sensory perception. *Zetetic Scholar*, 1979, **5**, 7–16.

WALKER, E. H. Quantum mechanics/psi: The theory and suggestions for new experiments. *Journal for Research in Psi Phenomena*, 1976, **1**, 38–52.

WHEELER, JOHN ARCHIBALD. Not consciousness, but the distinction between the probe and the probed, as central to the elemental quantum act of observation. Paper presented at the annual meeting of the American Association for the Advancement of Science, Houston, Texas, on January 8, 1979a.

WHEELER, JOHN ARCHIBALD. Parapsychology — A correction (Letter to the editor). *Science*, 1979b, **205**, 144.

J. B. Rhine and His Critics

K. Ramakrishna Rao

I believe that J. B. Rhine is one of the greatest scientists of this century. This belief is not prompted merely by the enormity of the implications psi has for an understanding of human nature. More important, it seems to me, are J.B.R.'s achievements, given the subject of his quest and the circumstances surrounding his longevity as a scientist. Science in its true sense is not a body of accumulated knowledge, but a *method* of knowing. It is inquiry. As Charles Peirce noted, science is something "living." It is "the concrete life of the men who are working to find out the truth" (7.50). It is the "concrete lives" of Galileos and Rhines that tell us what science is all about, for their lives illustrate the possibilities and pitfalls, the excitement as well as hazards one encounters in the pursuit of the truth, especially when that "truth" happens to conflict with the prevailing belief systems. J. B. Rhine sought the truth in an area that was more a province of occultists than a subject for scientific inquiry. In seeking to naturalize the supernatural he offended at once the scientific establishment that resented the occult associations of his subject matter and the spiritualist groups that could not stand the rigor of the scientific scrutiny of their sacred beliefs. To survive such a predicament could easily be the most severe challenge that one would willingly confront. It was the challenge of Rhine's life and work. It was a challenge as big as science itself.

It is important to keep in perspective that J. B. Rhine was a trained scientist and that he worked the better part of his life in a university that is acknowledged for its excellence in the academic world. His long and fruitful career there itself is enough to distinguish him from any cranks and pseudoscientists in this field. But this fact, however, did not prevent Haldeman-Julius, editor of the *American Freeman*, from calling Rhine a "charlatan," and Martin Gardner, the science writer, from including Rhine's work in his book on pseudoscience. Describing Duke University as a "yokel institution that is lousy rich with the money of a tobacco king who could hardly write his name," Haldeman-Julius (1938) wrote, "Prof. Rhine, aided by such zanies as Upton Sinclair, is putting over an immense hoax on the public." What is it that provoked this irrepressible man to make such a strong and irresponsible statement? We find his motivation in a condemnation of his fellow socialist Upton Sinclair, for dabbling in psychical research. "I am outraged," wrote Haldeman-Julius, "by his [Sinclair's] efforts to use his vast influence to lead workers into paths that are dangerous and lie-ridden as the worst forms of fundamentalist clericalism."

The chapter "ESP and PK" in Martin Gardner's book *Fads and Fallacies in the Name of Science* (1957), deals primarily with the work of J. B. Rhine, who, according to Gardner, is a "sane and reputable scientist." To quote Gardner:

> Rhine is clearly not a pseudo-scientist to a degree even remotely comparable to that of most of the men discussed in this book. He is an intensely sincere man, whose work has been undertaken with a care and competence that cannot be dismissed easily [p. 299].

Why then include him in the book devoted to crackpot research and pseudoscientists? Because, answers Gardner,

> of the great interest that centers around his findings as a challenging new "unorthodoxy" in modern psychology, and also because he is an excellent example of a borderline scientist whose work cannot be called crank, yet who is far on the outskirts of orthodox science [p. 299].

Unorthodoxy is hardly a justification for including one's work among pseudoscientists. Gardner admits that, to a certain extent, he shares the "enormous, irrational prejudice on the part of most American psychologists ... against even the possibility of extrasensory powers" (p. 299).

Dr. Rhine's credentials as a scientist and his faithful application of scientific method to the study of psychic phenomena were clearly embarrassing to psychologists. Incensed at the publication of an article by Rhine in the *American Magazine*, Columbia psychologist Henry Garrett (1944) wrote: "No one can possibly object to Dr. Rhine's search for the soul. But, like many other psychologists, I do wish that he would describe his activities under some other label than psychology" (p. 4). So it is clear that what these critics are objecting to is not Dr. Rhine's method but the subject matter of his study and its reach beyond the orthodox disciplines.

Like belief, skepticism has various grades of clarity and distinctness. The methods of reinforcing skepticism closely parallel those of fixing belief. Charles Peirce, for example, identifies four methods of fixing belief. The first is the method of tenacity. It consists in holding steadfast to any belief as an answer to a question and contemptuously rejecting anything that tends to disturb it. When men fear to face a problem, they choose to deliberately avoid the problem itself. When the individual beliefs give way to the beliefs held by the community, we find the method of authority taking over the method of tenacity. In reality, the method of authority is the method of tenacity practiced not by the individual but by the establishment such as the church or the state.

The third method of fixing belief is what Peirce calls the a priori method. If being "agreeable to reason" is what settles our belief, then we are dealing with the third method. Peirce finds that none of the above three methods is adequate for fixing stable beliefs because the beliefs so attained are either questioned by someone or disapproved by their manifest conflict with experience.

The only method which Peirce regards as completely adequate in fixing stable beliefs is the scientific method, which assumes that to every question there is *one* answer which is the *same* to *all* disinterested persons in all conceivable and relevant circumstances. Scientific method involves investigation. "Let any two minds investigate any question independently and if they carry the process far enough," says Peirce, "they will come to an agreement which no further investigation will disturb" (7.319).

Ideally, then, we should all be able to agree on an answer to a question, if we truly and sufficiently investigate that question. This ideal is easily reached when there is no manifest conflict between a belief resulting from investigation and other beliefs. But when there is a conflict, investigators become involved and interested and their investigation loses objectivity and gives way to one of the prescientific belief methods. Then communication among the participant investigators becomes difficult, controversy ensues, and stable belief eludes us.

Against this analysis of the way we settle our beliefs, I shall attempt to examine the controversy that surrounds Dr. Rhine's work. I wish to show that the controversy surrounding Rhine is in a large measure due to the use of prescientific methods in settling our opinion concerning psi. Since the critical literature on Rhine's work is too voluminous to cover, I will be content with discussing a few illustrative cases.

With the publication of J. B. Rhine's monograph *Extra-Sensory Perception* in 1934, a scientific claim was made for the existence of an ability that seemed to provide information through channels that did not involve sensory participation. Rhine was of course not the first to carry out a scientific experiment in this field or claim significant evidence in support of such an ability as ESP. Yet the orderly way he went about operationally defining his concepts, limiting the scope of his inquiry to researchable problems, systematically collecting empirical data and describing the conditions under which the data were collected, making it possible for other scientists to evaluate for themselves the significance of the evidence and to attempt independent replication of the findings, gave his findings a status and a significance that could no longer be ignored. In other words, he made a scientific claim for the existence of ESP.

The reaction of the scientific community in general was what one would have predicted. Those who believed that some of the sacred "laws" of nature were being threatened by this new evidence felt that there should be something wrong somewhere and proceeded to examine the evidence. These criticisms, 35 of them contained in 56 published reports, were summarized by Rhine in *Extra-Sensory Perception after Sixty Years* (hereafter *ESP-60*) which was first published in 1940, some six years after the publication of the first monograph. These criticisms are both specific and speculative. The specific criticisms that have empirical relevance broadly fall into two categories — those dealing with the collection of the data and those concerned with the analysis made and inferences drawn from the data.

Any data purporting to provide evidence for ESP should be collected under conditions that provide no opportunity for any sensory leakage of information; that is, the ESP target must be completely shielded from the subject for all possible sensory cues. Were the conditions of Rhine's research such that this necessary precaution was adequately observed? Skinner (1937), Wolfle (1938), and Kennedy (1938), among others, pointed out that the commercially produced ESP cards were so printed that under certain lighting conditions the symbols could be visually identified from the backs of cards. Rhine pointed out, however, that in the original experiments hand-printed ESP cards free from such defects were used, that "invariable use of screens" which prevented any visual cues from the cards had become routine in ESP tests, and that crucial evidence for ESP comes from those tests where no part of the test cards was exposed to subject's view.

Kennedy (1939), Kellogg (1936), and Leuba (1938) argued that an increase in the experimental rigor of ESP research had resulted in a corresponding decline in ESP results, implying that extrachance ESP scores were due to loose experimental conditions. The weakness of this argument, as pointed out by Rhine and his colleagues (Rhine et al., 1940), is that some of the rigorously controlled experiments gave highly significant results, a fact which rules out the possibility that all successful ESP results were due to experimental error. For example, the average run score in all of Rhine's work published in his monograph, it is pointed out, was 7.1 and the average in the Pearce-Pratt experiment which had the best safeguarding among all the experiments reported until then was 7.5. Also, in cases where there was in fact a decline in scores when extra precautions were taken, such a decline could have been due to distraction and loss of spontaneity that usually accompany such procedural changes.

Kennedy (1939) pointed out how undetectable recording errors might produce significant ESP deviations and reported (1938) an experiment in which a significant number of such errors were shown to occur. Murphy (1938), however, compared Kennedy's findings with published reports of successful ESP experiments and concluded that the recording error hypothesis is inadequate to explain away the significance of the results. Other ad hoc explanations such as unconscious whispering were also shown to be inadequate to explain away ESP results.

ESP research was also criticized as involving improper data selection. Willoughby (1935), Kellogg (1937), Gelles (1938), and Leuba (1938), objected to the selection of subjects. Jastrow (1939), Lemmon (1939), Leuba (1938), and Willoughby (1935) opposed the selection of arbitrary stopping points in experiments. Rhine and his colleagues agreed that "the elimination of low scores or series with low score averages either through accident, inadvertence, ignorance of statistical error involved, or deliberate intent to deceive" constitutes improper selection of data (Rhine et al., 1940, p. 193). But much of serious ESP research, they argued, is beyond such criticism. Again, the selection of subjects as special subjects with ESP capabilities, it is pointed out, is entirely proper if such a selection does not violate any of the statistical assumptions. The criticism of optional stopping, that is, stopping the series or the experiment at a point where the results meet a statistical criterion of significance, is countered by showing that such a criticism is not applicable to all published results and when applicable, is not adequate to explain away the significance of the results.

The second category of criticisms relate to mathematical and statistical procedures employed to show that a given result may not be attributed to chance or coincidence. Willoughby (1935), Kellogg (1936), Lemmon (1937), Heinlein and Heinlein (1938), and Herr (1938) criticized various features of the technique of analysis employed by Rhine and his workers, while Greenwood and Stuart (1937) had defended the technique. The historians Mauskopf and McVaugh (1979), who made a special study of the controversy over the use of statistics by parapsychologists, concluded that the statistical issues, unlike some other issues debated by psychologists and parapsychologists, were:

> concerned with matters of analytical technique rather than metaphysical issues. As a result, it was possible for the two groups to talk *to* rather than *through* one another and eventually resolve the problem. Despite the original difference of viewpoint, despite the occasional acrimonious exchange, this remains perhaps the most rational and carefully defined debate that parapsychologists have ever had with their critics [p. 121].

While statistical discussions relating to ESP research continued over the years to the advantage of both parapsychology and statistics, the central controversy on the appropriateness of the use of statistical procedures and their validity in parapsychological research was, however, largely abated. Burton Camp, president of the Institute of Mathematical Statistics, issued the following statement in 1937:

> Dr. Rhine's investigations have two aspects: experimental and statistical. On the experimental side mathematicians of course have nothing to say. On the statistical side, however, recent mathematical work has established the fact that assuming that the experiments have been properly performed, the statistical analysis is essentially valid. If the Rhine investigation is to be fairly attacked it must be on other than mathematical grounds [Camp, 1937].

Thus, the early controversy following Rhine's claim of the

reality of psi was fruitful in that it asked specific questions and elicited appropriate responses resulting in the raising of standards of research and minimizing the possibility of experimental errors and other artifacts in ESP research. Much of the early criticism was a serious attempt to find procedural flaws and inferential errors in Rhine's work, and therefore it was helpful in clarifying the issues and leading to an objective assessment of the evidence. There were a few scientists, however, who preferred other methods for fixing their beliefs. Rogosin (1938, 1939), for example, argued that ESP findings cannot be deduced from accepted scientific theories and that in fact they flatly contradict some of these deductions. Therefore, any attempt to demonstrate ESP is essentially nonscientific inasmuch as no science can carry out an investigation so opposed to its well-established theories. This view was not, however, shared by many. A survey by Warner and Clark (1938) showed that a majority of psychologists thought at the time that ESP was a legitimate topic for scientific investigation.

Following the publication of *ESP-60*, there was quiet for almost a decade. It appeared as though the parapsychologists had won their battle and silenced their critics on essential methodological issues. But in 1952 D. H. Rawcliffe felt that it was "time that the fallacies underlying psychical research were revealed in their entirety" (p. 12), and toward that end published his book *The Psychology of the Occult* hoping to expose "the methodological and psychological bias" lying behind parapsychological experiments and to demonstrate clearly their "pseudo-scientific status." But Julian Huxley, who contributed a foreword to this book was himself unconvinced. "I must confess," he wrote,

> that I cannot follow him in stigmatizing studies on telepathy, clairvoyance, etc., as 'occult research,' unfit to be admitted to our universities. Hypnotism was for long regarded as mere quackery, and if modern psychical research has some of its origins in superstition, it is also inspired by the desire for new knowledge [Rawcliffe, 1952, p. 6].

Most of Rawcliffe's criticisms were a rehash of the criticisms of Duke work that were made before 1940. Sensory cues through ideomotor movements, involuntary whispering, unconscious perception, unusual sensory acuity, and recording errors were among those discussed as sources of error in ESP experiments. While Rawcliffe accused parapsychologists of *glossing over in their reports* "the unfavorable features of experiments in ESP" (p. 434), he conveniently ignored the reasonable responses of parapsychologists to similar criticism before and failed to discuss those experiments which provided strong evidence for ESP, but were not subject to those criticisms. Acknowledging that the "thirty-five separate arguments against the validity of ESP experiments were stated and answered with varying degrees of success" by the authors of *ESP-60*, Rawcliffe argued that the one criticism which the authors neglected to answer fully was the question of the reliability of the experimenters themselves" (p. 454). He indicts Rhine and other parapsychologists as being unfit to carry out experiments.

> The continual stream of propaganda and special pleading conducted by Rhine with all the zest of a self-discovered prophet, do not supply the best conditions for scientific calm and judgment. Nor do such methods inspire much confidence in the intellectual integrity of those responsible (p. 453].

During the same year Martin Gardner published his book, *In the Name of Science*. Gardner was much more charitable to Rhine than Rawcliffe, and did not question his credentials as a scientist. But he was also unconvinced by the evidence and wondered whether by "treating high runs as evidence of ESP and PK, and finding plausible excuses for chance and low scores, is it possible Rhine has become the victim of an enormous self-deception?" (Gardner, 1952, p. 308). It may be recalled that about a dozen years earlier Rhine and his coworkers pointed out that these criticisms of data selection and recording errors were inapplicable to much of their research and that Burton Camp (1937) unequivocally declared that the evaluational procedures employed by Rhine were essentially valid.

In support of his contention against Rhine, Gardner refers to John E. Coover's work at Stanford University and credits Coover with making "extensive and carefully controlled ESP tests" which failed to support Rhine's results. Gardner goes on to argue:

> Rhine and others have gone over Coover's tables, looking for forward and negative displacement, etc. They insist that ESP is concealed in his figures.... You can always find patterns in tables of chance figures if you look deep enough [p. 308].

Usually careful and candid, Gardner appears to have become a victim of his own prejudice when he attempts to argue the case against psi. His enthusiasm for Coover's work has little justification. First of all, Coover's experiments are no better controlled than Rhine's. In fact, they look fairly primitive in comparison to the Pearce–Pratt series. Again, it was unfair to suggest that Rhine carried out too many analyses of Coover's data until he came up with something significant. This is what Rhine (1934) said about Coover's work:

> Prof. Coover seems to have regarded his own work as negative, and in many respects it was. But it seems pretty clear that he might have obtained more positive results and perhaps made considerable contribution by the very simple device of repeating the tests with those who succeeded best the first time. Even as it was, his 10,000 tests on "telepathy" ... and clairvoyance yielded 294 successes as against chance expectation of 250 (p equals 1/40). This deviation of 44 ... would be generally regarded as statistically significant. Prof. Coover does not appear to have discovered this contribution which he made to the subject [p. 26].

Rhine had previously shown that the subjects in ESP tests succeeded whether or not there was an agent looking at the target symbols. Consequently, Coover's control trials in which the agent did not look at target faces (imageless trials as he called them) were, in fact, clairvoyance trials. It is clear that Rhine did not overanalyze Coover's data, but made the right analysis and pointed out the basic fallacy of Coover in regarding clairvoyance data as control for telepathy.

I referred to the criticisms of Rawcliffe and Gardner to illustrate how bias and prejudice turn a scientific discussion into a rhetorical debate where winning an argument is valued more than knowing the truth. There is, however, another approach that skeptics have often taken. This does not involve any distorted look at the parapsychological evidence, but argues the assumed impossibility of paranormal phenomena. Scottish philosopher David Hume (1825) forcefully presented this argument in his essay entitled "Of Miracles":

> A miracle is a violation of the laws of nature; and as a firm and unalterable experience has established these laws, the proof against a miracle, from the very nature of the fact, is as entire as any argument from experience can possibly be imagined [p. 114].

Every miraculous event to merit that name presupposes a "uniform experience" against it. Since "uniform experience amounts to a proof, there is here a direct and full *proof* ... against the existence of any miracle" (p. 115). Consequently, "no testimony is sufficient to establish a miracle, unless the testimony be of such a kind, that its falsehood would be more miraculous than the fact which it endeavors to establish" (p. 115). I have attempted to show elsewhere that while Hume's argument has validity against those beliefs in the supernatural for which no empirical support is claimed, it has little validity when such support is claimed. Dr. Rhine's work did make such a claim in support of psi.

In 1955 *Science* published an article by G. R. Price entitled "Science and the Supernatural" which is by far the most explicit statement of Hume's position vis-à-vis Rhine and contemporary parapsychology. Price (1955) credited parapsychologists as winning a "decisive victory" and silencing the opposition as a "result of an impressive amount of careful experimentation and intelligent argumentation" (p. 359). Parapsychological phenomena, if valid, are of "enormous importance, both philosophically and practically," he conceded. He even admitted that he himself believed in ESP after reading *ESP-60*. But he changed his mind, we are told, when he became "acquainted with the argument presented by David Hume" (p. 360).

Pushed to its logical limits, the assumption of the absolute impossibility of "miraculous" events warrants our ascribing fraud and self-deception to anyone who makes a claim for the paranormal that cannot be dismissed on other mundane grounds. Price quotes rhetorically from Thomas Paine who asked, "Is it more probable that nature should go out of her course, or that a man should tell a lie?"

Some of the results of ESP experiments such as the Pearce–Pratt series, Price agreed, cannot be explained away by "clerical and statistical errors and unintentional use of sensory cues," but, he says, "ESP is incompatible with current scientific theory." Therefore, these results "are dependent on deliberate fraud or mildly abnormal mental conditions" on the part of those reporting them. Price's verdict, then, is that it is more probable that the best of psi results are due to "a few people with the desire and the ability artfully to produce false evidence for the supernatural" (p. 363) than that they demonstrate the existence of such an impossible phenomenon as ESP. This a priori judgment leads Price to examine some of the experiments and argue that the experimenters in these studies could have cheated if they so wished. He then goes on to suggest a fraud-proof experiment which would involve "a committee of 12 and design tests such that the presence of a single honest man on the 'jury' will ensure validity of the test even if the other 11 members should cooperate in fraud" (p. 366). Until the parapsychologists thus demonstrate ESP "to the most hostile, pig-headed, and skeptical of critics," Price hoped that his "fellow scientists will similarly withhold belief" (p. 367).

Strange as it may seem, Rhine, whom Price had accused of being among those with the "desire and the ability artfully to produce false evidence" welcomed Price's attack as a good event for parapsychology because (i) "it is better to be attacked than it is to be ignored" and (ii) Price's article portrayed "so vividly the potential importance of psi abilities" (Rhine, 1956, p. 11).

The most eloquent rebuttal to Price's attack came from psychologist Paul Meehl and the philosopher of science Michael Scriven (1956). They argued that Price's argument stands on two false premises, (i) "That extrasensory perception (ESP) is incompatible with modern science," and (ii) "that modern science is complete and correct" (p. 14). According to Meehl and Scriven,

> Price is in exactly the same position of a man who might have insisted that Michaelson and Morley were liars because the evidence for the physical theory of that time was stronger than that for the veracity of these experiments [p. 14].

Moreover, Price was unable to show that any specifiable laws of physics are violated by the parapsychological findings. Price's ideal experiments are only standard tests plus a skeptical jury. But the members of the jury need to do the preliminary study and get the necessary training in the field. Otherwise one might as well have "twelve clergymen as judges at a cardsharps' convention." Meehl and Scriven concluded:

> The allegations of fraud are as helpful or as pointless here as they were when they were made of Freud and Galileo by the academics and others who honestly believed that they *must* be mistaken. They are irresponsible because Price has not made any attempt to verify them (as he admits), despite the unpleasantness they will cause, and because it has been obvious since the origin of science that any experimental results, witnessed by no matter how many people, *may* be fraudulent [p. 15].

Something happened between 1955 and 1971: Price published a

letter in *Science* (1972) apologizing for what he said in his 1955 article. Price's retraction notwithstanding, fraud as an explanation for significant psi results, which are not flawed by other artifacts, continues to be advanced by skeptics. C. E. M. Hansel (1961), for example, attempted to show that Pearce, the subject in the Pearce–Pratt experiment, could have cheated. Hansel invents a scenario which makes it possible for Pearce to cheat if he so wished. Hansel provides no evidence that Pearce cheated, nor does he find any suspicious circumstances that raise doubts about his integrity. Even the *possibility* that Pearce could have cheated was questioned by Rhine and Pratt. The point, however, is that even if the conditions of the Pearce–Pratt experiment were such that Pearce could not have cheated without the involvement of Rhine and Pratt, it could still be argued that the three together could have conspired to falsely obtain the results. On the argument that ESP is impossible and conspiracy and collusion among three individuals is theoretically possible, it is more parsimonious to reject ESP than to believe in the genuineness of the experiment. It is this belief in the antecedent impossibility of psi that makes one treat ESP experiments differently from experiments in other areas. The problem is one of refusal to take an ESP experiment at its face value. As long as this attitude continues, there does not seem to be a way to do an ESP experiment that will convince skeptics. As Harry Collins (1980) points out, there is no experiment which, given sufficient time, cannot be criticized and made to look unscientific.

Given a strong negative attitude that a phenomenon is impossible and faced with a persisting claim of empirical evidence in its support, one finds oneself in such a dissonant situation that one may go to any length to reduce that dissonance. An example may be found in a savage attack on Rhine made recently by a distinguished physicist at a forum organized by a very prestigious scientific association.

At an AAAS symposium in Houston early in 1979, Dr. John A. Wheeler went out of his way to assail parapsychology, and to accuse parapsychologists of being pseduoscientists and frauds. In an appendix to his paper read at the symposium, Wheeler appealed to the AAAS to drive parapsychology out of the "workshop of science." To make his point, he discussed the Bermuda Triangle, occult chemistry, UFO's, Atlantis, and other such subjects, making no attempt to comment on the scientific studies of psi. When asked to relate his remarks to contemporary psi research, Wheeler responded with a story in which a post-doctoral assistant of William McDougall was depicted as intentionally altering conditions in a Lamarckian experiment to produce spurious results in support of the hypothesis. Wheeler concluded his story by saying, "The only thing that I haven't mentioned here is the name of the post-doctoral: It was Rhine. Rhine — he started parapsychology that way." (This was transcribed from the tapes of the symposium sold by the AAAS).

Coming from a man of Wheeler's stature, someone not expected to have any personal animosity against Rhine, and told before a forum of scientists such as the AAAS, this story carried with it an air of credibility even to those who did not share Wheeler's distrust of parapsychology. Therefore, it seemed important to me to check carefully the accuracy of his statements.

Wheeler's remarks may be reduced to the following seven assertions he made directly and two others implied by them. Each of these are given below along with what I have been able to find out about their accuracy.

1. *McDougall carried out experiments with rats to test whether acquired learning skills of one generation can be transmitted to the subsequent generations.* It is true that he carried out experiments to test the Lamarckian hypothesis of inherited learning.
2. *The task was to test rats in order to discover whether they could successfully learn to go through a maze, receive food, and avoid electric shock.* Wheeler did not get the experimental description right. There was no food involved. The task the rats were trained to perform was to escape from a water tank, without receiving an electric shock, to a platform connected by two gangways — one illuminated and the other unilluminated. If the rat went through the unilluminated gangway, it escaped without an electric shock. When the rat attempted to escape through the illuminated gangway, it received an electric shock.
3. *McDougall had to be away for the summer and entrusted the work to J. B. Rhine.* This statement is partially true. Rhine did train the rats in McDougall's absence. But this is not the only time that Rhine collaborated with McDougall in the Lamarckian experiments. Rhine had cooperated with McDougall from 1928 to about 1933 when he ceased taking "active part" because "his time and energy had been wholly absorbed in the direction and supervision of the work of the large sub-department of parapsychology..." (McDougall, 1938, p. 321).

4. *Rhine obtained such impressive results in support of the hypothesis that McDougall and he put the work together in a paper.* This apparently innocuous statement is the most misleading of all because it implies that Rhine alone obtained impressive results in support of the Lamarckian hypothesis. The truth of the matter is otherwise. It was McDougall who first obtained highly significant results. He did not leave any crucial aspects of the experiment to any of his assistants. As he says,

> In view of the importance of the question at issue, the many possibilities of subtle errors, and the desirability, in case of a positive result, of being able to meet all criticisms with first-hand knowledge of every detail of the procedure followed, I had decided to keep in my own hands every detail of the handling of half-stock T [i.e., the experimental rats]. (1927, p. 286)

5. *McDougall took the precaution to first submit the work to Tracy Sonneborn.* It was not at all true that McDougall submitted his work to Tracy Sonneborn for his comments before publication. But McDougall was familiar with the published criticism of Sonneborn and others. In a footnote to the 1933 paper, McDougall has this to say:

> My cordial thanks are due for helpful criticisms, especially to Drs. F. E. E. Crew, T. M. Sonneborn, J. B. S. Haldane, V. Hazlitt, W. E. Agar, and most especially to Dr. J. B. Rhine,' who, in addition to many helpful criticisms and suggestions, has given much skilled and laborious collaboration during the last four years [p. 235].

6. *Sonneborn became suspicious of the work and went to Duke to talk with McDougall and Rhine where he discovered that Rhine, who was so interested in proving the hypothesis, shocked the experimental rats for a longer time than the control rats to ensure the former did better than the controls.* I could find no evidence that Sonneborn had ever become suspicious of the Lamarckian experiments in the sense Wheeler implies. It is true Sonneborn had published a criticism of McDougall's experiments in *American Naturalist* in 1931, and had later visited Duke and talked with Rhine. But nowhere in the article did Sonneborn state, suggest, or imply any foul play by Rhine or anyone else. Sonneborn's criticism of McDougall's experiments was two-fold. First, the intensity and duration of the shock given to the rats was not

adequately controlled. Sonneborn refers approvingly to Rhine's experiments which were designed to test whether the intensity of shock had accelerative effects on the learning of rats in McDougall's experiments. Contrary to what Wheeler states, it was Rhine who reported the results indicating that the intensity of the shock could cause differences in the rate of learning (this was shown to be the case with both the experimental and control groups). And it was these results Sonneborn made use of in support of his criticism of McDougall's experiments. Sonneborn's second criticism emphasized the possibility of selecting favorable rats for training in the experimental group. Since results had shown large individual differences among rats, deliberate or unwitting selection of the rats could bias the results. These were constructive criticisms and McDougall suitably responded to them in his subsequent papers. Sonneborn does not recollect talking to McDougall at all. But as he says, he had very vivid impressions at the time of Rhine's "sincerity and enthusiasm and interests."

7. *Because of this discovery, the paper was never published.* This statement is patently false. McDougall published four reports on his Lamarckian experiments, one of them coauthored by Rhine.

The implications of Wheeler's statements are clear and unambiguous. They are: (1) Rhine manipulated the shocks to bias the results in favor of the Lamarckian hypothesis; and (2) McDougall became aware of this through the good offices of Sonneborn. The story is false on both counts. In fact, in his 1933 report, McDougall unequivocally stated: "My colleague Dr. Rhine and I have in many cases trained groups of the same stock quite independently and obtained closely similar results" (p. 234). Also, the results obtained by Rhine under conditions in which he did not know the origin of the rats, i.e., whether they belonged to the experimental or control groups, were comparable to the results obtained by McDougall.

There was no evidence whatsoever that McDougall was ever suspicious of Rhine. In fact, McDougall repeatedly praised Rhine for his honesty and objectivity. He saw in him "a well-trained biologist, a most careful worker" (1930, p. 210). McDougall (1934) wrote of Rhine:

> I found J. B. Rhine to be a ruthless seeker after truth, almost, I may say, a fanatical devotee of science, a radical believer in the adequacy of its methods and in their unlimited possibilities [p. xv].

Finally, Sonneborn himself has stated that he "never said or implied," either in his writings or conversations with anyone, what Wheeler makes the central point of his criticism against Rhine.

It is astonishing that a man like Wheeler should go to this length and make up this story so full of falsehoods with the sole purpose of discrediting parapsychological research. Apparently, it did not matter to Wheeler if, in the process, he falsely accused a fellow scientist of dishonesty. Like Price, Wheeler (1979) withdrew his allegations against Rhine, but with much less grace. "I unwisely repeated," wrote Wheeler in a letter published in *Science*, "a second-hand, and as it turned out, incorrect account of the experiments of Rhine and McDougall...."

Thus, the reception accorded to J. B. Rhine's work during his fifty years of active involvement in parapsychology illustrates at once not only the turbulance that a scientist who navigates in an unconventional area has to face, but also the fact that acceptance or rejection of a scientific claim is not simply a matter of the weight of evidence. Scientists who themselves make distinguished contributions to the advancement of science in one area may be content with prescientific ways of thinking in another area. Investigators do not always use the same standards in judging the claims of others as they do in judging their own. The strength and the kind of evidence they demand is often, it appears, a matter of their predisposition to believe or disbelieve. So, then, what happens to the belief we seem to share in the ultimate truth of the scientific method?

> There are real things, whose characters are entirely independent of our opinions about them...any man, if he have sufficient experience and he reason enough about it, will be led to the one true conclusion [Peirce, 5.384].

I do not believe the scientific situation is hopelessly solipsistic. The subjectivity of judgment can be traced in most cases to a regression to prescientific methods in settling our opinions. As pointed out earlier, the process of rejecting a scientific claim closely parallels the process of making such a claim. Consequently, the rules and criteria governing them are alike and we are fully justified in subjecting a critic's contentions to the same scrutiny the critic affords the claims he disputes. In a sense, the claim and its rejection are two sides of the same coin.

Paralleling Peirce's four methods of fixing belief, we have four methods of rejection. Tenacious rejection involves the refusal to look at evidence. It is a tendency to reject anything that disturbs a well entrenched belief. This method is simple, direct and even effective until a certain point. But when a claim persists over a period of time and gathers some momentum, it becomes increasingly difficult not to be disturbed by it. When such a disturbance is experienced, one has to resort to other methods of rejection. Since one no longer can handle it alone, one may appeal to the authority of the establishment in bringing about the rejection. Wheeler, for instance, could not contain his tenacious rejection when he found "honest work [in the quantum theory of observation] almost overwhelmed by the buzz of absolutely crazy ideas, put forth with the aim of establishing a link between quantum mechanics and parapsychology." He therefore appealed to the authority of the American Association for the Advancement of Science to disaffiliate the Parapsychological Association and thus dismiss parapsychological claims.

The third is what may be called the method of rhetorical rejection. This is about the most commonly used method. When one finds one's long-standing beliefs questioned by a claim one is unable to ignore or suppress, one resorts to rhetorical rejection of the claim. Rhetorical rejection takes various forms. In its ugliest form it is directed against the person or persons whose names are associated with the claim and is filled with innuendoes and abusive attacks. Another low-level rhetorical strategy is to attempt to establish guilt by association. It is not infrequently that critics attempt to assail parapsychology by its antecedent occult associations and by lumping it along with crazy cults, UFO's, Big Foot, Bermuda Triangle, and Pyramid Power. Again, Wheeler's attack on Rhine and parapsychology is a good example.

A more respectable form of rhetorical rejection of a claim is arguing from its a priori impossibility or manifest implausibility. Sometimes a claim is rejected on the ground that there is no theory capable of making sense of it. In metaphysical and nonempirical areas of discourse these arguments have validity and make sense. But when one is dealing with scientific claims that raise empirical questions of existence, such arguments become rhetorical and largely irrelevant to the issue of the claimed existence of a phenomenon.

The only proper way of rejecting an empirical claim is through scientific criticism which attempts to show that the claim is spurious by an examination of the evidence itself. It consists in pointing out errors of observation, evaluation, and inference. The critical difference between rhetorical rejection and scientific rejection lies in the fact that the former is independent of the data claimed to support the evidence and follows from a set of assumptions and generalities that are either unfalsifiable or irrelevant to the issues under discussion. Scientific rejection, on the contrary, is not argumentative, but investigative. It draws its force from the evidential data. Its assumptions are relevant to data and are falsifiable.

Inasmuch as scientific assessment is based on a set of criteria shared, we hope, by all scientists, the proponents and the opponents stand on a common ground that makes communication between them possible. While we may debate whether there are such universally applicable criteria for judging parapsychology's scientific claims (and indeed there are decisive differences on such matters as the role of replication and the levels of controls required to guard against fraud, and so on), much of the controversy concerning the existence of psi is not caused by a failure to agree on the criteria or the ground rules of the scientific method, but by a failure to follow those rules. Thus, a critic who selectively refers to experiments that can be criticized, ignoring evidence that cannot be so criticized, is doing no better than a scientist who selectively presents his data without adequately dealing with the negative results. Again, the tendency to accept evidence that supports one's position without adequate critical thought is clearly just as unacceptable when rejecting a claim as when accepting it. If suppression of information and data that do not support a researcher's claim is pseudoscience, ignoring data and information that contradict a critics argument is pseudocriticism. Some of the characteristics of pseudocriticism are (a) attacking the scientist instead of the evidence, (b) selective mention of weak evidence, (c) failure to acknowledge the best evidence and defense, and (d) uncritical acceptance of evidence supportive of the criticism.

I have not argued that all criticisms of J. B. Rhine are false, or without value. On the contrary, much of the early criticism was helpful in clarifying the issues of controversy and in suggesting possible sources of errors in observation and judgment. These criticisms in most cases led to an improvement in the way parapsychological experiments were done and reported. When the issues involved were clear and specific (for example, the statistical questions), there was a measure of agreement between parapsychologists and their critics. Only when the salient criticisms seem to have been adequately answered did a greater surge of rhetorical rejection of psi begin, criticism that only helped to cloud issues rather than clarify them. This led to a breakdown in the communication between psi researchers and outside critics, and in turn led to a situation in which parapsychologists themselves focussed increasingly on critical examination of each other's work. It now appears that the best critics of parapsychological research are parapsychologists themselves — as all of us can see from the dispassionate appraisals of each other's work in parapsychological journals, and as some of us as editors are privileged to see in referees' comments on articles submitted for publication in our scientific journals. This trend is something that had always cheered the man we honor here.

References

Camp, B. H. (Statement under "notes"), *Journal of Parapsychology*, 1937, 1, 305.

Collins, H. Comments on "Seven evidential experiments" by John Beloff. *Zetetic Scholar*, 1980, 6, 98–100.

Gardner, M. *Fads and fallacies in the name of science*. New York: Dover, 1957.

Garrett, H. E. Letter. Dispute on mind reading. *American Magazine*, 1944 (Oct.), 4.

Gelles, Manuel. Letter to editor. *American Scholar*, 1938, 7, 376–77.

Greenwood, J. A., & Stuart, C. E. Mathematical techniques used in ESP research. *Journal of Parapsychology*, 1937, 1, 206–25.

Haldeman-Julius, E. Questions and answers. *The American Freeman*, 1938 (Jan.), No. 1984.

Hansel, C. E. M. A critical analysis of the Pearce-Pratt experiment. *Journal of Parapsychology*, 1961, 25, 87–101.

Heinlein, C. P., & Heinlein, J. H. Critique of the premises and statistical methodology of parapsychology. *Journal of Psychology*, 1938, 5, 135–48.

Herr, D. L. A mathematical analysis of the experiments in extra-sensory perception. *Journal of Experimental Psychology*, 1938, 22, 491–96.

Hume, David. *Essays and treatises on several subjects*. Vol. 2. Edinburgh: Bell & Bradfute and W. Blackwood, 1825.

Jastrow, Joseph. ESP, house of cards. *American Scholar*, 1939, 8, 13–22.

Kellogg, C. E. Dr. J. B. Rhine and extra-sensory perception. *Journal of Abnormal and Social Psychology*, 1936, 31, 190–93.

Kellogg, C. E. The problems of matching and sampling in the study of extra-sensory perception. *Journal of Abnormal and Social Psychology*, 1937, 32, 462–79.

Kennedy, J. L. The visual cues from the backs of the ESP cards. *Journal of Psychology*, 1938, 6, 149–53.

Kennedy, J. L. A methodological review of extra-sensory perception. *Psychological Bulletin*, 1939, 36, 59–103.

LEMMON, V. W. Extra-sensory perception. *Journal of Psychology*, 1937, **4**, 227–38.

LEUBA, CLARENCE. An experiment to test the role of chance in ESP research. *Journal of Parapsychology*, 1938, **2**, 217–21.

McDOUGALL, W. An experiment for the testing of the hypothesis of Lamarck. *The British Journal of Psychology*, 1927, **17**, 267–304.

McDOUGALL, W. Second report on a Lamarckian experiment. *The British Journal of Psychology*, 1930, **20**, 201–18.

McDOUGALL, W. Fourth report on a Lamarckian experiment. *The British Journal of Psychology*, 1938, **28**, 321–45, 365–95.

MAUSKOPF, S., & McVAUGH, M. The controversy over statistics in parapsychology, 1934–1938. In S. H. Mauskopf (ed.), *The reception of unconventional science* (AAAS Selected Symposium 25). Boulder, Colo.: Westview Press, 1979.

MEEHL, P. E., & SCRIVEN, M. Compatibility of science and ESP. *Science*, 1956, **123**, 14–15.

MURPHY, G. On the limits of recording errors. *Journal of Parapsychology*, 1938, **2**, 262–66.

PEIRCE, C. S. *Collected papers of Charles Sanders Peirce.* Vols. I–VI, Hartshorne & Weiss (eds.); vols. VII–VIII, Burks (ed.); Cambridge, Mass.: Harvard University Press, 1931–1935, 1958 (numbers in text refer to volume and paragraph).

PRICE, G. R. Science and the supernatural. *Science*, 1955, **122**, 359–67.

PRICE, G. R. Apology to Rhine and Soal. *Science*, 1972, **175**, 359.

RAWCLIFFE, D. H. *The psychology of the occult.* London: Derricke Ridgway, 1952.

RHINE, J. B. *Extra-sensory perception.* Boston: Boston Society for Psychical Research, 1934.

RHINE, J. B. Comments on "Science and the supernatural." *Science*, 1956, **123**, 11–14.

RHINE, J. B., & McDOUGALL, W. Third report on a Lamarckian experiment. *The British Journal of Psychology*, 1934, **24**, 213–35.

RHINE, J. B.; PRATT, J. G.; STUART, C. E.; SMITH, B. M.; & GREENWOOD, J. A. *Extra-sensory perception after sixty years.* New York: Henry Holt, 1940.

ROGOSIN, H. Telepathy, psychical research, and modern psychology. *Philosophy of Science*, 1938, **5**, 472–83.

ROGOSIN, H. An evaluation of extra-sensory perception. *Journal of General Psychology*, 1939, **21**, 203–17.

SKINNER, B. F. Is sense necessary? (Review of *New frontiers of the mind*). *Saturday Review of Literature*, 1937 (Oct. 9).

SONNEBORN, T. M. McDougall's Lamarckian experiment. *The American Naturalist*, 1931, **65**, 541–50.

WARNER, L., & CLARK, C. C. A survey of psychological opinion on ESP. *Journal of Parapsychology*, 1938, **2**, 296–301.

WHEELER, J. A. Drive the pseudos out of the workshop of science. *The New York Review of Books*, 1979a (May 17), 40–41.

WHEELER, J. A. Letter. Parapsychology—a correction. *Science*, 1979b, 205 (13 July), 144.

WILLOUGHBY, R. R. A critique of Rhine's "Extra-sensory Perception."
Journal of Abnormal and Social Psychology, 1935, **30**, 199–207.
WOLFLE, D. L. A review of the work on extra-sensory perception.
American Journal of Psychiatry, 1938, **94**, 943–55.

The Place of J. B. Rhine
in the History of Parapsychology

BRIAN MACKENZIE

When we try to sum up a scientist's place in the history of his field, we often point to his discoveries or theories that had a lasting influence in that field. Thus, the importance of Kepler in the history of astronomy comes from his laws of planetary orbits, the importance of Einstein comes from the theory of relativity, that of Fleming from the discovery of penicillin, and that of McClelland from the theory of achievement motivation. Sometimes this is an oversimplified way of describing a scientist's importance, but it usually does not misrepresent his contribution to an unacceptable degree.

In some cases, however, this procedure can be actively misleading. The importance of Wilhelm Wundt in the history of psychology, for instance, surely does not rest on his tridimensional theory of feeling nor on his contributions to the theory of innervation. These theories have sunk almost, if not quite, without a trace, as have the specific methods of introspective analysis that he developed. These contributions on which Wundt labored so hard are today regarded as little more than side issues, dead ends in the history of psychology. Were his importance to be estimated on the basis of them, he would rank somewhere behind E. H. Weber* instead of in the forefront of the pioneers of experimental psychology.

Instead, what makes Wundt one of those pioneers whose influence is still being felt is not what he did so much as how he did it. His theories were not simply sent out to make their own way in the world. They were promulgated as part of an extensive social

---

*Weber's very restricted work on sensory magnitudes was revived by G. T. Fechner and made part of the basis for psychophysics.

endeavor of which Wundt oversaw every aspect. He established a laboratory, enrolled graduate students, founded a journal for the publication of experimental reports, and supervised enough dissertations that his students and his students' students dominated experimental psychology (especially in America) for almost fifty years (see Boring & Boring, 1948). Wundt's activities exemplified the rapidly growing system of scientific education in nineteenth-century Germany, combining the social and the scientific aspects of scientific innovation in such a way as effectively to establish experimental psychology as a scientific discipline (see Ben-David & Collins, 1966).

The case of parapsychology and the place of J. B. Rhine in its history are similar but even more pointed. Rhine's parapsychological theories were not his major, nor his most influential, work. More significantly, the main phenomena that parapsychology is concerned with did not need to be discovered when Rhine entered the field. They had been known, or at least talked about and reported, for a long time. Telepathy, clairvoyance, and various kinds of psychokinetic influence had been frequently described and ostensibly demonstrated since antiquity. Instead, what these phenomena, and the field of parapsychology as a whole, needed was to be *established*. This was the need that Rhine filled. The importance of J. B. Rhine in the history of parapsychology does not lie mainly in the many substantial technical contributions he made to the field. Instead, it lies in the establishment of a distinct scientific discipline of parapsychology to which these contributions could be made. Furthermore, it does not depend on the extent to which Rhine's views are currently accepted by psychologists or parapsychologists. It does not even depend on the extent to which they, or any related ones, are valid. This introductory point must be made strongly, because it is an important one. The achievement of establishing a scientific discipline cannot be evaluated in terms of any later judgments about the legitimacy or illegitimacy, the genuineness or illusoriness, of the subject-matter of that discipline. Even if the most extreme skeptics turned out to be right about parapsychology so that there was "nothing in it," that fact would not detract from Rhine's achievement of placing the study of parapsychology on a scientific footing.

This chapter will attempt to explain what it means to say that Rhine established a field of scientific parapsychology. By contrasting Rhine's work with the work of a few earlier workers in the field, it will also attempt to outline a few of the details of how he did it.

I. EARLY ATTEMPTS AT A SCIENTIFIC STUDY
OF PARANORMAL PHENOMENA

First, therefore, it is necessary to look at the work of a few people in the history of parapsychology and its precursors to see why none of them were successful in establishing their field as a science. By the precursors of parapsychology are meant mesmerism, spiritualism, and the kinds of methodical psychical research undertaken in the first fifty years of the Society for Psychical Research (SPR) after its founding in 1882. One of the noteworthy features of this history of parapsychology and its precursors, indeed, is the way that it neatly illustrates some contemporary ideas on what is required to establish a scientific speciality. The use by individuals of objective "scientific methods" as traditionally described is not sufficient; a social dimension is also necessary. The social dimension, furthermore, must be marked by a particular kind of intensive interaction between individuals. The mere shared commitment by a group to the standards and procedures of scientific method is also insufficient.

Mesmerism and Spiritualism: The Lack of a Community

That the use of scientific methods by individuals is not sufficient is shown by the examples of mesmerism and spiritualism. These were not for the most part scientific movements, of course. They were popular movements, and often quasi-religious ones. They were marked by mass enthusiasm for theatrical displays on the one hand, and by secret societies with occult doctrines on the other. But there were always a few individuals who, while more or less sympathetic to these movements, took a relatively sophisticated critical or experimental approach to the evaluation of mesmeric and spiritualist phenomena.

In reviewing the history of mesmerism, or animal magnetism, for instance, Alexandre Bertrand (1826) painstakingly tried to separate the wheat from the chaff in this movement. He showed how most of the phenomena could readily be accounted for by the power of suggestion, producing a state of heightened consciousness which he labelled "extase"; there remained, however, several apparently genuine cases of clairvoyance and thought-reading that called for further attention. Five years later, in 1831, the members of the Second French Commission to investigate animal magnetism showed themselves more than usually competent in experimentation. Their controls on the performance of clairvoyants were as good, or almost, as those of a hundred years later and, repeatedly insisting that it was facts and not theories they were after, they somewhat diffidently reported the successful performances of some of their subjects (*Report on the Magnetic Experiments*, 1844). J. C. Colquhoun, in his many pamphlets and books promoting animal magnetism, laid particular stress on the evidential value of experiments that could serve as textbook examples of ABA case study designs in clinical psychology (e.g., Colquhoun, 1838, p. 16).

Turning to spiritualism, the first major experimental investigation was that of Robert Hare, a chemistry professor at the University of Pennsylvania. His *Experimental Investigations of the Spirit Manifestations* (1855) describes many ingenious pieces of apparatus he invented for quantifying the force of physical phenomena and for isolating the medium from the recording equipment. Some of Hare's apparatus was the prototype for that later used by the British chemist William Crookes in his researches on spiritualism in the 1870s. Crookes refined Hare's equipment and procedures, emphasizing the need for precise instrumental control over the circumstances in which the phenomena were to be produced. He then proceeded to successful experiments with two of the best known mediums of the time, D. D. Home and Florence Cook (Medhurst, 1972).

All of these writers, and others such as Esdaile (1846) and Gasparin (1857), made at least a good start toward a careful scientific study of paranormal phenomena. By this it is not meant that their methodology was faultless or that it was as rigorous as can be found in modern experiments in psychology or parapsychology. But they were trying. They give the strong impression of doing the best they could to find out what was genuine in mesmerism and spiritualism and what was not. Their writings shine unmistakably through the mass of enthusiastic and naive tracts of the scoffers. When reading their works, one cannot help being struck at times by the cogency of their reasoning and the elegance of their experimental designs, and might well ask: Why were these not taken more seriously in their own time?

Unfortunately, there is a simple answer. They were not taken seriously because very few people were interested in a relatively sophisticated experimental approach to the study of these matters. Both the true believers and the scoffers already knew the truth about mesmeric and spiritualist phenomena. They were all true, and testified to the existence of transcendental cosmic forces (e.g., Cahagnet, 1850, Ballou, 1853); or they were all false, except for the ones that could be assimilated to orthodox nineteenth-century physiology (e.g., Bennett, 1851, Hammond, 1876).* The writers with idiosyncratic scientific aspirations tended, therefore, when they were noticed at all, to be pilloried both by the enthusiasts, because they did not accept everything, and by the medical and scientific establishments, because they did not reject or explain away everything. Thus, Bertrand was virtually ignored. The Report of the Second French Commission was suppressed by the Royal Academy of Medicine that had commissioned it (Inglis, 1977, p. 165). Hare was "howled down" when he presented his experiments to the American Association for the Advancement of Science at its meetings in Montreal in 1854 and was subsequently denounced for his "insane adherence to a gigantic humbug" (Fodor, 1933, p. 158). Crookes's writings likewise evoked a storm of vituperative criticism from his fellow scientists, and he eventually abandoned the field for the safety of his more respectable chemical researches (Medhurst, 1972, p. 6).

Such criticism of research on paranormal phenomena is not altogether unfamiliar to modern parapsychologists. But these individuals lacked something more important than general scientific acceptance. They lacked anyone to talk to. That is, they had no reference group to which they could submit their findings with the expectation that they would be critically but sympathetically assessed. Approval by the scientific community at large is a very nice thing to have, but what is essential for the growth of scientific knowledge—or even pseudoscientific knowledge—is a restricted community of practitioners, a reference group, that can assess one's work as part of a shared endeavor. Such a reference group not only assesses and criticizes an individual's work, but also, because its members are engaged in similar work, to some extent insulates the individual from the values and priorities of both the popular and the general scientific culture and thereby provides the basis for a professional identity.

Lacking such a reference group, these individual researchers were under great personal pressure to conform to the demands of one or the other of the reference groups that did exist, that of the

---

*There was also a third extremist viewpoint, holding that the phenomena were genuine and the work of the devil (e.g., Munger, 1857).

believers or that of the scoffers. In one way or another, many of them succumbed to this pressure. Thus, Colquhoun's methodological sophistication was highly variable. He quite cheerfully mixed his elegant experimental designs with blatant ad hoccery and special pleading for the truth and the glory of animal magnetism. Hare, after his researches were rejected by his scientific peers, abandoned his professorial and experimental work and spent the rest of his days in transcribing messages from his father in the spirit world; most of his *Experimental Investigations* (1855) is devoted to these. Crookes did not fare quite so badly, but vacillated in a significant and revealing way. He fell first into the arms of the true believers, writing and publishing encomiums and poems of praise to Katie King, Florence Cook's materialized companion from the spirit world (Medhurst, 1972, p. 139). Sensationalistic charges have also been levelled about his personal relationship with the medium (Hall, 1962), but these are irrelevant here. Whatever his private actions were, Crookes's public statements clearly showed that he had quite lost the objectivity and rigor with which he had approached the study of mediumship originally. Like Hare, he had become intensely involved on a personal and subjective level with the spiritualistic subject matter of his researches. When he abandoned studies of mediumship and returned to his respectable scientific field, he salvaged his reputation and went on to win many honors. But that was a return to the fold of his original scientific reference group. He never again seriously attempted to thread his way between the conflicting demands of the spiritualist and scientific communities.

Psychical Research: The Insufficiency of a Community

Again, what was lacking for these isolated individuals was an appropriate reference group, a body of sympathetic but critical readers and discussants of their parapsychological researches who could criticize the details while ratifying the attempt. Just such a reference group was provided by the founding and growth of the Society for Psychical Research in 1882 and, to a lesser extent, by the subsequent founding of similar bodies such as the American Society for Psychical Research and the Société Metapsychique. These societies were founded explicitly to make possible a wide-ranging scientific study of psychic phenomena. They attracted the interest and membership of a substantial number of accomplished scientists and intellectuals. The active members carried out a wide variety of careful methodical investigations, published them in their semiprofessional and specialist journals, and made detailed technical criticisms of each other's work. They thus made up an effective reference group of scientifically oriented psychical researchers, sharing a commitment both to rigorous standards of evidence and to the importance and legitimacy of investigating psychic phenomena. In doing so, however, they also showed that these are not enough, that the existence of a reference group with a shared methodological commitment is also an insufficient basis on which to found a science.

The researches of the SPR investigators were extremely, and intentionally, diverse. Their view was that careful scientific observations of all the classes of supposedly paranormal events would establish once and for all which ones were genuine and which ones were not, and that from observation of the genuine ones a general understanding of the paranormal would emerge by induction. Thus, they took their problems from the broad sweep of the paranormal as it was then conceived. In its opening manifesto of 1882, the SPR announced the formation of committees to investigate thought-reading or telepathy, or more generally "any influence which may be exerted by one mind upon another, apart from any generally recognized mode of perception"; mesmeric trance, mesmeric anaesthesia, clairvoyance, "and other allied phenomena"; odylic force, apparitions, and haunted houses, and the physical phenomena of spiritualism such as raps and materializations; and a further one to collate all the evidence already in existence on these subjects (Society for Psychical Research, 1882). These were the allegedly paranormal phenomena that commanded attention at the time, and it seemed reasonable — more, it seemed essential — to address them all. Some of these were investigated more intensively than others, but all were attempted and new ones were added. Furthermore, these investigations by the SPR and others were sometimes very careful and sophisticated. However, the wide range of their investigations led to a great dispersion of their attention and made it very difficult to relate the findings in one area to those in another except by reference back to the popular interest that was the source of all of them. As an inevitable result, the "map" of the paranormal that these investigators drew up and which guided their research was the map they inherited from the popular movements of mesmerism and spiritualism, rather than one drawn up bit by bit from the results of their own researches.

With the SPR and similar bodies, in short, the problem was not the lack of a reference group, a body of sympathetic but critical discussants. The problem was that the reference group was not sufficiently cohesive to provide a consistent direction and common focus for research. The explicit intent was rather to provide a forum for the investigation of all claimed paranormal events in a scientific manner. This aim was at times reasonably well fulfilled, but at the cost of a great dispersion of attention and, consequently, of the inability to bring the results together in a way that could permit the continuous, cumulative development of the field. For this reason, the investigations of the SPR and similar bodies, while sometimes seeming to be individually impeccable, never coalesced into a firm and continuous scientific movement in which data, theory, and method could all dovetail and support one another. Kuhn's remark (1962) on preparadigm science seems particularly applicable to psychical research of this period: "Though the field's practitioners were scientists, the net results of their activity was something less than science" (p. 13). They tried to do too much, to conquer all worlds at once. Viable scientific movements, however, do not conquer all worlds at once, but more modestly, only one at a time.

The personal consequences for the individuals in this later period were not nearly so severe as in the earlier one. They did not face so much pressure to conform to the views of either the enthusiasts or the conservatives, since they had a reasonably high status reference group to bolster their identity as dispassionate scientific investigators. The SPR's policy of recruiting famous men to act as president, whether they had made any major contribution to the field or not, served that body well in this regard. But while the individuals were able to maintain a relatively secure identity as scientific researchers, the lack of a common direction for their research prevented them from making that research a genuinely cooperative endeavor. They remained individuals, doing much research in the field, but essentially as amateurs, going off in a variety of directions determined for each of them by their personal predilections and their professional and educational backgrounds.

Psychical research in the United States displayed this same lack of integration up to the early 1930s. There was a variety of studies on mental and physical phenomena in mediumship, on tests of telepathy and clairvoyance in university students and others, on mind-reading horses and other trick animals, and more. Some of these were done well and some poorly, but they all remained separate and almost unrelated studies. In a nutshell, we can say that if the isolated scientific investigators in the earlier years of the nineteenth century had no one to talk to, the loose community of investigators in the later years were not quite sure what they wanted to talk about.

What was necessary for the field to achieve any scientific coherence was for the investigators to abandon the amateur pattern of studying any and all interesting paranormal phenomena. They needed instead to concentrate more modestly on the most workable, rather than the most interesting, of current problems. Parapsychology would necessarily lose some of its lay appeal and gain something in professionalism as a result. Future developments in the field would have to depend on the outcomes of these first intensive studies; the topics for future research would have to be those suggested by those outcomes, rather than by the previously existing body of parapsychological questions. Enough investigators would have to agree on these shared priorities to form a relatively cohesive group that could by example define the direction of progress in the field.

II. COMMUNITY FORMATION IN PARAPSYCHOLOGY

This was the situation in the field of psychical research when J. B. Rhine began his activity in it. It was only with the early — but not the earliest — work of Rhine that psychical research, redefined as parapsychology, began to acquire the unity of outlook necessary for any kind of cumulative development. This is what is meant in saying that Rhine established a distinct discipline of scientific parapsychology. He was the nucleus of what became a reference group of professional parapsychologists, ones who agreed not only on the application of scientific method in general, but also in detail on the choice of procedures, problems, standards, language, and audience. Through his influence, workers in the field came to share priorities and techniques, as well as a commitment to the field as a whole.

There were many factors that entered into Rhine's having such an influence. His early studies of extrasensory perception, published in the monograph of that title in 1934, used sophisticated and rigorous, but simple and easily copied, experimental methods (Rhine, 1934/1973). His data analysis emphasized the objective criteria of statistical significance, rather than subjective ones of similarity or personal meaningfulness. Working at Duke University, with the full support of the professor of the psychology department and the president of the university, he had a strong university backing. And of course, in that first major set of experiments, he had some dramatically successful results to report. All of these factors undoubtedly helped Rhine, through that book, to have a major influence.

But these were not sufficient. They were, after all, not new. If all philosophical ideas can be found in the ancient Greeks, as someone has said, likewise all parapsychological ideas can be found in the publications of the SPR. The use of careful, controlled experimental methods, card-guessing as a technique for investigating telepathy and clairvoyance, statistical analysis of the data, and impressively significant results are all to be found in the SPR *Proceedings* in the fifty years prior to the publication of Rhine's *Extra-Sensory Perception*. Some of the earlier researchers also had secure university positions, and while these were not solely in parapsychology, neither was Rhine's until long after publication of his monograph in 1934.

Instead, what was crucial to Rhine's influence was something that is easy to describe but more difficult to put into practice. It was his restriction of attention to a small subset of paranormal phenomena and his commitment to making an extensive investigation of them. Those problems—the experimental study of telepathy and clairvoyance, soon combined as ESP—and the specific approach taken to working on them, were not chosen adventitiously or randomly. They were isolated as the most readily interpretable and operationally specifiable of paranormal phenomena. Again, it was not the development of the specific methods used in the Duke Laboratory that gained it preëminence in the field, but the persistence of Rhine and a few collaborators in using them, the making of a long series of closely linked studies with them that could serve as an example to others in the field. This restriction of attention to a small set of related problems and methods, and the persistence in concentrating on them, made the research that each person was doing in that restricted area able to be related to the research that everybody else in the area was doing. The common focus on a small number of related issues forced a degree of cohesiveness in the small group at Duke that had been notably lacking in the larger psychical research communities. As a result, the research that Rhine initiated at Duke gradually acquired a systematic status that attracted others to replicate and extend it.

It did not happen overnight. Popular acclaim followed quickly after the publication of his *Extra-Sensory Perception* in 1934, but professional acceptance was slower. Replication was neither easy nor guaranteed, and the existing psychical research societies were naturally inclined to see Rhine's experimental work as an interesting but narrow sideline to their main concerns. But within five to ten years of the publication of *Extra-Sensory Perception*, its influence was being fully felt. The *Journal of Parapsychology* was established in 1937 to provide a vehicle for Rhine's kind of behavioral studies of ESP, and the SPR and American SPR had, by the early 1940s, come to emphasize the same kind of experimental approach in their own publications. Throughout the 1940s and later, the parapsychological journals acted as professional organs devoted to the kind of inter-related, restricted behavioral studies of the kind Rhine had emphasized. It was due to this kind of influence that McVaugh and Mauskopf (1976) rightly judged Rhine's monograph of 1934 to be a paradigmatic work for parapsychology.

If this chapter were concerned solely with the history of para-psychology as a scientific specialty, it could stop here, having pointed out the systematic influence that Rhine's work had on the develop-ment of the field and the different nature of his contribution from that of earlier investigators who attempted to make a scientific study of paranormal phenomena. But even paradigms can have a personal history, and in a book that proposes to discuss J. B. Rhine as well as the specialty he established, it is appropriate to consider how Rhine was able to have the influence he did. His own early professional history is in any case a fascinating case study in the development of research methods.

III. PERSONAL AND PROFESSIONAL FACTORS IN THE INFLUENCE OF J. B. RHINE

J. B. and Louisa E. Rhine first committed themselves to para-psychology, or psychical research, in 1926.* They had recent PhD degrees in botany from the University of Chicago and an aggressive confidence in the power of scientific method. They also, however, had religious-cum-metaphysical doubts about the place of human beings in the universe, the implications of reductionist biology, and the existence of the soul. They hoped to resolve these doubts by

*All biographical details, except where otherwise noted, are from Rhine & Rhine (1978).

scientific studies of phenomena that, on the surface, seemed to challenge the materialism they had been steeped in at Chicago. To turn their backs on their professional training and forsake their careers for such a cause was a bold step. It was a comprehensible one, however. It was the same kind of step, though more extreme, as the early workers in the SPR had taken, and was taken for the same kind of reasons. Like those earlier workers, the Rhines entered the field as dedicated amateurs. There was, after all, no other way to enter it.

The Rhine's first-hand experience in the field began with an informal study of Mrs. Mina Crandon, a renowned Boston medium known professionally as "Margery," whose séances were widely acclaimed in the ASPR and elsewhere as positive proof of survival. This choice also was not surprising. The Rhines' initial interest in psychical research had been excited by Oliver Lodge and Arthur Conan Doyle, both of them champions of different varieties of spiritualism. Furthermore, the Rhines began their active involvement in the field as protégés, in a minor way, of the spiritualistically inclined leadership of the ASPR (Mauskopf & McVaugh, 1980).

Indeed, the only surprising thing about the Rhines' investigation of Margery was its results. They "came to Boston," as they wrote, "with a favorable notion of the case already formed" (Rhine & Rhine, 1927, p. 401). Nevertheless, while witnessing phenomena that, they were told, had been shown to satisfied sitters scores of times, they were appalled to find widespread trickery in the séance room. Organizing their observations systematically, they found six "conditions which permitted fraud and which were not necessary for genuine mediumship," nine "inconsistencies which look suspicious and which fraud alone will explain satisfactorily," and four pieces of "positive evidence of fraudulent action" (Rhine & Rhine, 1927, pp. 406, 409, 412). Their report was published in the *Journal of Abnormal and Social Psychology* in January 1927, and the Rhines ended their cordial relationship with the ASPR leadership, which was still actively promoting Margery. Interestingly, while the ASPR officers replied heatedly in their *Journal* to critiques of Margery by Dingwall, Hoagland, Houdini, and others of the time (e.g., Bird, 1926), they never responded to the Rhines' report.

The Rhines' exposé of Margery exemplified the strengths they brought to psychical research. Those included keen powers of analytical observation, moderate skepticism, and hard-headed common sense, sharpened by their scientific training in the no-

nonsense fields of botany and plant physiology. These were sufficient to permit them to see through Margery because her activities were all in the range of ordinary human action. The question to be addressed in studying her was not exactly a scientific question requiring specialized scientific knowledge in psychology, any more than in botany. It was instead a kind of judicial question, a question of truth or falsity, bona fides vs. fakery, requiring the testimony of competent witnesses. This the Rhines were able to provide in good measure. There were psychological questions involved, too, regarding Margery's motivations and thought processes, but these were not the Rhines' concern.

In their next piece of research, however, the Rhines displayed the limitations that went along with their strengths. When the question at issue required the sophisticated application of scientific knowledge in a field outside their own, they were, inevitably, not able fully to resolve it. They showed this in their study of Lady, a mind-reading horse (Rhine & Rhine, 1929a). They were attracted to the study of telepathy in this animal for a number of reasons. The main one was that telepathy had always been the counterhypothesis to survival in accounting for the information delivered by successful mediums, and it was clear that it needed study for its own sake. A secondary reason was that telepathic animals, unlike humans, would be unlikely to try to commit fraud. In addition, J. B. Rhine (1925) had recently reviewed Bechterev's experiments with telepathic dogs and was very impressed by them; the procedures that the Rhines used for studying Lady were very largely based on Bechterev's.

Lady made her guesses by touching her nose to alphabet or number blocks to answer questions addressed to her mentally or verbally. The main question in assessing her performance was not one of fraud, although fraud on the part of the owner/trainer was considered. It was rather one of eliminating the counterhypothesis that she was guided by minute movements indicative of expectant attention made by her owner or by the questioners. A great deal was known on the subject from the research of Pfungst (1911/1965) on the horse known as "Clever Hans," and from other sources.

It has sometimes been alleged that the Rhines were quite ignorant of Pfungst's research and similar studies and were therefore easily taken in and tricked by Lady's owner. This seems quite untrue. They were well read in the literature, cited Pfungst's research as well as others, and introduced what seemed to be adequate controls on movements of the observers, including sending Lady's owner out of the tent where the performances were taking place. Lady's performance on trials with her owner absent was significantly better than chance. Indeed, from the standpoint of the critical common sense that had served them so well with Margery, the controls were adequate. It was only from the standpoint of the psychological methodology and theory of the day that the controls were clearly insufficient.

The Rhines' rationale for their controls was that "the theory of unconscious guidance ... assumes involuntary gestures, but the same psychologic assumption must grant also voluntary control over them" (Rhine & Rhine, 1929a, p. 462). They therefore usually had the owner and themselves sit motionless and avoid eye movements while Lady was making her choices of blocks, and found that her success rate remained high under these conditions. This procedure was inadequate, however. Pfungst had found that the questioners could *not* refrain from making minute guiding movements. After prolonged self-training, he could take the part of the horse and respond to mental questions even when the questioners were intent to avoid giving any cues (Pfungst, 1911/1965, Ch. 4). But Pfungst did not dwell at length on the impossibility of controlling such movements. He did not need to. His psychological readers in the early part of the century would have shared with him a familiarity with and general acceptance of what was called a motoric theory of consciousness. The experimental demonstration that, in a particular case, conscious expectations would express themselves in minute motor acts would therefore have been immediately understood. It was merely the successful application of an established theory to a new instance.

Lacking that theoretical and methodological background, the Rhines relied on common sense in controlling for signals, and thus failed to do all that was necessary. To be sure, there were practical difficulties. They had to keep on good terms with Lady's rather tempermental owner and were thus limited in the controls they could impose. Nevertheless, the methodologically appropriate controls would have been procedurally simpler and less intrusive than the most rigorous one that they did successfully impose, that of sending Lady's owner out of the tent. That control eliminated fraud as the sole explanation. To eliminate the "Clever Hans" effect, however, it should instead have been J. B. Rhine who went out of the tent, on some of the 21 trials when he alone knew the target. (Of the visitors, it was usually J. B. Rhine who mentally "controlled" the horse; the

other members of his party, including Louisa Rhine, William Mc-
Dougall, and John Thomas, were less successful.) If Rhine's complete removal was impractical, he could have approximated it by
blocking his view of the horse with a screen, or even by closing his
eyes while she was choosing the target. There were a number of tests
in which the *horse's* view of all those who knew the target was more
or less restricted: by hats pulled down over their faces, by a small
screen, and by a larger screen. Her performance deteriorated as the
extent of visual blockage increased. The relevant control, however,
was to prevent the *questioners*, those who knew the target on a given
trial, from seeing *her*. It was their uncontrollable movements, indicative of expectant attention, that would provide the signalling
function — according to the motoric theory of consciousness as applied to the "Clever Hans" phenomenon. Control of the horse was
secondary. However, lacking the necessary technical background,
the Rhines did not appreciate that fact; and so they addressed their
controls instead to the announced or suspected performers, the horse
and her owner. It thus remained not certain but highly possible that
Lady was responding to small motor movements despite the Rhines'
best efforts to eliminate them. Their apparently cautious conclusion,
that "no other hypothesis [than telepathy] ... seems tenable in view
of the results" (Rhine & Rhine, 1929a, p. 463) was incorrect as a result.
The counterhypothesis was not ruled out. When Lady's sensitivity,
from whatever source, declined some months later so that she
required obvious signals in order to perform, they could only report
regretfully that her abilities had vanished (Rhine & Rhine, 1929b).

The intent of this discussion is not simply to find fault with this
53-year-old study. It is more serious than that. The difference between the Margery and the Lady studies shows clearly the difference
between fact-finding in a structured social context, however bizarre,
and testing a scientific hypothesis. For the former, an intelligent and
critical application of the observational procedures of daily life is often sufficient. The question, again, is a kind of judicial one. Scientific
training may be helpful, especially if it is not related to the matter
being investigated, but it is not essential. For the latter, however, a
precise technical methodology, appropriate to the hypothesis and the
specific problem situation, is essential. It does not have to be
procedurally complex, as we have seen; but it does have to take close
account of the relevant knowledge and theories already existing in
the field. Judicial procedures, based on the codification of common
sense, are inadequate.

Had the Rhines followed the lead of many earlier psychical researchers at this point, then, disappointed with Lady, they might have gone on to look for other diverse instances of inexplicable behavior and reported them hopefully as demonstrations of a new force. Had they followed the lead of Pfungst and other psychologists in his tradition, they might have studied human and animal psychology deeply enough to become experts in the interpretation of performing animals such as Lady and Clever Hans. Instead, they did something quite different, avoiding both the dilettantism that threatened seekers of the unexplained and the narrowness that would have resulted from concentrating on a technical area only tangentially relevant to their own goals. What they did was to develop the needed technical proficiency, from the ground up, in their own subject area. They began, that is, to construct the technical methodology and conceptual framework for a science that did not yet exist.

The careers of J. B. and Louisa E. Rhine began to diverge at this point. Louisa Rhine took mainly a supportive role in developing the basic methodology of parapsychology and later began the mammoth and optimistic task of analyzing the distribution and patterns of spontaneous cases, a task which is still in progress (e.g., Rhine, L. E., 1949, 1981). The task was a mammoth one because of the volume of material. It was an optimistic one because it laid the groundwork for a natural history of psi, a groundwork that could be built upon only after the experimental studies had provided firm guidelines for making judgments on the presence of psi in the spontaneous cases. In the meantime, however — and this was the original basis for undertaking the study — it could usefully serve as a source of research hypotheses.

J. B. Rhine took the lead in developing workable methods. Although he was originally sent to Duke with private funding to analyze some mediumistic records, his interests even before the Margery affair had tended to focus on studies of telepathy and clairvoyance as being more easily interpretable. As soon as he could, therefore, he began looking for appropriate techniques for the experimental study of these. Knowing what he was after, he was able implicitly to follow the simple rule: keep trying until you find something that works, and then stick with it. A number of more-or-less successful experiments of the time involved the supposedly telepathic transmission of playing cards or pictures. So, in the summer of 1930, Rhine tested groups of children in summer camp, having them guess the number from 0 to 9 printed on a card concealed in his hand. There were no interesting results. In the fall of 1930, Helge Lundholm, a new member of the Duke psychology department, suggested that he hypnotize students to test their telepathic ability in the hypnotic state. Lundholm and Rhine tested 30 students in this way, with no results. Also in the fall of 1930, another member of the psychology department, Karl Zener, suggested that they print numbers or letters on cards, seal them in envelopes, and give them to students to guess. No results followed — except for the discovery of one high-scoring subject who was retained for later study (Rhine, J. B., 1934/1973). Rhine then asked Zener to design cards with more distinctive symbols than ordinary numbers or letters (Mauskopf & McVaugh, 1980). Zener, whose field was the psychology of perception, accordingly designed the ESP cards that for a time, and to his distaste, bore his name.

With these they began to get results. Tests involving over 800 trials by unselected undergraduates in the winter of 1930–1931 yielded results significant at well beyond the .001 level. The one high-scoring subject discovered previously did even better with the new cards. Throughout 1931 and into 1932, Rhine worked out the techniques used with these cards in collaboration with other members of the faculty, students, and friends. They developed the "Down-Through" and "Before-Touching" techniques and variants on these, made the operational distinction between clairvoyance and clairvoyance-plus-telepathy, became surer of their use of the probability calculus, identified a number of additional high-scoring subjects, and began to try to identify the psychological correlates of successful performance (Rhine, J. B., 1934/1973). These early studies culminated in Rhine's first paper on ESP in 1932, which he delayed publishing for two years, however, to make sure that he was not taking another false step (Rhine, J. B., 1934).

In these early and exploratory studies, Rhine displayed, individually and with a few collaborators, the same pattern of persistence and systematic restriction of attention that marked the Duke group in the years after 1934 when the work started to become known. The genesis of that group cohesiveness that enabled parapsychology to become a scientific speciality was evident from the beginning of Rhine's own experimental work at Duke, before there was much of a group to be cohesive or not.

IV. Conclusion

The personal and professional factors involved in J. B. Rhine's major contribution to parapsychology—establishing it as a coherent scientific specialty—were thus those that enabled him to serve as the nucleus of an intensive and restricted research community. These of course included experimental skills, a commitment to the importance and legitimacy of the field, confidence in the applicability of scientific methods to its problems, a favorable institutional setting, and—an important factor that has not been dealt with here—a forful personality that inspired enthusiasm and commitment in many of his coworkers. These were all necessary, but were neither unprecedented in the field nor sufficient for the purpose. The additional crucial factor was a combination of flexibility and dogged persistence. It was a willingness to try a variety of approaches to investigating the field, followed by an unprecedented persistence and narrowing of focus once a workable approach had been identified. The first part led Rhine to hop from mediums to trick horses to card-guessing, and from one technique to another in the study of card-guessing. The second led him to stop once he had found something that worked, to devote more energy—both his own and that of the researchers working under his leadership—to studies of a highly restricted topic than had ever before been expended on any experimental topic in the field. The initial flexibility was necessary at first to prevent premature closure before a successful approach had been identified. Once it was identified, however, it was the subsequent persistence that paid off. Additional research topics and extensions of the original ones would be introduced slowly and cautiously, and would be based as far as possible on the work already done.

In 1977, I asked J. B. Rhine how he might account for his early success in parapsychology. How, in his view, had he been so much more successful than others in building up a systematic body of evidence? Rhine replied that he had always been fairly confident that if there was anything to be found, he would have a good chance of finding it. It was not because of any special brilliance or gifts on his part, he emphasized, that he had had this confidence. It was rather because he had the doggedness and determination to push on with the methods of science until they supplied the answers to his questions, one way or another.

These comments may seem to reflect only a becoming modesty

in an elder statesman in the field. To a considerable extent, however, they appear to be justified. Whatever "special brilliance or gifts" J. B. Rhine might have possessed, it was his doggedness and determination, supplemented by his eye for the selection of workable problems, that largely transformed psychical research into experimental parapsychology. It is in this sense that the establishment of parapsychology's scientific status, grudging though that status often still is, has an intensely personal history. That history, more than in most sciences, is the history of the work and the influence of one individual. That work, and what it led to, made parapsychology into a scientific discipline and, along with the numerous technical and professional contributions he went on to make in the field, assured J. B. Rhine a key place in the history of parapsychology.

REFERENCES

BALLOU, A. *An exposition of views respecting the principal facts, causes and peculiarities involved in spirit manifestations*, 2d ed. Boston: Bela Marsh, 1853.

BEN-DAVID, J., & COLLINS, R. Social factors in the origins of a new science: The case of psychology. *American Sociological Review*, 1966, 31, 451–465.

BENNETT, J. H. *The mesmeric mania of 1851, with a physiological explanation of the phenomena produced*. Edinburgh: Sutherland & Knox, 1851.

BERTRAND, A. *Le magnetisme animal en France*. Paris: J. B. Bailliere, 1826.

BIRD, J. M. The Margery mediumship. *Journal of the American Society for Psychical Research*, 1926, 20, 385–406

BORING, M., & BORING, E. G. Masters and pupils among the American psychologists. *American Journal of Psychology*, 1948, 61, 527–534.

CAHAGNET, L. A. *The celestial telegraph, or secrets of the life to come revealed through magnetism*. London: George Pierce, 1850.

COLQUHOUN, J. C. *Hints on animal magnetism addressed to the medical profession in Great Britain*. Edinburgh: Maclachlan & Stewart, 1838.

ESDAILE, J. *Mesmerism in India and its practical application in surgery and medicine*. London: Longmans, Brown, Green, & Longmans, 1846.

FODOR, N. *Encyclopedia of psychic science*. London: Arthurs Press, 1933.

GASPARIN, COMTE A. DE. *A treatise on turning tables, the supernatural in general, and spirits*. New York: Higgins & Kellogg, 1857.

HALL, T. H. *The spiritualists: The story of Florence Cook and William Crookes*. London: Duckworth, 1962.

HAMMOND, W. A. *Spiritualism and allied causes and conditions of nervous derangement*. New York: G. P. Putnam's Sons, 1876.

HARE, R. *Experimental investigations of the spirit manifestations*. New York: Partridge & Brittan, 1855.

INGLIS, B. *Natural and supernatural: A history of the paranormal from earliest times to 1914*. London: Hodder & Stoughton, 1977

KUHN, T. S. *The structure of scientific revolutions.* Chicago: University of Chicago Press, 1962.

McVAUGH, M. R., & MAUSKOPF, S. H. J. B. Rhine's *Extra-Sensory Perception* and its background in psychical research. *Isis*, 1976, 67, 161–189.

MAUSKOPF, S. H., & McVAUGH, M. R. *The elusive science: A history of experimental parapsychology 1915–1940.* Baltimore: Johns Hopkins University Press, 1980.

MEDHURST, R. B. (ed.), *Crookes and the spirit world.* New York: Taplinger, 1972.

MUNGER, C. *Ancient sorcery, as revived in modern spiritualism, examined by the divine law and testimony.* Boston: Henry V. Oegen, 1857.

PFUNGST, O. *Clever Hans: The horse of Mr. Von Osten.* New York: Holt, Rinehart & Winston, 1965. (Originally published, 1911.)

Report on the magnetic experiments, made by a committee of the Royal Academy of Medicine, at Paris. In J. C. Colquhoun, *Isis Revelata: An inquiry into the origin, progress, and present state of animal magnetism,* 3d ed. Edinburgh: William Wilson, 1844.

RHINE, J. B. Current periodicals. *Journal of the American Society for Psychical Research,* 1925, 19, 663–666.

RHINE, J. B. Extra-sensory perception of the clairvoyant type. *Journal of Abnormal and Social Psychology,* 1934, 29, 151–171.

RHINE, J. B. *Extra-sensory perception.* Boston: Branden Press, 1973. (Originally published, 1934).

RHINE, J. B., & RHINE, L. E. One evening's observation on the Margery mediumship. *Journal of Abnormal and Social Psychology,* 1927, 21, 401–421.

RHINE, J. B., & RHINE, L. E. An investigation of a "mind-reading" horse. *Journal of Abnormal and Social Psychology,* 1929, 23, 449–466. (a)

RHINE, J. B., & RHINE, L. E. Second report on Lady, the "mind-reading" horse. *Journal of Abnormal and Social Psychology,* 1929, 24, 287–292 (b)

RHINE, J. B., & RHINE, L. E. A search for the nature of the mind. In T. S. Krawiec (ed.), *The psychologists,* Vol. 3. Brandon, Vt.: Clinical Psychology Pub. Co., 1978.

RHINE, L. E. Case books of the last quarter century. *Journal of Parapsychology,* 1949, 13, 292–296.

RHINE, L. E. *The invisible picture: A study of psychic experiences.* Jefferson, N.C.: McFarland, 1981.

Society for Psychical Research. Objects of the Society. *Proceedings of the Society for Psychical Research,* 1881, 1, 3–4.

Bibliography of
Works by J. B. Rhine

FARILLA A. DAVID*

1924

The clogging of the stomata of conifers in relation to smoke injury and distribution. *Botanical Gazette*, 1924, **78**, 226–32.

1925

Current periodicals. *Journal of the American Society for Psychical Resear-* 1925, **19**, 663–66.
Translocation of fats as such in germinating fatty seeds. Unpublished doctoral dissertation, University of Chicago, 1925.

1927

One evening's observation on the Margery mediumship. *Journal of Abnormal and Social Psychology*, 1927, **21**, 401–21.

1929

An investigation of a mind-reading horse. *Journal of Abnormal and Social Psychology*, 1929, **23**, 449–66.
Religion, an illusion? Review of *The future of an illusion*, by Sigmund Freud. *Duke University Archive*, 1929, **41**(5), 15–19.
Second report on Lady, the "mind-reading" horse. With L. E. Rhine. *Journal of Abnormal and Social Psychology*, 1929, **24**, 287–92.

Grateful thanks to Mrs. Dorothy H. Pope, Miss Rhea White and many others without whose help this bibliography would have been far less complete and accurate.

1933

Third report on a Lamarckian experiment. With William McDougall. *British Journal of Psychology*, 1933, **24**, 213–35.

1934

Are we "psychic" beings? *Forum*, 1934, **92**(6), 369–72.

Extra-sensory perception. Boston: Boston Society for Psychic Research, 1934. (Also: Boston: Bruce Humphries, 1935; Boston: Bruce Humphries, 1964 paperback revised; Boston: Branden Press, 1973 paperback.)

Extrasensory perception of the clairvoyant type. *Journal of Abnormal and Social Psychology*, 1934, **29**, 151–71.

Telepathy and clairvoyance in the normal and trance states of a "medium." *Character and Personality*, 1934, **3**, 91–111.

1935

After death — what? *Forum*, 1935, **93**(2), 114–18.

Don't fool yourself. Pitfalls in psychic research. *Forum*, 1935, **94**(3), 187–89.

The evidence for prophecy. *Forum*, 1935, **94**(2), 120–23.

The gift of prophecy. *Forum*, 1935, **94**(1), 50–53.

Note on Professor Thouless's review of *Extra-sensory perception*. *Proceedings of the Society for Psychical Research*, 1935, **43**, 542–44.

The practical side of psychism. *Forum*, 1935, **93**(1), 51–54.

Telepathy and clairvoyance in a trance medium. *Scientific American*, July 1935, **153**, 12–14.

1936

The Pratt-Garrett study of mediumistic trance utterances. In J. G. Pratt, *Towards a method of evaluating mediumistic material*. Boston: Boston Society of Psychic Research, 1936, 54–59.

Some selected experiments in extrasensory perception. *Journal of Abnormal and Social Psychology*, 1936, **31**, 216–28.

1937

Editorial comment. *Journal of Parapsychology*, 1937, **1**, 81–83.

Editorial comment. *Journal of Parapsychology*, 1937, **1**, 159–62.

Editorial comment. *Journal of Parapsychology*, 1937, **1**, 231–33.

Editorial introduction. *Journal of Parapsychology*, 1937, **1**, 1–9.

The effect of distance in ESP tests. *Journal of Parapsychology*, 1937, **1**, 172–84.

Foreword. In C. E. Stuart and J. G. Pratt (eds.), *A handbook for testing extrasensory perception*. New York: Farrar & Rinehart, 1937.

New frontiers of the mind. New York: Farrar & Rinehart, 1937. (Also London: Faber & Faber, 1938. In German: *Neuland der Seele*, Stuttgart: Deutsche Verlags-Anstalt, 1938. Cleveland: World Publishing Co., 1942; Harmondsworth, England: Penguin Books, 1950 paperback. In Italian: *Nuove frontiere della mente*, Milan: Arnoldo Mondadori Editore, 1950. Westport, Conn.: Greenwood Press, 1972.)

The question of sensory cues and the evidence. *Journal of Parapsychology*, 1937, **1**, 276–91.

Some basic experiments in extrasensory perception: A background. *Journal of Parapsychology*, 1937, **1**, 70–80.

1938

Comments on Dr. Wolfle's review. *American Journal of Psychiatry*, 1938, **94**, 957–960.

Editorial comment. *Journal of Parapsychology*, 1938, **2**, 1–4.

Editorial comment. *Journal of Parapsychology*, 1938, **2**, 77–83.

Editorial comment. *Journal of Parapsychology*, 1938, **2**, 155–59.

Editorial comments. *Journal of Parapsychology*, 1938, **2**, 242–46.

ESP: What precautions are being taken to forefend against error in the extrasensory perception research as conducted at Duke University? *Scientific American*, June 1938, **158**, 328.

ESP tests with enclosed cards. *Journal of Parapsychology*, 1938, **2**, 199–216.

Experiments bearing on the precognition hypothesis: I. Preshuffling card calling. *Journal of Parapsychology*, 1938, **2**, 38–54.

Experiments bearing on the precognition hypothesis: II. The role of ESP in the shuffling of cards. With B. M. Smith and J. L. Woodruff. *Journal of Parapsychology*, 1938, **2**, 119–31.

Extrasensory perception. *Sigma Xi Quarterly*, 1938, **26**, 170–174.

The hypothesis of deception. *Journal of Parapsychology*, 1938, **2**, 151–52.

Letter re commercial ESP cards. *Journal of the Society for Psychical Research*, 1938, **30**, 257–58.

Psychical research of parapsychology during 1937. *Aryan Path*, April 1938, 194–97.

Requirements and suggestions for an ESP test machine. *Journal of Parapsychology*, 1939, **3**, 3–10.

Rothera experiments. *Journal of Parapsychology*, 1938, **2**, 325–26.

Symposium on ESP methods, at the meeting of the Southern Society for Philosophy and Psychology. With T. N. E. Greville, J. A. Greenwood, J. G. Pratt, C. E. Stuart, and V. W. Lemmon. *Journal of Parapsychology*, 1939, **3**, 85–115.

William McDougall (1871–1938). *Journal of Parapsychology*, 1938, **2**, 239–41.

1940

Experiments bearing upon the precognition hypothesis: III. Mechanically selected cards. *Journal of Parapsychology*, 1941, 5, 1–57.

Extrasensory perception: A review. *Scientific Monthly*, 1940, 51, 450–59.

Extrasensory perception after sixty years. With J. G. Pratt, B. M. Smith, C. E. Stuart and J. A. Greenwood. New York: Henry Holt, 1940. (Also Boston: Bruce Humphries, 1966, with a new foreword by J. B. Rhine.)

1941

It follows from ESP. *Journal of the American Society for Psychical Research*, 1941, 35, 179–95.

Letter in reply to Saul B. Sells, chairman, Board of Review. *Journal of Parapsychology*, 1941, 5, 92–95.

Letter in reply to S. B. Sells and others. *Journal of Parapsychology*, 1941, 5, 255–59.

Terminal salience in ESP performance. *Journal of Parapsychology*, 1941, 5, 183–244.

1942

A check on salience relations in ESP data. With J. G. Pratt (first author) and B. M. Humphrey (second author). *Journal of Parapsychology*, 1942, 6, 44–51.

A confirmatory study of salience in precognition tests. With B. M. Humphrey (first author). *Journal of Parapsychology*, 1942, 6, 190–219.

Editorial: Change in editorship and the new program. *Journal of Parapsychology*, 1942, 6, 1–4.

Editorial: Hypnotism, "graduate" of parapsychology. *Journal of Parapsychology*, 1942, 6, 159–63.

Editorial: Progress of parapsychology as a university study. *Journal of Parapsychology*, 1942, 6, 237–42.

Editorial: Whose field is parapsychology? *Journal of Parapsychology*, 1942, 6, 79–84.

Evidence of precognition in the covariation of salience ratios. *Journal of Parapsychology*, 1942, 6, 111–43.

Exceptional scores in ESP tests and the conditions: I. The case of Lillian. With Margaret Pegram Reeves (first author). *Journal of Parapsychology*, 1942, 6, 164–73.

An experiment in precognition using dice. With J. L. Woodruff (first author). *Journal of Parapsychology*, 1942, 6, 243–62.

The present status of extrasensory perception. *Aryan Path*, April 1942, 147–59.

A single subject in a veriety of ESP test conditions. With W. R. Russell (first author). *Journal of Parapsychology*, 1942, 6, 284–311.

A transoceanic ESP experiment. With B. M. Humphrey. *Journal of Parapsychology*, 1942, 6, 52–74.

Unusual types of persons tested for ESP: I. A professional medium. With W. R. Birge (first author). *Journal of Parapsychology*, 1942, 6, 85–94.

1943

A comparison of three sizes of dice in PK tests. With Homer Hilton, Jr. (first author) and George Baer. *Journal of Parapsychology*, 1943, 7, 172–90.

Dice thrown by cup and machine in PK tests. *Journal of Parapsychology*, 1943, 7, 207–17.

Editorial: ESP, PK and the survival hypothesis. *Journal of Parapsychology*, 1943, 7, 223–27.

Editorial: The mind has real force! *Journal of Parapsychology*, 1943, 7, 69–75.

Editorial: "Physical phenomena" in parapsychology. *Journal of Parapsychology*, 1943, 7, 1–4.

Editorial: Significance of the PK effect. *Journal of Parapsychology*, 1943, 7, 139–43.

A large series of PK tests. With E. P. Gibson (first author) and L. H. Gibson (second author). *Journal of Parapsychology*, 1943, 7, 228–37.

The PK effect: The McDougall one-die series. With B. M. Humphrey. *Journal of Parapsychology*, 1943, 7, 252–63.

The PK effect: II. A study in declines. With M. P. Reeves (first author). *Journal of Parapsychology*, 1943, 7, 76–93.

The PK effect: III. Some introductory series. With E. P. Gibson (first author). *Journal of Parapsychology*, 1943, 7, 118–34.

Position effects in the large Gibson series. With B. M. Humphrey (first author). *Journal of Parapsychology*, 1943, 7, 238–51.

The psychokinetic effect: I. The first experiment. With L. E. Rhine (first author). *Journal of Parapsychology*, 1943, 7, 20–43.

A second comparison of three sizes of dice in PK tests. With Homer Hilton, Jr. (first author). *Journal of Parapsychology*, 1943, 7, 191–206.

1944

Are you a mind reader? *American Magazine*, September 1944, 32–33.

The contribution of Mr. H. E. Saltmarsh on the problem of survival. *Journal of the American Society for Psychical Research*, 1944, 38, 62–71.

Editorial: Is parapsychology a profession? *Journal of Parapsychology*, 1944, 8, 173–76.

Editorial: Parapsychology and the government of men. *Journal of Parapsychology*, 1944, 8, 247–51.

Editorial: PK research at the point for decision! *Journal of Parapsychology*, 1944, 8, 1–2.

Editorial: The practice of fake telepathy. *Journal of Parapsychology*, 1944, 8, 251–53.
Editorial: Ten years retrospect of ESP research. *Journal of Parapsychology*, 1944, 8, 89–94.
The evaluation of salience in Dr. Schmeidler's ESP data. With B. M. Humphrey (first author). *Journal of Parapsychology*, 1944, 8, 124–26.
Letter in reply to Soal and Goldney. With B. M. Humphrey. *Journal of Parapsychology*, 1944, 8, 318–20.
"Mind over matter" or the PK effect. *Journal of the American Society for Psychical Research*, 1944, 38, 185–201.
Parapsychology and religion. *Christian Register*, August 1944, 291.
The PK effect: Early singles tests. *Journal of Parapsychology*, 1944, 8, 287–303.
The PK effect: Mechanical throwing of three dice. With E. P. Gibson (first author) and L. M. Gibson (second author). *Journal of Parapsychology*, 1944, 8, 95–109.
The PK effect: Special evidence from hit patterns: I. Quarter distributions of the page. With B. M. Humphrey. *Journal of Parapsychology*, 1944, 8, 18–60.
The PK effect: Special evidence from hit patterns: II. Quarter distributions of the set. With B. M. Humphrey. *Journal of Parapsychology*, 1944, 8, 254–71.
PK tests with six, twelve and twenty-four dice per throw. With B. M. Humphrey. *Journal of Parapsychology*, 1944, 8, 139–57.
Position effects in the Soal and Goldney experiment. With B. M. Humphrey (first author). *Journal of Parapsychology*, 1944, 8, 187–213.
The subject-experimenter relation in the PK test. With Margaret M. Price (first author). *Journal of Parapsychology*, 1944, 8, 177–86.

1945

Early PK tests: Sevens and low dice series. *Journal of Parapsychology*, 1945, 9, 106–15.
Editorial: A consistent standard of significance. *Journal of Parapsychology*, 1945, 9, 4–6.
Editorial: On the further reconsideration of telepathy and clairvoyance. *Journal of Parapsychology*, 1945, 9, 228–29.
Editorial: Parapsychology and dualism. *Journal of Parapsychology*, 1945, 9, 225–28.
Editorial: Parapsychology and religion. *Journal of Parapsychology*, 1945, 9, 1–4.
Editorial: A proposed basis for choosing terms in parapsychology. *Journal of Parapsychology*, 1945, 9, 147–49.
Editorial: The question of practical application of parapsychological abilities. *Journal of Parapsychology*, 1945, 9, 77–79.
The effect of alcohol upon performance in PK tests. With R. L. Averill

(first author). *Journal of Parapsychology*, 1945, 9, 32–41.

An exploratory experiment on caffeine upon performance in PK tests. With B. M. Humphrey and R. L. Averill. *Journal of Parapsychology*, 1945, 9, 80–91.

An exploratory investigation of the PK effect. With C. J. Herter (first author). *Journal of Parapsychology*, 1945, 9, 17–25.

Fantastic flights of the London prophet's mind. *American Weekly*, April 1, 1945, 20.

Letter: Re Tyrrell's "Is measurement necessary in psychical research?" *Journal of the American Society for Psychical Research*, 1945, 39, 126.

The PK effect: The first doubles experiment. With M. P. Reeves (first author). *Journal of Parapsychology*, 1945, 9, 42–51.

The PK effect: Special evidence from hit patterns: III. Quarter distributions of the half-set. With B. M. Humphrey and J. G. Pratt. *Journal of Parapsychology*, 1945, 9, 150–68.

The PK effect with sixty dice per throw. With B. M. Humphrey. *Journal of Parapsychology*, 1945, 9, 203–18.

PK tests with two sizes of dice mechanically thrown. With B. M. Humphrey. *Journal of Parapsychology*, 1945, 9, 124–32.

Position effects in the six-by-six series of PK tests. With B. M. Humphrey. *Journal of Parapsychology*, 1945, 9, 296–302.

Precognition reconsidered. *Journal of Parapsychology*, 1945, 9, 264–277.

Telepathy and clairvoyance reconsidered. *Journal of Parapsychology*, 1945, 9, 176–93. Condensed version reprinted in *Proceedings of the Society for Psychical Research*, 1946–1949, 48, 1–7.

Will power wins — even with dice. *American Weekly*, November 11, 1945, 14.

1946

Book review: The case for telepathy. *Thought transference* by Whately Carington. New York: Creative Age Press, 1946. In *Saturday Review*, June 22, 1946, 32.

Comment on Mr. Parson's letter. *Journal of Parapsychology*, 1946, 10, 63–64.

A digest and discussion of some comments on "Telepathy and clairvoyance reconsidered." *Journal of Parapsychology*, 1946, 10, 36–50.

Dr. J. B. Rhine's reply [to Carington, Hettinger, Thouless, Tyrrell, Broad, and Parsons]. *Proceedings of the Society for Psychical Research*, 1946, 48, 27–28.

Editorial: Are psi phenomena paranormal or normal? *Journal of Parapsychology*, 1946, 10, 149–53.

Editorial: Confirmatory experiments in PK research. *Journal of Parapsychology*, 1946, 10, 71–74.

Editorial: ESP and PK as "psi phenomena." *Journal of Parapsychology*, 1946, 10, 74–75.

Editorial: The first ten years of the *Journal*. *Journal of Parapsychology*, 1946, **10**, 221–23.

Editorial: Telepathy — will history repeat itself? *Journal of Parapsychology*, 1946, **10**, 1–4.

Have you second sight? *American Magazine*, November 1946, 38–39.

Hypnotic suggestion in PK tests. *Journal of Parapsychology*, 1946, **10**, 126–40.

La percezione extrasensoriale. *Metapsichica*. 1946, 1(3), 129–44.

The psychokinetic effect: A review. *Journal of Parapsychology*, 1946, **10**, 5–20.

The Schwartz PK experiment. *Journal of Parapsychology*, 1946, **10**, 208–12.

Scientific evidence. *American Weekly*, August 25, 1946, 4.

The source of the difficulties in parapsychology. *Journal of Parapsychology*, 1946, **10**, 162–68.

Two groups of PK subjects compared. With William Gatling (first author). *Journal of Parapsychology*, 1946, **10**, 120–25.

1947

Book review: *Personality of man* by G. N. M. Tyrrell. Harmondsworth, England: Penguin Books, 1946. In *Journal of Parapsychology*, 1947, **11**, 313–15.

Editorial: Charles Stuart (1907–1947): memorial. *Journal of Parapsychology*, 1947, **11**, 71–75.

Editorial: Parapsychology and ethics. *Journal of Parapsychology*, **11**, 1–3.

Editorial: Pierre Janet's contribution to parapsychology. *Journal of Parapsychology*, 1947, **11**, 155–59.

Editorial: Proposed symposium on a program for parapsychology. *Journal of Parapsychology*, 1947, **11**, 241–43.

Impatience with scientific method in parapsychology. *Journal of Parapsychology*, 1947, **11**, 283–95.

The reach of the mind. New York: William Sloane, 1947. (Also: London: Faber & Faber, 1948. In Danish: *Sjaelens Evner*, Coperhagen: H. Hagerup, 1949. In Italian: *I poteri dello spirito*, Rome: Casa Editrice Astrolabio, 1949. In Japanese: [trans. Aido Segawa] Tokyo: Hokuryukan, 1950. In German: *Die Reichweite des menschlichen Geistes*, Stuttgart: Deutsche Verlags–Anstalt, 1950. In French: *La double puissance de l'esprit*, Paris: Payot, 1952. Harmondsworth, England: Penguin Books, 1954. In Spanish: *El alcance de la mente* [trans. Dora Ivnisky], Buenos Aires: Editorial Paidos, 1956. In Portuguese: *O Alcance do espirito*, São Paulo: Bestseller, 1965. Condensed version of the book in *Reader's Digest*, February 1948, 129–142, translated and reprinted in the French edition April, 1948; and in the Danish, Finnish, Japanese, Swedish editions, May, 1948.)

A second Zagreb–Durham ESP experiment. With E. A. McMahan (first author). *Journal of Parapsychology*, 1947, **11**, 244–53.

1948

Can your dog read your mind? *American Weekly*, December 5, 1948, 20–21.
Conditions favoring success in psi tests. *Journal of Parapsychology*, 1948, 12, 58–75.
Editorial: Parapsychology and *The Reconstruction of Humanity* (book by P. A. Sorokin). In *Journal of Parapsychology*, 1948, 12, 157–61.
Editorial: The value of reports of spontaneous psi experiences. *Journal of Parapsychology*, 1948, 12, 231–35.
Foreword: In Betty M. Humphrey, *Handbook of tests in parapsychology*. Durham, N.C.: Parapsychology Laboratory of Duke University, 1948, 1–5.
Letter to Pitirim A. Sorokin. *Journal of Parapsychology*, 1948, 12, 158–59.
Research aims for the decade ahead. *Journal of Parapsychology*, 1948, 12, 101–07.

1949

Der sechstesinn. *Amerikanische Rundschau*. August/September, 1949, 13, 44–53.
Editorial: The limiting factor in parapsychology. *Journal of Parapsychology*, 1949, 13, 75–78.
Editorial: Parapsychology and psychiatry. *Journal of Parapsychology*, 1949, 13, 143–50.
Editorial: The relation between parapsychology and general psychology. *Journal of Parapsychology*, 1949, 13, 215–24.
Editorial: The value of reports of spontaneous psi experiences. *Journal of the Society for Psychical Research*, 1949, 35(652), 63–66.
Editorial: The Washington symposium. *Journal of Parapsychology*, 1949 13, 1–2.
ESP and prognosis. *Journal of Insurance Medicine*, 1949, 4, 16–17.
How good are your hunches? *Mechanix Illustrated*, April 1949, 82–84; 162–63.
The nature of psi processes (round table discussion). With R. A. McConnell, R. B. Roberts, J. A. Greenwood, C. B. Nash, L. E. Rhine, J. Ehrenwald, and M. Ullman. *Journal of Parapsychology*, 1949, 13, 47–62.
Parapsychology and psychopathology. (Abstract.) *Digest of Neurology and Psychiatry*, 1949, 17, 266.
Parapsychology (psychical research). In *Americana annual*. New York: Americana Corporation, 1949. (Revised in 1950, 1951, 1952, 1954, 1956, and 1960.)
The question of spirit survival. *Journal of the American Society for Psychical Research*, 1949, 43, 43–58.
Things I can't explain. *American Weekly*, January 1949, 42–43; 144–45.

1950

Editorial: Mid-century inventory of parapsychology. *Journal of Parapsychology*, 1950, **14**, 227–43.
Editorial: Parapsychology and biology. *Journal of Parapsychology*, 1950, **14**, 85–94.
Editorial: Publication policy. *Journal of Parapsychology*, 1950, **14**, 1–8.
Editorial: The shifting scene in parapsychology. *Journal of Parapsychology*, 1950, **14**, 161–67.
How does your dog find his way home? *American Weekly*, November 26, 1950, 4–5.
Impressions of a recent visit abroad. *Journal of the American Society for Psychical Research*, 1950, **44**, 161–62.
An introduction to the work on extrasensory perception. *Transactions of the New York Academy of Sciences*, 1950, **12**, 164–68.
Nuove frontiere della mente (trans. Gastone De Boni). Milan: Mondadori, 1950.
Miracles yesterday, experiments today. *Student Prince* (Heidelberg College), Spring 1950.
Parapsychology and the study of altruism. In Pitirim A. Sorokin (ed.), *Explorations in altruism and behavior*. Boston: Beacon Press, 1950, 165–80.
Parapsychology (psychical research). In *Americana annual*. New York: Americana Corporation, 1950.
Psi phenomena and psychiatry. *Proceedings of the Royal Society of Medicine*, 1950, **43**, 804–14.
Some exploratory tests in dowsing. *Journal of Parapsychology*, 1950, **14**, 278–86.
Telepathy and human personality. In Tenth Frederic W. H. Myers Memorial Lectures. London: Society for Psychical Research, 1950. (Reproduced in The *Journal of Parapsychology*, 1951, **15**, 6–39.)
Western science and communism. *Tomorrow*, October 1950, 4–8.

1951

Can your pet read your mind? *American Magazine*, June, 1951, 46–47.
The central question about man. In Alson J. Smith (ed.), *The psychic source book*. New York: Creative Age Press, 1951, 45–52.
Editorial: The outlook in parapsychology. *Journal of Parapsychology*, 1951, **15**, 151–63.
Editorial: Parapsychology and the biology of purpose. *Journal of Parapsychology*, 1951, **15**, 1–5.
Editorial: Parapsychology and physics. *Journal of Parapsychology*, 1951, **15**, 81–88.
Editorial: Proposals for a new symposium and for a parapsychology forum. *Journal of Parapsychology*, 1951, **15**, 227–29.
Experiments bearing on the precognition hypothesis: Preshuffling card

calling. In Alson J. Smith (ed.), *The psychic source book*. New York: Creative Age Press, 1951, 367–85.

The Forwald experiments with placement PK. *Journal of Parapsychology*, 1951, **15**, 49–56.

Hvaŏ varŏar vísindin um sálraena reynslu? *Morgunn*, 1951, **32**, 68–84.

Letter to Edmund W. Sinnott re the biological implications of psi in connection with his book, *Cell and psyche*. *Journal of Parapsychology*, 1951, **15**, 2–3.

Parapsychology (psychical research). *Americana annual*. New York: Americana Corporation, 1951.

The present outlook on the question of psi in animals. *Journal of Parapsychology*, 1951, **15**, 230–51.

The Rhine–Sorokin letters. In Alson J. Smith (ed.), *The psychic source book*. New York: Creative Age Press, 1951, 410–14.

The uncanny power that leads a dog home. *Magazine Digest*, September 1951.

What can science do about psychic experiences? *Tomorrow*, March, 1951, 1–8.

1952

Editorial: The challenge of the dowsing rod. *Journal of Parapsychology*, 1952, **16**, 1–10.

Editorial: Editorials, a forum, and a symposium. *Journal of Parapsychology*, 1952, **16**, 77–79.

Editorial: Parapsychology and scientific recognition. *Journal of Parapsychology*, 1952, **16**, 225–32.

Editorial: What kind of interest sustains the psi researchers? *Journal of Parapsychology*, 1952, **16**, 157–64.

Extrasensory perception and hypnosis. In L. M. LeCron (ed.), *Experimental hypnosis*. New York: Macmillan, 1952, 359–68.

Ghosts. *American Weekly*, May 4, 1952, **11**, 20.

Heimsmyndarkenningin nýja og spíritisminn. *Morgunn*, 1952, **33**, 59–64.

The mystery of the animal mind. *American Weekly*, March 30, 1952, 9, 27.

The mystery of "bewitched" muscles. *American Weekly*, March 23, 1952, 14; 20.

Mystery of echoes from the past. *American Weekly*, August 10, 1952, 9.

The mystery of the medium. *American Weekly*, June 15, 1952, 11.

The mystery of mind over matter. *American Weekly*, April 20, 1952, 16–17.

The mystery of telepathy. *American Weekly*, March 16, 1952, 16–18.

The mystery of warning dreams. *American Weekly*, March 9, 1952, 14–15, 17.

Parapsychology. *Americana annual*, New York: Americana Corporation, 1952.

The problem of psi-missing. *Journal of Parapsychology*, 1952, **16**, 90–129.

Über Hans Driesch. In Hans Driesch (ed.), *Parapsychologie* (Die Wissenschaft von den "okkulten" Erscheinungen, mit Beitragen von Dr. J. B. Rhine). Zürich: Rascher Verlag, 1952.

1953

Book review. *The psychology of the occult.* by D. H. Rawcliffe. London: Derricke Ridgway, 1952. In *Journal of the American Society for Psychical Research*, 1953, 47, 125–27.

Editorial: Parapsychology and its personnel. *Journal of Parapsychology.* 1953, 17, 1–5.

Editorial: The pattern of history in parapsychology. *Journal of Parapsychology*, 1953, 17, 247–58.

Editorial: The prospect for further exploration. *Journal of Parapsychology*, 1953, 17, 161–67.

New world of the mind. New York: William Sloane Associates, 1953. (Also: Toronto: George J. McLeod, 1953; London: Faber & Faber, 1954. In French: *Le noveau monde de l'esprit*, Paris: Librarie Adrien–Maisonneau, 1955. In Japanese: [trans. Aiko Segawa] Tokyo: Nihon Kyobunsha, 1958. In Spanish: *El nuevo mundo de la mente* [trans. Dora Ivnisky de Kreiman] Buenos Aires: Paidos, 1958. New York: William Sloane, 1962 paperback; New York: William Morrow, 1971 paperback.)

A scientific approach to the problems of religion. In *Main currents in modern thought*, November 1953, 34–36.

1954

Editorial: Perspective in transverse. *Journal of Parapsychology*, 1954, 18, 1–9.

Editorial: Rational acceptability of the case for psi. *Journal of Parapsychology*, 1954, 18, 184–94.

Editorial: The research is the thing! *Journal of Parapsychology*, 1954, 18, 241–44.

Editorial: Some considerations of methods in parapsychology. *Journal of Parapsychology*, 1954, 18, 69–81.

Letter in reply to Professor Hornell Hart. *Journal of Parapsychology*, 1954, 18, 198.

Letter to Professor L. C. Wilbur. *Journal of Parapsychology*, 1954, 18, 196.

The new world beyond physics. *Tomorrow*, Winter 1954, 41–72.

A review of the Pearce–Pratt distance series of ESP tests. With J. G. Pratt. *Journal of Parapsychology*, 1954, 18, 165–77.

The science of nonphysical nature. *Journal of Philosophy*, 1954, 51, 801–12.

1955

The controversy in *Science* over ESP: Comments on "Science and the Supernatural." *Journal of Parapsychology*, 1955, 19, 242–43.

The controversy in *Science* over ESP: The experiment should fit the hypothesis. *Journal of Parapsychology*, 1955, 19, 246.

Do animals have strange mental powers? *Atlanta Journal and Constitution Magazine*, February 6, 1955, 12–13.

Do dreams come true? *Everybody's Weekly*, February 5, 1955. (Reprinted in *Reader's Digest* Canadian edition, March 1955; German and Italian editions April 1955; and Australian, Brazilian, Danish, Finnish, French, Norwegian, Swedish editions May 1955.)

Editorial: The controversy in *Science* over ESP: The balance of the view. *Journal of Parapsychology*, 1955, 19, 267–71.

Editorial: The controversy in *Science* over ESP: The critical background. *Journal of Parapsychology*, 1955, 19, 236–38.

Editorial: Some present impasses in parapsychology. *Journal of Parapsychology*, 1955, 19, 99–110.

Editorial: Spontaneous psi reconsidered. *Journal of Parapsychology*, 1955, 19, 180–89.

New world of religion. *Science of Mind*, January, 1955, 20.

Objetivos inmediatos de la parapsicología (trans. Benjamin E. Odell). In *Tomorrow. Revista de Parapsicología*, 1955, 2, 3–11.

Parapsychology. In A. A. Roback (ed.), *Present-day psychology*. New York: Philosophical Library, 1955, 471–85.

Períodos en la historia de la parapsicología (trans. Benjamin E. Odell). *Revista de Parapsicología*, 1955, 1, 10–22.

Value of a "negative" experiment in extrasensory perception. *Science*, June 3, 1955.

What use can parapsychology make of spontaneous psi experiences? (Abstract.) *Proceedings of four conferences of parapsychological studies*. Parapsychology Foundation, 1955, 124–26.

1956

El alcance de la mente (trans. Dora Ivnisky). Buenos Aires: Paidos, 1956.

Book review: *The interpretation of nature and the psyche* by C. G. Jung and W. Pauli. New York: Pantheon Books, 1955. In *Tomorrow*, 1956, 4(2), 43–49.

Comments on "Science and the Supernatural." *Science*, Jan. 6, 1956, 11–14.

Did you live before? *American Weekly*, April 8, 1956.

Editorial: Parapsychology's reliance on a free press. *Journal of Parapsychology*, 1956, 20, 266–68.

Editorial: The journal's first twenty years. *Journal of Parapsychology*, 1956, 20, 263–66.

The experiment should fit the hypothesis. *Science*, 1956.

The laboratory's task. *Tomorrow*, Autumn 1956, 26–33.

The need for research workers in parapsychology. *Journal of Parapsychology*, 1956, 20, 184–96.

Parapsychology. In Alan Pryce–Jones (ed.), *The new outline of modern knowledge*. New York: Simon & Schuster, 1956, 193–211.

Research on spirit survival re-examined. *Journal of Parapsychology*, 1956, 20, 121–31.
Something worth-while in ways of excitement over new things in comments by M. Bernstein, *The search for Bridey Murphy*. Garden City, N.Y.: Doubleday, 1956. In *Tomorrow*, Summer 1956, pp. 26–27.

1957

Editorial: Order in the findings of parapsychology. *Journal of Parapsychology*, 1957, 21, 147–53.
Editorial: Parapsychology in a forward perspective. *Journal of Parapsychology*, 1957, 21, 66–72.
Foreword. In K. Ramakrishna Rao, *Psi cognition*. Tenali, India: Tagore Pub. House, 1957.
Introduction to parapsychology. *Yale Scientific Magazine*, 1957, 32, 8–16.
The laboratory's task. In Eileen Garrett (ed.), *Does man survive death?* New York: Helix Press, 1957, 72–80.
El mecanismo es un hermoso ídolo (trans. Julio C. di Liscia). *Revista de Parapsicología*, 1956. 3/4, 31–34.
Parapsychology: Frontier science of the mind. With J. G. Pratt. Springfield, Ill.: C. C. Thomas, 1957. (Also Oxford: Blackwell Scientific Publications, 1957; Toronto: Ryerson Press, 1957; Springfield, Ill.: Charles C. Thomas, 1962 revised edition. In German: *Grenswissenschaft der Psyche* (with J. G. Pratt), Switzerland: Francke Verlag, 1962. In Spanish: *Parapsicología* (trans. Adolfo Jasca), Buenos Aires: Edición Troquel. In Portuguese: São Paulo: Liviania Editora, 1966. In Japanese: Tokyo: Shukyo-Shinnugaku-Kenkyujo, 1964.)
Survival. *American Weekly*, December 8, 1957, 7–8, 28.
Why national defense overlooks parapsychology. *Journal of Parapsychology*, 1957, 21, 245–58.

1958

The goings on at Seaford (letter). *New Republic*, October 1958, 2–13.
El nuevo mundo de la mente (trans. Dora Ivnisky de Kreiman). Buenos Aires: Paidos, 1958.
On the nature and consequences of the unconsciousness of psi. *Journal of Parapsychology*, 1958, 22, 175–86.
Your hidden psychic powers. *American Weekly*, Feb. 16, 1958, 4–6, 30–31.

1959

ESP—can it influence teaching? *Education Summary*, September 12, 1959, 4–5.
How does one decide about ESP? *American Psychologist*, 1959, 14, 606–08.

Some avoidable misconceptions in parapsychology. *Journal of Parapsychology*, 1959, **23**, 30–43.
What do parapsychologists want to know? *Journal of the American Society for Psychical Research*, 1959, **53**, 3–15.

1960

Chairman's opening remarks and introduction of the first speaker. *Journal of Parapsychology*, 1960, **24**, 1–7.
Incorporeal personal agency: The prospect of a scientific solution. *Journal of Parapsychology*, 1960, **24**, 279–309.
Introducción a la parapsicología (trans. by O. Poblete and B. Onetto). *Revista de Parapsicología*, 1960–1962, 1–20.
On parapsychology and the nature of man. In Sidney Hood (ed.), *Dimensions of mind*. New York: New York University Press, 1960, 71–77.

1961

Book review: *William James on psychical research* by G. Murphy and R. O. Ballou (eds.), New York: Viking Press, 1960. In *Journal of Parapsychology*, 1961, **25**, 59–62.
Careers in parapsychology. *Tomorrow*, Spring 1961, 38–44.
Editorial introduction: A controversy over charges of fraud in ESP. *Journal of Parapsychology*, 1961, **25**, 86.
Extra-sensory perception: A review. In Fabian Gudas (ed.), *Extrasensory perception*, New York: Charles Scribner's Sons, 1961, 111–117.
Introduction: In Rosalind Heywood, *Beyond the reach of sense*. New York: E. P. Dutton, 1961, 7–8 (originally *The Sixth Sense*).
Die Parapsychologie und die zukünftige Entwicklung der Menschheit. In Ernst Benz (ed.), Zürich: Rhein–Verlag AG, 1961.
A quarter-century of the *Journal of Parapsychology*: A brief review. *Journal of Parapsychology*, 1961, **25**, 237–246.
A reply to the Hansel critique of the Pearce–Pratt series. With J. G. Pratt. *Journal of Parapsychology*, 1961, **25**, 92–97.
Science discovers what makes people lucky (as told to Isobel Aronin). *This Week*, May 1961, 28.

1962

The future of parapsychology: A symposium. *International Journal of Parapsychology*, 1962, 4(2), 5–26.
Parapsychology. *Shiksha*. 1962, 15(2), 69–82.
The precognition of computer numbers in a public test. *Journal of Parapsychology*, 1962, **26**, 244–51.
The shifting scene in parapsychology. *Journal of Parapsychology*, 1962, **26**, 293–307.

The study of cases of "psi trailing" in animals. With Sara R. Feather. *Journal of Parapsychology*, 1962, **26**, 1–22. (Reprinted in *Zeitschrift für Parapsychologie und Grenzgebiete der Psychologie*, 1963, **6**, 1–27.)

1963

Clairvoyance. In *Encyclopedia Americana*. New York: Americana Corporation, 1963.

Comparison of some exceptionally high ESP test performances. (Abstract.) *Journal of Parapsychology*, 1963, **27**, 274.

The implications of parapsychology for religion. *Wesleyan Studies in Religion*, 1962–63, **55**(8), 23–36.

Parapsychology at Duke: Retrospect and prospect. *Parapsychology Bulletin*. May 1963, 1–6.

Science and the spiritual nature of man. *Fate*, July, 1963, 74–81.

1964

Editorial: Parapsychology today. *Journal of Parapsychology*, 1964, **28**, 233–38.

Motivación especial en actuaciones excepcionales de ESP (trans. Dora Ivnisky). *Cuadernos de Parapsicología*, 1964, **1**(6), 1–11.

Policy and program of the Stone Fund for Parapsychological Education. Seventh Parapsychological Association convention. *Journal of Parapsychology*, 1964, **28**, 274–75.

Special motivation in some exceptional ESP performances. *Journal of Parapsychology*, 1964, **28**, 42–50.

1965

Advancement toward control and application. In J. B. Rhine and associates, *Parapsychology from Duke to FRNM*. Durham, N.C.: Parapsychology Press, 1965, 45–56.

Beginnings in the Department of Psychology: ESP established. In J. B. Rhine and associates, *Parapsychology from Duke to FRNM*. Durham, N.C.: Parapsychology Press, 1965, 57–58.

Cuestiones corrientes acerca de la parapsicología (trans. Dora Ivnisky). *Cuadernos de Parapsicología*, 1965, **2**, 3:8–11.

Editorial: Current questions about the field of parapsychology. *Journal of Parapsychology*, 1965, **29**, 223–29.

Editorial: *FRNM Bulletin*, no. 1, Summer 1965, 2.

Editorial: *FRNM Bulletin*, no. 2, Autumn 1965, 2.

ESP — What can we make of it? In *Guildhall lectures*. Manchester, England: Granada Television, 1965.

The field of parapsychology. *Journal of the Mississippi State Medical Association*, 1965, 6(10), 373–74.

Hvaö er maöurinn? *Morgunn*, 1965, 46, 93–106.

Introductory remarks. In J. B. Rhine and associates, *Parapsychology from Duke to FRNM*. Durham, N.C.: Parapsychology Press, 1965, 3–4.

Letter. *Journal of Parapsychology*, 1965, 29, 275–76.

O alcance do espirito (trans. E. Jacy Monteiro). São Paulo: Bestseller, 1965.

Parapsicología. With J. G. Pratt (eds.). (Trans. Adolfo Jasca). Buenos Aires: Troquel, 1965.

Parapsychology and medicine. *Journal of the Mississippi State Medical Association*, 1965, 6(10), 378–81.

Parapsychology becomes a branch of science. In J. B. Rhine and associates, *Parapsychology from Duke to FRNM*. Durham, N.C.: Parapsychology Press, 1965.

Parapsychology from Duke to FRNM. With associates. Durham, N.C.: Parapsychology Press, 1965.

The place of psi in the natural order. In J. B. Rhine and associates, *Parapsychology from Duke to FRNM*. Durham, N.C.: Parapsychology Press, 1965.

Preface. In J. B. Rhine and associates, *Parapsychology from Duke to FRNM*. Durham, N.C.: Parapsychology Press, 1965, v–vii.

The status and prospect of parapsychology today. In J. B. Rhine and associates, *Parapsychology from Duke to FRNM*. Durham, N.C.: Parapsychology Press, 1965.

1966

The bearing of parapsychology on human potentiality. *Journal of Parapsychology*, 1966, 30, 243–58.

Editorial: On conventions. *FRNM Bulletin*, no. 4, Autumn 1966, 2.

Editorial: Suggestions regarding personnel. *FRNM Bulletin*, no. 3, Spring 1966, 2.

ESP—What can we make of it? *Journal of Parapsychology*, 1966, 30, 84–105.

Fjarskyggnigáfan. *Morgunn*, 1966, 34, 107–17.

An introduction to parapsychology. *Probe*, 1966, 7–12.

Kurze Einführung in die parapsychologie (trans. Helga Wollenweber). In Hans Bender (ed.), *Parapsychologie*. Darmstadt: Wissenschaftliche Buchgesellschaft, 1966.

Psi-trailing bei tieren. With Sara A. Feather. In Hans Bender, *Parapsychologie*. Darmstadt: Wissenschaftliche Buchgesellschaft, 1966.

Two incredible experiments. In Daniel McDonald (ed.), *Controversy*. San Francisco: Chandler Pub. Co., 1966.

Zum Problem der spiritischen. In Hans Bender (ed.), *Parapsychologie*. Darmstadt: Wissenschaftliche Buchgesellschaft, 1966.

1967

Book review. *The world of Ted Serios* by Jule Eisenbud. New York: William Morrow, 1967. In *Journal of Parapsychology*, 1967, 31, 297–300.

Editorial: *FRNM Bulletin*, no. 6, Summer 1967, 2.

Editorial: Long-range support for psi research. *FRNM Bulletin*, no. 8, Winter 1967, 3.

Editorial: Prospects. *FRNM Bulletin*, no. 5, Spring 1967, 2.

Editorial: Public interest — a problem. *FRNM Bulletin*, no. 7, Autumn 1967, 2.

1968

The bearing of parapsychology on human potentiality. In Herbert A. Otto (ed.), *Human Potentialities*. St. Louis: Warren H. Green, 1968.

Clairvoyance. In *American People's Encyclopedia*. New York: Grolier, 1968.

Editorial: Hard letters to answer. *FRNM Bulletin*, no. 10, Autumn 1968, 2.

Editorial: The role and value of practice research. *FRNM Bulletin*, no. 9, Spring 1968, 2.

Introduction: In J. B. Rhine and Robert Brier (eds.), *Parapsychology today*. New York: Citadel Press, 1968.

Parapsychology. In *American People's Encyclopedia*. New York: Grolier, 1968.

Parapsychology Today. With Robert Brier (eds.). New York: Citadel Press, 1968. (In Portuguese: *Novas perspectivas de parapsicologia*. São Paulo: Editora Cultrix, 1971 paperback.)

Psi and psychology: Conflict and solution. *Journal of Parapsychology*, 1968, 32, 101–28.

The science of parapsychology. In G. Pat Powers and Wade Baskin (eds.), *New outlooks in psychology*. New York: Philosophical Library, 1968.

Some guiding concepts for parapsychology. *Journal of Parapsychology*, 1968, 32, 190–218.

1969

Book review. Lecture forum honoring Chester F. Carlson (*Proceedings of the American Society for Psychical Research*, 1969, 28.) In *Journal of Parapsychology*, 1969, 33, 272–73.

Editorial: The financing problem again. *FRNM Bulletin*, no. 14, Fall 1969, 2.

Editorial: How is parapsychology progressing? *FRNM Bulletin*, no. 11, Winter 1969, 2.

Editorial: The problem of economic independence. *FRNM Bulletin*, no. 13, Summer 1969, 2.

Editorial: Psi in the university department of psychology. *FRNM Bulletin*, no. 12, Spring 1969, 2.

An outline of the history of parapsychology. *Proceedings, 77th Annual Convention, American Psychological Association*, 1969, 841–42.

Position effects in psi test results. *Journal of Parapsychology*, 1969, **33**, 136–57. (Reprinted in Rhea A. White, *Surveys in Parapsychology*. Metuchen, N.J.: Scarecrow Press, 1976.)

Psi-missing re-examined. *Journal of Parapsychology*, 1969, **33**, 1–38.

Psychical Research. In *Encyclopedia Americana*. New York: Americana Corporation, 1969.

Psychical research, or parapsychology. In David Knight (ed.), *The ESP reader*. New York: Grosset & Dunlap, 1969.

A reply to the Hansel critique of the Pearce-Pratt series. With J. G. Pratt. In Gertrude R. Schmeidler (ed.), *Extrasensory perception*. New York: Atherton Press, 1969, 47–57.

Spiritualism. In David Knight (ed.), *The ESP reader*. New York: Grosset and Dunlap, 1969.

1970

A brief look at parapsychology. *Conditional Reflex*, 1970, **5**(1), 1–5.

Clairvoyance. In *Collier's Encyclopedia*. New York: Crowell-Collier Educational Corp., 1970.

Editorial: Repeatability and reliability. *Parapsychology Bulletin*, no. 18, Autumn 1970, 2.

Editorial: Some problems linked with progress. *Parapsychology Bulletin*, No. 15, Winter 1970, 2.

Editorial: A time for more efficiency. *Parapsychology Bulletin*, No. 17, Summer 1970, 2.

Editorial: Where to draw the line. *Parapsychology Bulletin*, No. 16, Spring 1970, 2.

ESP tests in mine location by man-dog team. (Abstract.) *Journal of Parapsychology*, 1970, **34**, 69–70.

Pastoral dimensions. *The Journal of Pastoral Counseling*, 1970, **5**(1), 9.

1971

Book review. *A century of psychical research: The continuing doubt and affirmation*, by Allan Angoff and Betty Shapin (eds.). In *Journal of Parapsychology*, 1971, **35**, 290–92.

Editorial: Apollo test. *Parapsychology Bulletin*, no. 20, Summer 1971, 2.

Editorial: Reflections after a success. *Parapsychology Bulletin*, No. 19, Winter 1971, 2.

Eileen J. Garrett as I knew her. *Journal of the Society for Psychical Research*, 1971, **46**(747), 59–61.

Guiding concepts for psi research. In J. B. Rhine (ed.), *Progress in Para-*

psychology. Durham, N.C.: Parapsychology Press, 1971.

The importance of parapsychology to William McDougall. *Journal of Parapsychology*, 1971, **35**, 169–88.

An interview with Dr. Rémy Chauvin. *Journal of Parapsychology*, 1971, **35**, 132–37.

Introduction: Dimensions of progress. In J. B. Rhine (ed.), *Progress in parapsychology*. Durham, N.C.: Parapsychology Press, 1971.

Location of hidden objects by a man-dog team. *Journal of Parapsychology*, 1971, **35**, 18–33.

McDougall's contribution to parapsychology. In J. B. Rhine (ed.), *Progress in parapsychology*. Durham, N.C.: Parapsychology Press, 1971.

News and comments. *Journal of Parapsychology*, 1971, **35**, 242–49.

News and comments. *Journal of Parapsychology*, 1971, **35**, 302–10.

Parapsychology and man. In E. Laszlo and J. B. Wilbur (eds.), *Human values and the mind of man*. New York: Gordon, 1971.

Progress in parapsychology (ed.). Durham, N.C.: Parapsychology Press, 1971. (Also second printing 1973 paperback.)

Psi and psychology: Conflict and solution. In J. B. Rhine (ed.), *Progress in parapsychology*. Durham, N.C.: Parapsychology Press, 1971.

1972

News and comments. *Journal of Parapsychology*, 1972, **36**, 78–87.

News and comments. *Journal of Parapsychology*, 1972, **36**, 167–76.

News and comments. *Journal of Parapsychology*, 1972, **36**, 241–50.

News and comments. *Journal of Parapsychology*, 1972, **36**, 314–27.

Parapsicología: una nueva rama de estudio médico. *Tribuna Médica* (Madrid), February 1972, 16–17.

Parapsychology. *New Zealand Medical Journal*, 1972, **75**, 36.

Parapsychology. *Raleigh Times*, March 25, 1972, 5A.

Parapsychology and man. *Journal of Parapsychology*, 1972, **36**, 101–21.

The poltergeist (interview conducted by Jean S. Bolen). *Psychic Magazine*, July 1972, 1–11.

Psi and psychology: Conflict and solution. In Raymond Van Over (ed.), *Psychology and extrasensory perception*. New York: New American Library, 1972, 161–87.

1973

Book review: *The welcoming silence* by D. Scott Rogo. *Journal of Parapsychology*, 1973, **37**, 349–50.

La ciencia de la naturaleza no-física (trans. Brenio Onetto B. with a short biographic note from J. Philos). *Revista de Parapsicología*, 1973, **1**(3), 23–32.

Letter in reply to McConnell. *Journal of Parapsychology*, 1973, **37**, 54.

News and comments. *Journal of Parapsychology*, 1973, **37**, 57–70.

News and comments: *Journal of Parapsychology*, 1973, 37, 137–50.
News and comments: *Journal of Parapsychology*, 1973, 37, 227–40.
News and comments: *Journal of Parapsychology*, 1973, 37, 351–66.

1974

Can parapsychology help religion? *Spiritual Frontiers*, 1974, 6, 3–20.
Comments: A new case of experimenter unreliability. *Journal of Parapsychology*, 1974, 38, 215–25.
Comments: Security versus deception in parapsychology. *Journal of Parapsychology*, 1974, 38, 99–121.
Informe anual sobre parapsicología (trans. Dora Ivnisky Kreiman). *Cuadernos de Parapsicología*, 1974, 1, 1–7.
Introduction: How to cope with a mystery. In Richard Cavendish (ed.) and J. B. Rhine (consultant), *Encyclopedia of the unexplained*. New York: McGraw-Hill, 1974.
Letter. To my fellow members on the Board of Directors (and other friends) of the FRNM. *Journal of the Society for Psychical Research*, 1974, 47(762), 520–21.
Man's nonphysical nature. In J. W. Cullen (ed.), *Legacies in the study of behavior*. Springfield, Ill.: Charles C. Thomas, 1974.
Telepathy and other untestable hypotheses. *Journal of Parapsychology*, 1974, 38, 137–53. (Reprinted by Rhea A. White in *Surveys in Parapsychology*. Metuchen, N.J.: Scarecrow Press, 1976.)
La telepatía y otras hipótesis no comprobables (trans. Dora Ivnisky Kreiman). *Cuadernos de Parapsicología*, 1974, 4, 23.

1975

Comments: Psi methods re-examined. *Journal of Parapsychology*, 1975, 39, 38–58.
Comments: Publication policy regarding nonsignificant results. *Journal of Parapsychology*, 1975, 39, 135–42.
Comments: Second report on a case of experimenter fraud. *Journal of Parapsychology*, 1975, 39, 306–25.
Introduction. In J. L. Randall, *Parapsychology and the nature of life*. New York: Harper & Row, 1975.
Introductory remarks (Abstract). *Journal of Parapsychology*, 1975, 39, 36–37.
National acceptability of the case for psi. In Peter French (ed.), *Philosophers in wonderland*. St. Paul, Minn.: Llewellyn, 1975, 347–354.
The parapsychology of religion: A new branch of inquiry. *The centrality of science and absolute values*. Proceedings of the Fourth International Cultural Foundation. New York: 1975.
Perry Bentley as I know him. *Journal of Texas Society for Psychical Research*, 1975, 9–10.

Presentación: In Enríque Novillo Pauli, S. J. (ed.), *Los fenómenos para-psicológicos*. Buenos Aires: Kapelusz, 1975.
Revisión de los métodos parapsicológicos (trans. Dora Ivnisky Kreiman). *Cuadernos de Parapsicología*, 1975, 4, 25–27.
Security versus deception in parapsychology. In Stanley Dean (ed.), *Psychiatry and mysticism*. Chicago: Nelson-Hall, 1975.

1976

Comments: Publication policy on chance results: Round two. *Journal of Parapsychology*, 1976, **40**, 64–68.
Occultism. In *Encyclopedia Americana*. New York: Americana Corporation, 1976.
Parapsychology and psychology: The shifting relationship today. *Journal of Parapsychology*, 1976, **40**, 115–35.
Position effects in psi test results. (Reprinted from *Journal of Parapsychology*, 1969, 33, 136–57.) In Rhea W. White's *Surveys in parapsychology: Reviews of the literature with updated bibliographies*. Metuchen, N.J.: Scarecrow Press, 1976, 204–26.
Psi-missing re-examined. (Reprinted from *Journal of Parapsychology*, 1969, 33, 1–38.) In Rhea A. White's *Surveys in parapsychology: Reviews of the literature with updated bibliographies*. Metuchen, N.J.: Scarecrow Press, 1976, 142–79.
A review of current needs and expectations. In Betty Shapen and Lisette Coly (eds.), *Education in parapsychology. Proceedings of an International Conference held in San Francisco, August 14–16, 1975*. New York: Parapsychology Foundation, 1976.

1977

A backward look on leaving the *Journal of Parapsychology*. *Journal of Parapsychology*, 1977, **41**, 89–102.
Extrasensory perception. In B. Wolman (ed.), *Handbook of parapsychology*. New York: Van Nostrand Reinhold, 1977.
History of experimental studies. In B. Wolman (ed.), *Handbook of parapsychology*, New York: Van Nostrand Reinhold, 1977.
Parapsychology and religion. *Journal of the Texas Society for Psychical Research* (1976–77), 1977, 9–20.

1978

A century of parapsychology. In Martin Ebon (ed.), *The Signet handbook of parapsychology*. New York: New American Library, 1978.
Comments on "Science and the Supernatural." In Jan Ludwig (ed.), *Philosophy and parapsychology*. Buffalo, N.Y.: Prometheus Books, 1978.

The experiment should fit the hypothesis. In Jan Ludwig (ed.), *Philosophy and parapsychology*. Buffalo, N.Y.: Prometheus Books, 1978. (Reprinted from *Science*, 1956, **123**, 19.)

The parapsychology of religion: A new branch of religion. *Journal of the Texas and Oklahoma Society for Psychical Research* (1977–78) 1978, 1–23.

The science of nonphysical nature. In Jan Ludwig (ed.), *Philosophy and parapsychology*. Buffalo, N.Y.: Prometheus Books, 1978.

A search for the nature of the mind. With L. E. Rhine. In T. S. Krawiec (ed.), *The psychologists*, Vol. 3. Brandon, Vt.: Clinical Psychology Pub. Co., 1978.

The study of cases of "psi trailing" in animals. With Sara A. Feather. In Martin Ebon (ed.), *The Signet handbook of parapsychology*. New York: American Library, 1978.

Twentieth anniversary (Abstract of round table discussion.) With C. T. Tart, R. A. McConnell, G. R. Schmeidler, J. G. Pratt, C. B. Nash, Karlis Osis. In W. G. Roll (ed.), *Research in Parapsychology*, Metuchen, N.J.: Scarecrow Press, 1978, 3–5.

1979

Letter. Parapsychology — a correction. *Science*, July 13, 1979, **205**, 144.

1980

Afterword. With L. E. Rhine. In S. M. Mauskopf and M. R. McVaugh, *The elusive science*. Baltimore: Johns Hopkins University Press, 1980.

My partner, Gardner Murphy. *Journal of the American Society for Psychical Research*, 1980, **74**, 62–65.

In Press

The development of parapsychology. Frank Nelson Doubleday lecture given at the Smithsonian Institution on April 19, 1978. To be published by Doubleday in their forthcoming volume, *Frontiers of the Mind*.

Bibliography of
Works about J. B. Rhine

Bolen, J. S. Interview: J. B. Rhine. *Psychic*, 1972, 3(6), 6–10, 30–34.

Brian, Denis. *The enchanted voyager: The life of J. B. Rhine.* Englewood Cliffs, N.J.: Prentice-Hall, 1982.

Ebon, M. J. B. Rhine at 80. *Parapsychology Review*, 1975, 6(5), 1–5.

Hall, M. H. Interview: J. B. Rhine. *Psychology Today*, 1969, 2(10), 20–26, 67–68.

McVaugh, M. R., & Mauskopf, S. H. J. B. Rhine's extra-sensory perception and its background in psychical research. *Isis*, 1976, 67, 161–189.

Mauskopf, S. H., & McVaugh, M. R. *The elusive science: A history of experimental parapsychology 1915–1940.* Baltimore: Johns Hopkins University Press, 1980.

Moore, R. L. Joseph Banks Rhine and the first ten years of parapsychology at Duke University. In *In search of white crows.* New York: Oxford University Press, 1977, 184–203. (See also 237–242.)

Murphy, G. Dr. Rhine and the mind's eye. *American Scholar*, 1938, 2, 189–200.

Nilsson, I. The paradigm of the Rhinean school. *European Journal of Parapsychology.* Part I, 1975, 1, 45–59; part II, 1976, 1, 57–71.

Sloane, W. M. Letter to his [Sloane's] father entitled Jung and Rhine. *Quadrant*, 1975, 8(2), 72–76.

Stevens, C. C. Parapsychology and modern science. *Journal of Parapsychology*, 1950, 14, 127–139.

Thouless, R. H. Dr. Rhine's recent experiments on telepathy and clairvoyance and a reconsideration of J. E. Coover's conclusion on telepathy. *Proceedings of the Society for Psychical Research*, 1935, 43, 24–37.

Index

257